AMERICAN
OIL OPERATIONS
ABROAD

The quality of the materials used in the manufacture of this book is governed by continued postwar shortages.

AMERICAN
OIL OPERATIONS
ABROAD

by

Leonard M. Fanning

Author of
The Rise of American Oil
Editor of
Our Oil Resources

McGRAW-HILL BOOK COMPANY, INC.

NEW YORK AND LONDON

1947

AMERICAN OIL OPERATIONS ABROAD

COPYRIGHT, 1947, BY THE
McGRAW-HILL BOOK COMPANY, INC.

PRINTED IN THE UNITED STATES OF AMERICA

PREFACE

"American Oil Operations Abroad" tells the story of the search for oil and the development of markets by Americans in foreign countries. It tells how, after the First World War, when the government of the United States gave the petroleum industry the mandate "Go abroad and find oil as a protection to the American economy and national defense," American oil companies carried the search to practically every country, even to remote corners of the earth, despite great obstacles and hardships. It gives the extent and scope of American investments abroad, made over the years—tells of the political and economic risks and of expropriation and seizure.

The building of oil camps that grew into cities, the training of nationals to become oil drillers and technicians, and the beneficial effect on the economy of nations and on social and educational standards are among the subjects treated.

The problems brought about by the trend toward nationalization in many countries—more acute in the postwar world than even during the prewar period—are set forth. Problems in international oil are presented in relationship to the position of American petroleum investment and activities abroad and to the interest therein of the American people.

The purpose of the book is to present the facts and thus give the reader a true insight into a most vital issue before the world and the American nation today—the international oil situation.

The information contained herein is based upon the Report of the Group on American Petroleum Interests in Foreign Countries [1] to the Special Committee Investigating Petroleum Resources, Senator Joseph C. O'Mahoney, Chairman.

LEONARD M. FANNING.

NEW YORK, N. Y.,
February, 1947.

[1] See Appendix, p. 183.

CONTENTS

CONTENTS

AMERICAN
OIL OPERATIONS
ABROAD

AMERICAN OIL OPERATIONS ABROAD

CHAPTER I

AMERICA LOOKS ABROAD FOR OIL

The United States looks more and more to foreign oil. Why is this so? Where do we stand in the matter of world oil reserves so closely related to our defense in war and to our high peacetime living standards? What must we do to maintain and strengthen our place in foreign oil? These and many other questions are answered in a Report on American Petroleum Interests in Foreign Countries recently presented to the Special Senate Committee Investigating Petroleum Resources.[1]

Above all, we are revealed with a vigilant petroleum industry, an industry that despite obstacles (in the form of political trends) and high venture (in the form of economic hazards) increased its total investment abroad in the period 1919–1939 from 399 million dollars to about 2½ billion dollars.[2]

[1] Report of the Group on American Petroleum Interests in Foreign Countries to Special Senate Committee Investigating Petroleum Resources, Senator Joseph C. O'Mahoney, chairman. U. S. Government Printing Office, 1946.

[2] From the returns of the 11 American oil companies reporting for themselves, their subsidiaries, and affiliates in answer to a questionnaire distributed by the Group on American Petroleum Interests in Foreign Countries. The companies that reported follow: Amerada Petroleum Corp., Atlantic Refining Co., Cities Service Co., Continental Oil Co., Gulf Oil Corp., Socony-Vacuum Oil Co., Standard Oil Co. of California, Standard Oil Co. (New Jersey), Sun Oil Co., The Texas Co., and Tide Water Associated Oil Co. These companies represent 93 per cent of the total net worth of the investment of all American oil companies in foreign countries. The figures also indicate that 29 per cent of the combined net worth of these same 11 companies in 1939 (totaling about $4,400,000,000) was invested in foreign operations. (Investment data were incomplete for some foreign countries for the years 1940–1944 because of war conditions. However, the incomplete figures for 1944 showed total assets employed of 2.3 billion dollars.)

The accumulative amount invested abroad up to the end of 1944 as arrived at on the basis of total amount invested at the end of 1944, plus all amounts written off or revalued since the end of 1918, showed the grand total amount of total assets employed of nearly 3.2 billion dollars, net assets of 2.2 billion dollars, and net worth of investment 1.7 billion dollars.

See also Appendix Tables 1–7.

It would be erroneous to fix American participation in foreign production and marketing as starting in 1919—the first year after the First World War—as indicated by the tidy amount of close to 400 million dollars in it at that time. Nevertheless, it was in that year that American oil companies were given a mandate by their government to go out and find and develop oil abroad. It was the beginning of a short-lived era of strong diplomatic support. It marked a reversal of the policy of the early 1910's—the "dollar-diplomacy" days—when the State Department told oil companies they were strictly on their own in alien countries. It began the broadest search—and the most resultful—ever undertaken by American oil interests.

Prior to the outbreak of the First World War, American interests were represented in the producing columns of only two foreign countries, Mexico and Rumania,[1] although American drilling equipment and methods were being adopted as superior in all the old producing fields of Rumania, Poland, and Russia. During the war period, 1914–1918, Americans extended their oil-producing interests into Peru, made refining investments in Argentina and Austria, and held shares, leases, or concessions in Russia, Poland, Colombia, and Argentina. They also made a costly expedition in search of oil into interior China where they had pioneered in marketing kerosene.

But it was immediately after the First World War that American interests really extended themselves abroad. It is a striking fact that, largely because of diplomatic backing given them in this period, American oil companies today have a foothold and are active in foreign countries all over the globe. Indeed, much of the available knowledge of oil prospects in many inaccessible and undeveloped regions of the earth stems back to far-flung American exploration ventures of the early and middle twenties. American geologists went into virtually every country believed to have oil possibilities—if they were permitted entry.

---

[1] The earliest known effort by Americans to develop oil resources abroad was in 1876 in Mexico. Shortly after the 1900's the first American-owned production abroad was brought in, this also in Mexico. It was followed almost immediately by the appearance of an American operator in Rumania. These two countries remained the only sites of American producing activity up to the First World War, at the beginning of which, in 1914, a total of 18 foreign countries were producing oil with American participation amounting to approximately 13 per cent. During the First World War, the intensive development of Mexico's "Golden Lane" by American as well as British companies, accompanied by the prostration of the Russian oil industry as the result of the Russian military collapse and the Bolshevist Revolution of 1917, sharply raised the American percentage to 32 per cent in 1918 (see Table 5, p. 15).

Many new producing areas in which American capital participated were discovered during the first postwar decade. American participation in foreign petroleum production, already rising rapidly during the war years, reached an all-time peak in 1922, amounting to some 50 per cent of total foreign production.

American Interests in Foreign Countries Defined.—Where American interests or American oil companies are referred to in this book, the reader should understand that this may mean either an American corporation or a subsidiary foreign corporation of an American interest.

In most cases American oil companies have to work in foreign lands through locally incorporated subsidiaries in which there may or may not be a material minority interest.

Fear of an Oil Shortage in Early 1920's.—Fear of an oil shortage in the United States—a holdover from a narrow escape from scarcity in 1917–1918 when we were in the midst of war—was uppermost in everyone's mind. What might have happened as a result of the tremendous drain on American oil supply had the war been prolonged into 1919 and 1920? That a case of national jitters developed is not surprising in view of the fact that the military importance of oil in modern war had just been demonstrated.

Oil supply truly took on a vital national-defense complexion. Figures —estimates of oil reserves—tended to support shortage fears. In a bulletin on the world's oil supply the U. S. Geological Survey said the United States was using twice as much oil as the rest of the world put together but that "the rest of the world, according to geological information as to where and what quantities of oil might be found, had about seven times as much oil upon which to draw as the United States."

"Even though we glory in the fact that we contributed 80 per cent of the great quantity needed to meet requirements of the Allies during the war [First World War], is not our world leadership more spectacular than safe?" said Dr. George Otis Smith, director of the Survey. "And even though the United States may today be the largest oil producer and though it consumes nearly 75 per cent of the world's output of oil, it is not a minute too early to take counsel with ourselves and call the attention of the American geologists, engineers, capitalists, and legislators to the need of an oil supply for the future."

United States production would reach a maximum in two to five years, said Dr. Van H. Manning, director of the U. S. Bureau of Mines, "and from that time on we will face an ever-increasing decline. We thus see domestic oil fields unable to meet our home demands under present methods of utilization and manufacture. This startling fact cannot be ignored." Both the Democratic and Republican parties and officials urged that American citizens acquire and develop oil properties abroad.

Fear of Foreign Oil Control.—The First World War had scarcely ended before fear of world oil control in the hands of a British-French-Dutch combination began to be voiced in the United States, with consequent strain between our country and our former Allies. Washington echoed with alarms. It was imperative that our own oil companies develop petroleum resources in lands other than our own.

The "almost hysterical outbursts" of Senators in debating the Naval Appropriations bill on Apr. 28, 1920, served to call attention to the "near strangle hold the British government has upon the undeveloped oil areas of the world, to the indifference the administrative officers have held toward the subject, and to the outstanding fact that the American industry is not at all to be blamed for the position in which this nation finds itself, immediately after a war in which it furnished the deciding factors in a flood of oil that carried the Allies to victory over Germany."

As a remedy, Senator Phelan of California introduced a bill in the Senate on May 18, 1920, to incorporate the "United States Oil Corporation." This corporation would develop oil resources of foreign countries by exploration, refining, transportation, and storing through capital supplied by American oilmen and oil companies but with the backing and sanction of the government. The government would have prior right to take any or all of the oil produced by the corporation on payment of the market price.

The bill would give control of the corporation to a board of nine directors appointed by the President. The corporation would have the right to solicit stock subscriptions and to organize subsidiaries. The theory was that American oilmen would be willing to furnish capital for an oil company promoted by the U. S. government and also that the government would use its diplomatic good offices to help such a corporation obtain sources of oil in other countries.

Secretary of State Bainbridge Colby pointed out objections to the proposed American government petroleum company. He told Senator Phelan it seemed not unlikely that foreign nations might refuse such a company the right to carry on business. As against the argument of precedence in British government stock ownership in the Anglo-Persian Oil Company (Anglo-Iranian Oil Company, Limited), the question of

One of first wells at Ebano, 1901.

"Prior to outbreak of the First World War, American interests were represented in the producing columns of only two foreign countries—Mexico and Rumania." See page 2.

Photographs on this and next seven pages are reprinted by the courtesy of the Standard Oil Company (Indiana). From "Mexican Petroleum," Pan American Petroleum & Transport Company, 1922.

Oil exude at base of Cerro de la Pez, Ebano.

Americans Started Ebano Development in 1901

Headquarters building on hill at Ebano.

General view of camp at Ebano.

First indication of oil at Cerro Azul No. 4.

Oil exude at Cerro Azul which prompted drilling.

Mexican Petroleum Company's great gusher came in Feb. 9, 1916, and on February 19 had reached 260,858 barrels in 24 hours—the biggest daily flow ever recorded for any

well—before being shut in. On February 11 the column of oil attained a height of 598 ft.

Valve partially over well.

Some of the men who closed in Cerro Azul No. 4.

Valve completely over well. Although Cerro Azul No. 4 blew in unexpectedly, it was fully controlled within ten days. More than half a million barrels were saved in temporary reservoirs.

Cerro Azul No. 4 Brought under Control

On Feb. 19, 1916, everything was ready to make the attempt to close the well. The table was clamped to the casing, and 30 ft. away men began to turn the screw that advanced the valve slowly over the casing. When the valve touched the casing, it held true in its place, and the body of oil was diverted slightly from the vertical. Gradually the entire body of oil was rushing through the valve, no longer uncontrolled. Fittings were made secure. Cerro Azul No. 4 was tamed!

American Drillers Introduce American Drilling Methods in Rumania

Test well drilled by American driller A. P. Lieser near Polesti, Rumania, 1912.

". . . American drilling equipment and methods were being adopted as superior in the old producing fields of Rumania, Poland, and Russia." See page 2.

Photographs by courtesy of A. P. Lieser.

The wells were originally drilled to 2,000 ft. with the Alianta (German drilling rig), requiring a year each to complete. Around 1916 A. P. Lieser and associates took over the wells, installed American drilling machinery, and in about 30 days for each well deepened them to a good oil sand at 6,000 ft.

Sold American Oil-drilling Equipment Abroad

Photograph from Oil Trade Journal, February, 1919.

Captain J. F. Lucey (*third from right, front row*) with staff, many of whom sold American oil-drilling equipment or drilled for oil in foreign countries.

Photograph by courtesy of Standard-Vacuum Oil Company.

One of the early American cable tool rigs with wooden derrick in Dutch East Indies.

American drillers at Baku, 1916–1917.

Bailing a hand-dug well at Baku. George McMurry and L. W. Danner, American drillers, "at the wheel," and Mrs. McMurry center. McMurry and Danner also are in the opposite photograph.

Photographs from Oil Trade Journal, July, **1917.**

Flowing well completed at Baku with American rotary rig. In the picture are Lon Allison, R. L. Dobbs, J. D. Stewart, Dave Simmons, American drillers, and their interpreter and nationals who formed part of their drilling crew.

Americans Helped Drill for Oil in England during First World War

Dr. A. C. Veatch, American geologist, was in charge of the geological work for S. Pearson & Sons, Ltd., which drilled on 11 locations in the British Isles during and immediately following the war. Mr. Conaghan of Muskegee, Okla., was proud of his American drillers and American drilling equipment.

Hardstoft No. 1 well.   Victor L. Conaghan, American drilling superintendent.

Photographs from Oil Trade Journal, October, 1919.

Another view of the Hardstoft well.

the ethics and practicability of such government participation was debated on both sides of the Atlantic.

Postwar Complications—Mandates.—Mandates assumed by Britain and France over Middle East petroliferous countries came up for airing during the 1919 Peace Conference, and oil was the heart of the debate at the Lausanne Near East Peace Conference in 1922 and 1923. Indeed, by this time oil had become a diplomatic issue of first rank.

The San Remo Agreement on Apr. 24, 1920, between Britain and France fed American suspicions. This agreement, in which Britain cut only France into a share of Mesopotamian (Iraq) oil, seemed by its general provisions to bar the United States from participating in the field. On May 12, 1920, the American ambassador to London, John W. Davis, presented a note to Lord Curzon, British Foreign Secretary, protesting against a policy of exclusion in Mesopotamia. This note was part of a diplomatic correspondence initiated under Secretary of State Colby in which the United States demanded the privilege first of participating in discussions on the Mesopotamian concessions and then of sharing in the concessions.

Secretary of State Charles Evans Hughes, who succeeded Mr. Colby, continued the attacks on Allied mandates as invalid except when American assent was given.

The Lausanne Near East Peace Conference of 1922 and 1923 nearly failed because of the oil stakes in the Turkish boundary question. An agreement was finally reached in November, 1923. The Mesopotamian dispute went to the League of Nations.

Open Door versus Closed Door Debated.—The diplomatic battle over mandates was accompanied by exchange of documents between the governments involved and also by exhaustive reports by U. S. government bureaus in response to Congressional queries. The public took up the debate on the question: open door versus closed door.

The State Department sent to the Senate on May 17, 1920, a report on the restrictions imposed by foreign governments upon American enterprises in development of oil fields in other lands. It showed that Great Britain maintained rigid restrictions except as to the occupied regions of the Turkish Empire, including Armenia, for which the Allies wished the United States to accept a mandate.

Closed Door in the United States?—Demands that we ourselves exclude foreign nationals from participation in United States oil were made by government officials and legislators. Meantime, there had been injected into the picture a bill for an embargo on oil shipped from the

United States, introduced Jan. 17, 1921, by Senator Phelan. Under it oil supplies from the United States to any country discriminating against American oil interests could be cut off at the discretion of the President.

Failure of American interests to secure a share in concessions to the Djambi oil fields in Netherlands India heaped fuel on the controversy and brought new American State Department protests. Official and public opinion in America held that Dutch interests were combined with British in an effort to exclude Americans, and a series of reports submitted to the Senate clearly documented the fact that, even while American oil interests were excluded from or restricted in British and Dutch territories, British and Dutch companies were acquiring extensive new resources in the United States.

The concern felt in the United States was reflected in the Minerals Leasing Act of Feb. 25, 1920, which authorized the Secretary of the Interior to reject applications for leases on public lands to citizens of foreign countries that deny "similar or like privileges to American citizens or corporations."

Foreign-ownership Report.—When the Netherlands government confirmed the Djambi concession to the Bataafsche Petroleum Company, a subsidiary of the Royal Dutch–Shell Company, Congress asked the Federal Trade Commission to investigate the whole subject of foreign ownership in the foreign and domestic oil industry. The Commission's report dated Feb. 12, 1923, showed the Royal Dutch interests controlling 11 per cent of the world's oil production and conditions of discrimination and exclusion against American interests in British, Dutch, and French territories.

A month after this report there was confirmation from Washington that Secretary of the Interior Albert Fall had denied the application of the Roxana Petroleum Company, a Royal Dutch subsidiary, for permission to lease oil lands of the Creek Indians in Oklahoma. The action was taken on the grounds that the Netherlands government refused like opportunity to American oil enterprise and that American oil interests were subjected to discriminations and burdens in various portions of the British Empire. This was one of the last decisions made by Mr. Fall before retiring as Secretary of the Interior.

State Department Action Bears Fruit.—In reply to a Senate resolution, President Calvin Coolidge on May 1, 1924, made public a covering letter by Secretary of State Hughes and correspondence since Mar. 4, 1921, with various foreign governments on the subject of oil concessions.

The year 1923, however, marked the climax of the prolonged tension over oil supplies among the former Allies, Britain, France, and the United States, and the excitement died down because of the opening of large new oil fields in the United States. The Netherlands government relaxed its policy of exclusion and granted to the N. V. Nederlandsche Koloniale Petroleum Maatschappij, a Dutch company in which the Standard Oil Company (New Jersey) then had a majority interest, concessions in Sumatra and other Dutch East Indies islands. The balance of the shares in this company was held by Dutch nationals. Eventually President Coolidge rescinded the exclusion of the Roxana Petroleum Company from United States held Indian lands.

Our State Department's intervention in the Middle East bore fruit in 1927, when an American company, the Near East Development Corporation, gained a 23¾ per cent interest in the Iraq Petroleum Company, successor to the Turkish Petroleum Company. The State Department invited wide participation in Iraq among American oil companies. The original shareholders numbered five: Atlantic Refining Company, Pan American Petroleum and Transport Company, Gulf Oil Corporation, Standard Oil Company of New York, and Standard Oil Company (New Jersey). The Atlantic, Gulf, and Pan American companies subsequently withdrew.

Overproduction and World Conservation.—By 1924 all talk of oil shortage, all immediate fears, had ended, submerged in a flood of oil from new United States fields. From an annual production of around 350 million barrels during the years 1917–1918, U. S. production had gone to 732 million barrels in 1923, and in 1929 it was to cross the billion-barrel mark for the first time. Many American companies that had gone into foreign exploration withdrew in favor of home operations. The problem now was one of overproduction, not underproduction. It was one of conservation of a valuable, irreplaceable natural resource and of reducing the physical and economic waste entailed in overproduction.

The U. S. oil industry voluntarily adopted proration methods, *i.e.*, reducing well and pool production in flush fields. A series of research projects was launched to bring about greater engineering efficiency in the production of oil. These studies and practices were soon to revolutionize production methods.

Results of Strong Diplomatic Support.—Meantime the strong diplomatic support given American companies in foreign countries had had significant results.

Exploration and development abroad by American capital actually had trailed many years behind its employment in the export and foreign-market business because American oil producers, with characteristic initiative and energy and favored by the abundance of oil in their homeland, outstripped all foreign petroleum industries in production, refining, and marketing methods and did not have to seek oil abroad to meet domestic and foreign-market needs. As exporters, Standard Oil, Tide Water Oil, Pure Oil, Vacuum Oil, and scores of other American companies with refineries in the Pennsylvania oil region and along the Atlantic seaboard had marketed their products all over the globe since shortly after the birth of the industry in 1859.

When American companies launched their drive for foreign oil sources in 1919, probably the bulk of their approximately 400-million-dollar investment abroad was in marketing and refining properties.[1] By 1925 so seriously had the mandate to find foreign oil been taken that at least 40 American companies were active in foreign exploration and production work.

In the close-by countries of Mexico and Venezuela, Americans increased their efforts after the First World War. They initiated new exploration and development programs in Argentina, Peru, and Ecuador. Separate expeditions were sent to Panama by the Sinclair, Gulf Oil, and Standard Oil interests; to Costa Rica by Sinclair. In 1919 there was a rush into Colombia with 49 American companies holding concessions.

For a short time in the twenties an American organization, the International Barnsdall Corporation, actually operated in Russia under a contract to drill and produce oil in the Baku area. Another near penetration on Russian soil was made by Sinclair Oil, which obtained a concession for the development of oil on the island of Sakhalin, lying

---

[1] Foremost among American companies exporting petroleum products in the 1920's were the Standard Oil Co. (New Jersey) and the Standard Oil Co. of New York, both having been pioneers in extending foreign markets. Other large companies that exported oil included the Vacuum Oil Co., Sinclair Oil Corp., The Texas Co., Sun Oil Co., Atlantic Refining Co., Tide Water Oil Co., and Pure Oil Co. Practically all the large California companies were active in export trade, including the Union Oil Co., Shell Co., General Petroleum Corp., Associated Oil Co., and Standard Oil Co. of California. Many other companies either directly shipped and marketed petroleum products abroad or were interested in export trade through manufacture of products for export. In many of the European countries where the American companies marketed, they built up marketing and distributing equipment and operated as partners with local capital.

"American geologists went into virtually every country believed to have oil possibilities—if they were permitted entry."

Photographs on this and next three pages by courtesy of Fred B. Ely.

The "three musketeers" in Yenen, Arabia, 1923; typical American geological surveying party. *Left to right:* R. M. McGovern, Pierre Lamare, French geologist, and Fred B. Ely. McGovern and Ely, American geologists.

"American oil companies were given a mandate by their government to go out and find and develop oil abroad. . . . it was immediately after the First World War that American interests really extended themselves abroad. . . . they have gained footholds, sometimes against almost insuperable odds, in most (although by no means all) of the great strategic oil-reserve areas of the earth." See pages 2, 3, 57.

Ely party on the march in Arabia.　　　Dhow in which party crossed Red Sea.

Meeting with Arab governor at Sana, 1923. *Left to right:* Son of Said Hussein; Turkish officer; Said Hussein, Arab governor of Sana; Georges Ghericich, operator of factory at Sana; McGovern; Colonel Rouhi, in command of Iman's troops; Cherruau.

Dugout canoe carrying Ely party on Sarangan River, North Sumatra, 1923.

Group at the Petak field, Java, 1923. *Left to right:* Ely, McGovern, Hilgers (geologist for the N.K.P.M.) and Buchanan, field superintendent.

Fred Ely at Red Sea.   Abyssinian escort.

Trouble in Tunisia.

Help on survey in Tunisia.

American geologists in Siberia. Taken by J. P. McCulloch on the ice of the Amur River near Nikolaiersk, Jan. 30, 1924.

Secured oil concession in Northern Sakhalin, 1923. *Left to right:* Secretary Zens; Chester Naramore, American geologist; Peter Rathvon.

Americans Explored and Drilled for Oil in Africa in the 1920's

Portuguese East Indies topographical helpers, 1921.

Dr. A. C. Veatch and Chester Naramore inspect seepage in Angola, 1925.

Landing freight for oil well at Cato Ledo, 100 miles south of Loanda, Angola, West Africa.

Photographs by courtesy of Chester Naramore and J. P. McCulloch.

Raft for landing freight through surf, Cato Ledo, Angola.

Above: Doctor examining nationals for sleeping sickness in tsetse fly area, Angola.

Right: Drilling rotary mud for Angola operations, 1925.

Below: Carrying drilling pipe to No. 8 well, Angola.

Photographs by courtesy of Chester Naramore.

Panama: geologist's "piragua" on the Tuira, October, 1926.

Colombia—American geologists' camp, 1925.

Colombia—geologists outfitted for week's trip, 1925.

Photographs by courtesy of J. P. McCulloch.

Costa Rica: J. P. McCulloch after three hours on the Olivia trail, January, 1923.

off Siberia. The same company secured a large concession to develop oil in Angola, a Portuguese colony on the west coast of Africa.

Further evidence that American oil enterprise searched the remote ends of the earth was the granting of a concession to a U. S. company to prospect and operate in Abyssinia, and another in Siam. In Palestine, the Standard Oil Company of New York had obtained a concession from the Turkish government before the First World War covering a considerable area between the Dead Sea and the Mediterranean and had built a road south from Jerusalem for the transport of its machinery and other needed material.

But by far the most significant development was the diplomatic victories resulting in American participation in petroleum production in Iraq and in the Dutch East Indies.

Thus did American oil companies respond to the call of their government to find oil in other parts of the world and to the opportunities that seemed to be offered to develop oil abroad. By 1929 they had increased their total investment by 1 billion to 1.4 billion dollars. Much of the increase was in exploration and production. As previously stated, the impetus of this period carried into the next decade.

From 1929 to 1939 investment increased an additional billion to nearly 2½ billion dollars.[1] The remarkable thing is that this was done despite only passive support from the government, particularly in the last decade. American oil companies that had expanded into foreign countries in some cases enlarged their holdings in their attempt to protect their earlier investments. Indeed, even in the face of an oversupply at home right up to the outbreak of the Second World War, American oil companies persisted in their foreign activities, a fact that served the United Nations well in ensuring oil where it was needed for military operations.

Growth of American Oil Investment Abroad.—To summarize, at the end of 1919 total assets (investment) employed by American companies in foreign countries were 399 million dollars and at the end of 1929 reached 1,406 million dollars, an increase of 1,007 million dollars, or 252 per cent. During the next decade another billion dollars to nearly $2,500,000,000 was invested. That is, during the period 1919–1939, the increase was slightly over 2 billion dollars, or 526 per cent. It will be noted that the amount of expansion was the same for each of the 10-year periods, 1 billion dollars, or at an average rate of 100 million dollars per annum (Tables 1 and 2).

[1] See Appendix, Table 1, Part I.

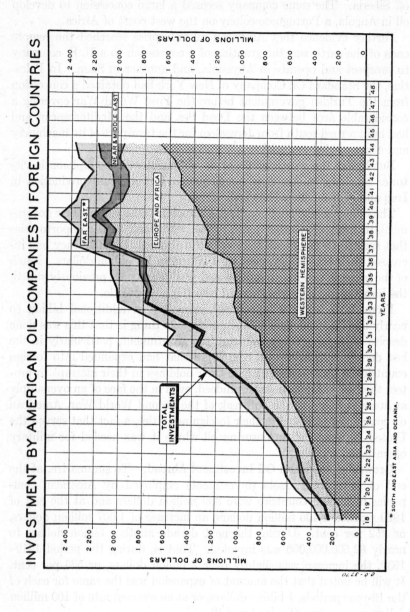

INVESTMENT BY AMERICAN OIL COMPANIES IN FOREIGN COUNTRIES

FAR EAST *

NEAR & MIDDLE EAST

EUROPE AND AFRICA

WESTERN HEMISPHERE

TOTAL INVESTMENTS

* SOUTH AND EAST ASIA AND OCEANIA.

YEARS

MILLIONS OF DOLLARS

G.G.-3770

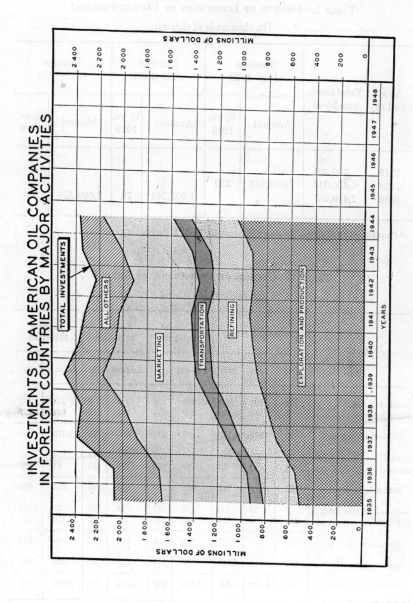

INVESTMENTS BY AMERICAN OIL COMPANIES
IN FOREIGN COUNTRIES BY MAJOR ACTIVITIES

MILLIONS OF DOLLARS

TOTAL INVESTMENTS

ALL OTHERS

MARKETING

TRANSPORTATION

REFINING

EXPLORATION AND PRODUCTION

YEARS

1935 1936 1937 1938 1939 1940 1941 1942 1943 1944 1945 1946 1947 1948

MILLIONS OF DOLLARS

TABLE 1.—GROWTH OF INVESTMENT BY 10-YEAR PERIODS [1]

(In thousands of dollars)

As at end of	Total assets employed	Increase 1919–1929		Increase 1929–1939		Increase 1919–1939	
		Amount	% vs. 1919	Amount	% vs. 1929	Amount	% vs. 1919
1919	399,431						
1929	1,406,014	1,006,583	252				
1939	2,499,257			1,093,243	78	2,099,826	526

[1] Complete detailed figures are shown in Appendix Table 1, Part I.

TABLE 2.—GROWTH OF INVESTMENT, BY AREAS [1]

(In millions of dollars)

Area	Amount end of year			Increase 1919–1929		Increase 1929–1939		Increase 1919–1939	
	1919	1929	1939	Amount	%	Amount	%	Amount	%
North America	113	303	297	190	168	6 [2]	2 [2]	184	163
South America	67	476	1,058	409	614	582	122	991	1,487
Western Hemisphere	180	779	1,355	599	333	576	74	1,175	654
Europe	91	338	715	247	270	377	112	624	682
Africa	11	39	72	28	260	33	85	61	567
Subtotal	102	377	787	275	269	410	109	685	670
Near and Middle East	7	10	93	3	57	83	800	86	1,314
Far East	111	240	264	129	117	24	10	153	138
Asia	118	250	357	132	113	107	42	239	203
Eastern Hemisphere	220	627	1,144	407	186	517	82	924	421
Grand total foreign	400	1,406	2,499	1,006	252	1,093	78	2,099	526

[1] See Appendix Table 1, Part I.
[2] Decrease.

State Department Action Bears Fruit

"It is a striking fact that largely because of diplomatic backing given them in this period (after First World War) American oil companies today have a foothold and are active in foreign countries all over the globe." See page 2. *". . . have invested 2½ billion dollars abroad."* See page 9.

Photograph by Vachon, courtesy of Standard Oil Company (New Jersey).

Oil well in jungle, Quiriquire field, Eastern Venezuela.

Photograph by courtesy of Imperial Oil Review.

Talara, Peru. The oil fields in the distance were developed by the International Petroleum Company, Ltd. This company built a modern town and refinery here.

Americans developed over-water drilling in Venezuela. Tia Juana field in Lake Maracaibo

Andean National pipe line near Barrancabermeja, Colombia.

Western Venezuela.

Bahrah No. 1 well of Kuwait Oil Company, Limited, jointly owned by Gulf Oil Corporation and Anglo-Persian Oil Company, Limited.

The Bahrah oil seepage.   The Sheik watches road scraper.

Photographs by courtesy of Kuwait Oil Company, Limited.

Inspection trip of the Sheik of Kuwait, Oct. 26, 1938, at Burgan No. 2 well. *Left to right:* Abdulla Mulla Saleh, Colonel Dickson, Maj. Harry G. Davis; H.H. The Sheik of Kuwait, Maj. Frank Holmes, and L. D. Scott, general superintendent.

"*At the end of 1919 total assets (investment) employed by American companies in foreign countries were $399,000,000 and at the end of 1939 reached $2,500,000,000.*" *See page* 9.

Photographs by courtesy of The Bahrein Petroleum Company, Limited

His Highness Sheik Sir Salman bin Hamed al Khalifa visits the refinery of The Bahrein Petroleum Company, Limited.   Oct. 21 1944   Lower right, his falcon bearer.

Aerial view of Arabian American Oil Company's refinery and marine terminal at Ras Tanura, Saudi Arabia.

Photographs on this and opposite page by Robert Yarnell Richie, by courtesy of Arabian American Oil Company.

Night view of Ras Tanura refinery.

The Arabian American Company's refinery at Ras Tanura on the Persian Gulf cost 40 million dollars and produces approximately 85,000 bbl. daily of fuel oil, diesel oil, and gasoline. Ras Tanura obtains its crude oil from pipe lines that connect it with the producing fields at Abquaiq, Damman, and Qatif. Dhahran, shown below, is in the heart of the producing field of Damman, where oil was first discovered in Saudi Arabia.

H.M. Abdul Aziz ibn Saud and H.R.H. the Amir Saud at Rigadh.

Aerial view of Arabian American Oil Company's community at Dhahran, in heart of the producing field of Damman where oil was first discovered in Saudi Arabia.

Photographs by courtesy of R. Leibensperger, Standard-Vacuum Oil Company.

Operations in the Dutch East Indies by the N.V. Nederlandsche Koloniale Petroleum Maatschappiz.

The percentage of total assets employed by American oil companies in foreign countries varied considerably in each major area in the years 1919, 1929, and 1939 (Table 3). It is interesting to note that the decline in American investment in Mexico culminating in the expropriation of foreign properties by the Mexican government in 1938 was more than offset by the increase in South America, largely reflecting the rise of American investment in Venezuela.

TABLE 3.—PER CENT OF INVESTMENT EMPLOYED IN DIFFERENT AREAS [1]

Areas	1919	1929	1939
North America	28	21	12
South America	17	34	42
Europe	23	24	29
Africa	3	3	3
Near and Middle East	1	1	4
South and east Asia	23	8	3
Oceania	5	9	7
Total	100	100	100

[1] See Appendix Table 1, Part I.

American Oil Investment in Practically Every Country in the World.

Today there is scarcely a country in the world where American oil companies have not made investments directly or through subsidiaries or affiliates. Although virtually excluded from participating in producing operations, in certain countries they are often represented in marketing activities [1] (Table 4).

[1] From the replies of American oil companies, it is possible for the first time to give an indication of the investment of American oil companies abroad by major activities. Of the total assets employed at the end of 1939 of nearly $2,500,000,000, 876 million dollars, or 35 per cent, was in exploration and production; nearly 791 million dollars, or 31 per cent, in marketing; over 365 million dollars, or 15 per cent, in refining; about 145 million dollars, or 6 per cent, in transportation; and 322 million dollars, or 13 per cent, in "all others." The last classification includes certain investments by some of the oil companies in foreign subsidiary and affiliated companies for which a breakdown by functional activities is not available.

See also Appendix Tables 1–7.

Downward Trend of American-owned Share in Foreign Oil.—Nevertheless, despite the continuing and expanding activities of American companies abroad in the interwar period, the percentage of foreign production controlled by them has declined since the twenties (see Table 5). This reflects the deterioration in the position of foreign oil companies in

TABLE 4.—TOTAL INVESTMENT BY HEMISPHERES [1]

(In thousands of dollars)

| Year | Western Hemisphere | | | Eastern Hemisphere | | | Total foreign | |
	Amount	% increase vs. 1919	% total	Amount	% increase vs. 1919	% total	Amount	% increase vs. 1919
1919	179,689		45	219,742		55	399,431	
1929	778,615	333	55	627,399	186	45	1,406,014	252
1939	1,355,376	654	54	1,143,881	421	46	2,499,257	526
1944	1,685,894	838						

[1] See Appendix Table 1, Part I.

certain Latin-American countries, notably Mexico, Bolivia, and Argentina. Another reason lies in the interwar revival of Russian production from which U. S. interests are excluded. Thus, while production in the United States about doubled from 1923 to 1943, foreign production increased by 180 per cent, chiefly because of the increase in Soviet output from 107,000 bbl. daily in 1923 to 675,000 bbl. daily in 1943.

However, even excluding Soviet-controlled production, the United States–owned share of all other foreign production declined from 57 per cent in 1922 to 39 per cent in 1941. This is a reflection of another factor, the relatively small interest the American companies secured in certain areas such as Iran, Iraq, and Trinidad, which underwent great expansion, but where other nationalities obtained preferential standing in concession and development rights.

Concern over Foreign Oil Policy.—The downward trend of the American-owned share of foreign oil production is causing concern to

American officials who are trying to establish a foreign oil policy and are exploring what our State Department might do to help combat the trend.

TABLE 5.—ESTIMATED AMERICAN-OWNED PRODUCTION IN FOREIGN COUNTRIES, 1860–1918

(In million barrels daily)

| Year | Total world | Total United States | % of world | Foreign | | | | | |
				Total foreign	Russia	Total foreign excluding Russia	American-owned foreign	% of total foreign	% of total foreign excluding Russia
1857–1860	*	*	96	*	...	*			
1870	16	14	91	2	1	1			
1880	82	72	88	10	8	2			
1890	210	126	60	84	79	5			
1900	409	174	43	234	208	26			
1910	898	574	64	324	193	131	9	2	6
1912	965	609	63	356	186	170	30	8	18
1914	1,113	728	65	385	179	206	50	13	24
1918	1,380	975	71	404	72	332	130	32	39
1920	1,905	1,210	64	695	76	619	330	48	53
1922	2,365	1,528	65	837	98	739	422	50	57
1923	2,793	2,007	72	787	107	680	311	40	46
1926	3,008	2,112	70	896	175	721	276	31	38
1929	4,079	2,760	68	1,320	282	1,038	392	30	38
1932	3,579	2,145	60	1,433	422	1,011	328	23	33
1935	4,524	2,730	60	1,794	498	1,296	462	26	36
1938	5,456	3,327	61	2,129	580	1,549	507	24	33
1941	6,076	3,842	63	2,234	647	1,587	610	27	39
1943	6,326	4,118	65	2,207	675	1,532	438	20	30

* Less than 500 bbl. daily.

A State Department memorandum on U. S. foreign petroleum policy dated Feb. 10, 1944, and prepared by Charles Rayner, petroleum adviser for the Special Senate Committee Investigating the National Defense Program (Truman Committee), gives the impression of vigilant and aggressive State Department activity in the interwar period. A "picture differing from that advanced by the State Department itself of consistent and effective diplomatic support of American nationals is unfolded by the record of the last decade which shows serious reverses suffered by

American interests in certain countries," says the report of the Foreign Oil Group.

It quotes Joseph E. Pogue as referring to "a change in the foreign oil policy of our government some 10 years ago, when the official attitude became one of indifference and neglect, if not discontinuance."

It cites the expropriation of foreign oil properties by the Mexican and Bolivian governments in 1938 and the rise of restrictive nationalizing governmental policies in other Latin-American countries.

Diplomatic Intervention Usually Post Facto.—"It is significant to note that United States diplomatic intervention in the last decade has been largely post facto and not one associated with a strong, established foreign oil policy," the report states. This is evidenced in the State Department's own memorandum of Feb. 10, 1944. The report quotes as follows from Henry Ozanne in "U. S. Foreign Oil Policy": "Government intervention in behalf of industry interests, it is clear from the State Department's own record, has been confined almost exclusively to consultation service *after* an issue has evolved. The expression 'good offices' figures prominently in the department statement. There was a growing awareness (from 1941) in the department [U. S. State Department] that government help has been extended only *after* a crisis had arisen, and too late to deal with it effectively. The anticipation of such situations of conflict would be one way of preventing them."

The Report of the Group on American Petroleum Interests in Foreign Countries also quotes from the testimony of Edward F. Johnson before the Special Senate Committee Investigating Petroleum Resources on June 27–28, 1945, to the effect that from Mr. Rayner's report it would appear "that during the periods mentioned when the public felt the need of foreign oil supplies, government was vigorous in its oil policies; otherwise, lacking the pressure of seeming necessity, governmental attention to oil developments abroad was less marked."

CHAPTER II

NUMBER ONE RISK—POLITICS

Political trends abroad have been referred to as "obstacles." The record shows this to be a mild characterization when applied to the risks encountered by American oil companies in many foreign countries during the last decade and a half. Expropriation of properties in Mexico and Bolivia, described fully later, is only part of the story. But highly important is the fact that the trend before the Second World War toward nationalization and confiscation is even more pronounced in the postwar world.

Those venturing into foreign fields must—and expect to—take the economic and physical risks involved on their own responsibility, and it will be seen that such risks in petroleum activities are considerable and unusual (Chap. III). But great as they are, they are less a risk factor in foreign investment than the political, which, being less predictable, offers the greatest uncertainty. Furthermore, political risks are compounded since they involve both the country whence the capital is derived and that in which it is being invested.

It is interesting to note, however, that despite the increasing political risks of recent years—in some countries converted into actual loss through confiscation and expropriation—American companies have persisted in seeking and hanging on to a foothold in foreign countries wherever possible.

One source of political risk greatly affecting foreign operations in the last two decades was the trend toward the nationalization both of national resources and of industries (cartelization).

Nationalization of the Subsoil.—As to natural resources, no foreign country, generally speaking, recognizes the surface landowner as the owner of the subsoil as does the United States. There are exceptions in some limited private titles existing in Canada, Colombia, Mexico, Trinidad, Rumania, and Poland. Excepted, also, are certain private titles belonging to native princes in India, Burma, and the two parts of British-controlled Borneo. Save for these, mineral rights in virtually all countries outside the United States belong to the sovereign nation

17

or to the state. The fact is that, to obtain oil rights in the foreign countries of the world, American companies must deal primarily with the sovereigns and not with private owners of land.

In other words, in foreign countries, generally the trend over a period of the last 25 years has been increasingly from private ownership of mineral rights to government ownership and control. This trend is traced in the testimony of Charles W. Hamilton, Edward F. Johnson, Laurence B. Levi, and others before the Special Senate Committee Investigating Petroleum Resources.

In countries where nationalization has occurred, a foreign corporation such as an American company often is either prohibited from doing business or can do business only as a minor stockholder of a national corporation.

Right in the Western Hemisphere nationalization of the subsoil has taken place on an ascending scale. This is true in Argentina, Uruguay, Chile, and Brazil, to name but a few, and has been far from conducive to American participation in the development of oil reserves in these countries.

Participation Difficult in Many Latin American Countries.—For instance, after commercial oil production had been developed by private companies including American concerns in several areas in Argentina, the government organized Yacimientos Petroliferos Fiscales (subsequently incorporated by an Act of Congress in 1932), which entered the oil business, and at that point, discriminations against the private companies began. By decree, reserve areas open only to Y.P.F. were established. The company also exerted pressure on the provincial governments to cancel existing titles held by private companies and to refuse further grants. Though not successful in canceling existing rights, the securing of further grants was blocked. Special privileges were granted to Y.P.F., including exemption from all federal taxes except the road tax, and free postage and reduced freight rates. Duties on imported material were eliminated. The private companies had to meet all these burdens.

Reserves in federal territory may be granted to Y.P.F. only. While theoretically private companies may obtain petroleum rights in the provinces, in practice there has been successful obstruction of the acquisition by private companies since before 1935—the date of the general oil law.

In 1936 the government by decree gave complete control of the importation of crude and products to the Y.P.F. Thus the private companies, with declining production and the necessity of clearing all import permits through it, were completely in the hands of Y.P.F. The situation reached the point in 1936 where one American company gave an option on its properties to Y.P.F. This option was never exercised because Y.P.F. did not get the approval of the Argentine Congress within the option period.

Unless the private companies obtain the right to explore for and to produce oil in Argentina or to import it to the extent of their requirements, their continuation in business is precarious indeed. The Argentine situation has been discussed almost continuously with the U. S. State Department, which has made repeated efforts to straighten it out. However, the status of the American petroleum industry in that country has steadily deteriorated.[1]

Uruguay in 1931 enacted a law that authorized the government to erect a refinery. On completion of the refinery the government was empowered to require all importers to refine their oil in the government refinery and to distribute under a system whereby the government fixed quotas and prices.

While private industry continues in business in this manner in Uruguay, the government may, under the law, create a complete oil monopoly for itself. Here again the U. S. State Department was unable to overcome the determination of Uruguay to handle its petroleum affairs on the basis outlined, but it was successful in preserving the position of American companies to some extent.

Petroleum recently has been discovered in Tierra del Fuego, Chile. The law of Chile permits only the state to search for and to develop the oil resources of the country. However, there has been before the Chilean Congress a bill that would permit private Chilean capital to participate in a Chilean company and allow foreign capital to hold a minority interest.

The Congress of Chile by law has reserved all refinery operations as a state monopoly. Furthermore, in 1932 Chile by law provided that state and Chilean capital should have a complete monopoly over the importation, distribution, and sale of petroleum products and authorized the president to fix the date when it should go into effect. After long negotiations with the foreign oil companies, the Chilean government decided not to put the law into effect, since two foreign-owned oil companies, one of which was American-controlled, operating in the market yielded almost half of their long-established distributing business to a Chilean company owned by national capital.

---

[1] Testimony of Edward F. Johnson before Special Senate Committee Investigating Petroleum Resources, June 28–29, 1945.

The law, though continuing in suspense, hangs over the heads of the foreign oil companies, subject to being placed in effect at any time by executive decree. The U. S. State Department has tried to help the oil companies in this situation but has been faced with the unyielding viewpoint of Chile.

Brazil is considered to be a likely prospect for the discovery of oil in large quantities. However, the government of Brazil does not look favorably on foreign participation in the country's petroleum industry. In 1931 the government issued a decree suspending all alienation of mineral deposits or lands on which a deposit was known to exist. In 1934 a new constitution was adopted requiring federal authorization to work mines and mineral deposits and declaring that such authorization would be granted exclusively to Brazilians or concerns organized in Brazil. In 1937 another constitution was adopted in which it was provided that mineral-deposit concessions could only be issued to Brazilians or enterprises constituted of Brazilian stockholders. This constitution was followed by a decree issued in 1938, which declared that there could be no private ownership of deposits of petroleum and natural gases. This decree eliminated rights that an American company had acquired in potential oil acreage from private owners in Brazil prior to the decree of 1931 against alienation.

In 1938 a law was passed making the petroleum industry a public utility and placing it under the direction and control of a national council on petroleum. This law placed oil refining entirely in the hands of native-born citizens, thus causing an American company immediately to stop construction of a small refinery at São Paulo. The Brazilian national council on petroleum has control over importation, transportation, and distribution and is empowered to fix maximum and minimum prices.

While American interests market petroleum products in Brazil, it will be seen that the official attitude in Brazil is not encouraging to American development of petroleum reserves there.

Trade Barriers and Monopolies in Marketing Abroad.—During the period of world depression when there were "dumping" of petroleum products and ruinous price wars, many European governments felt it necessary to attempt market stabilization for the protection of their internal economies.[1] Nationalistic restrictions sprang up in such coun-

[1] Laurence B. Levi, testifying at the joint hearing before the Special Senate Committee Investigating Petroleum Resources and the Subcommittee on Foreign Contracts of the Committee on the Judiciary on May 21, 1945.

The discovery well in the Itaparich field, State of Bahia, Brazil.

Derrick erected on coral reef well, Macio, Alagoas, Brazil.

Photographs by courtesy of J. E. Brantly.

Setting derrick corners coral reef well.

The above operations were carried on by American drilling contractors for the Brazilian government. Left to right in upper right picture: Paulo Sardinho (Brazilian), driller; Bob Evans, mechanic; Albert Scherera, driller; and Virgil McGathin (latter three Americans).

Trade Barriers Promoted Synthetic Plants and Forced Building of "Uneconomic" Refineries in Many Foreign Countries. See Page 20.

A Nazi Rothensee oil refinery near Magdeburg, summer of 1945, after RAF and AAF bombing. Approximately 35,000,000 lb. of gasoline and diesel-engine fuel oil per month flowed from this plant—4 per cent of Germany's synthetic oil output.

"Among the measures used to induce or force Americans to build refineries abroad are tariff differentials, foreign exchange restrictions, licensing of imports and refineries, and government participation in refining." See page 22.

Photographs by courtesy of Standard Oil Company (New Jersey).

Port Jerome refinery, Rouen, France.

tries in which American oil companies were carrying on a marketing and refining business, as Spain, Italy, France, Rumania, Czechoslovakia, Hungary, and Yugoslavia.

In fairness to the British, it might be pointed out that, while the British government has sought to restrict foreign including American operations in certain spheres of British influence, it has never in any way discriminated against American-owned operating companies doing business within the British Isles. In this connection its attitude has been very different from that of the other European countries referred to.

Serious marketing problems were imposed in those countries by restrictions in the nature of exchange controls and by the wide fluctuations that occurred in the relative value of the foreign currencies.

Many of the foreign governments, noting the adverse effects of these conditions upon their nationals engaged in the business and upon internal labor and economic conditions, became restive. Some countries enacted legislation providing for some form of market control; others were planning to adopt such measures; still others used pressure upon the industry to put its house in order. From all this evolved the making of trade agreements.

Local Trade Agreements.—The attitude of foreign governments toward local trade agreements varied only in degree, ranging from acquiescence or encouragement to compulsion by threat or by decree. In several instances, the government itself cartelized the industry or set up a petroleum regime in which the government was represented by direct or indirect ownership or control of a local oil company.

Agreements that affected the oil industry in foreign countries may be classified under two general headings:

1. By law, *i.e.*, government monopoly or compulsory cartel.
2. Trade agreements.

    a. By government direction or pressure.
    b. Organized by private initiative in accordance with the law of a country and permitted or encouraged by its government.

As has been seen, the American oil industry invested a very considerable amount of capital in refineries in foreign countries. Some of these refineries are economically justified because of the existence of indigenous production or near-by sources of supply. Others are not sound from a business standpoint, and in constructing them the oil companies, in most instances, were not free agents. They were obliged to conform with the policies that foreign governments considered to be in the national interest; and where refinery construction is based on political, military, or national considerations only, economic factors are usually ignored. The operation of these units often results in higher costs to the consumer, consequent restriction in demand, and unbalanced output that is out of line with internal consumption.[1]

Among the measures used to induce or force Americans to build refineries abroad are tariff differentials, foreign-exchange restrictions, licensing of imports and refineries, and government participation in refining.

Substitute Fuels Stimulated.—Foreign governments often imposed discriminatory excise taxes on imported commodities in order to stimulate the production and consumption of domestic products such as alcohol made from grain and other synthetic fuels.

Naturally this promotion and subsidizing of substitute fuels increased the cost and hazard of American investment in these countries.

Government promotion of substitute fuels took several forms, one or more of which might obtain at the same time. These may be listed as follows:

1. Compulsory purchase of such fuels by petroleum marketers as percentage of import or domestic manufacture of petroleum fuels.

2. Compulsory mixing law prescribing percentage of substitute fuel to be added to petroleum fuel.

3. Compulsory mixing to certain grades of fuel, these mixed fuel grades to be favored by lower excise taxes.

4. *Ad hoc* percentages for compulsory mixing or purchase that vary with harvests or other conditions.

5. Tax differentials to encourage use of substitute liquid fuels, gas, or coal in prime movers; for example, steam engines and turbines versus diesels, coal versus fuel oil for boilers.

6. Tax and duty exemptions or preferences on machinery or material imported for the production of substitutes and for vehicles using substitute fuels, such as wood-gas automobiles, etc.

This government promotion entailed two adverse developments for the marketer of petroleum as represented by American companies doing business in these countries. First, since companies operating in foreign countries plan and make their investments in anticipation of expansion rather than on a current sale basis, the arbitrary reduction of market

---

[1] Walter L. Faust in his testimony before the Special Senate Committee Investigating Petroleum Resources on June 28, 1945.

through substitute fuels resulted not only in a reduction of total turn-over profit but in unrecovered fixed costs as a penalty for long-term investment planning. Second, in acting as marketer at cost or less for the manufacturer of the substitute fuel the petroleum marketer undertook a large unprofitable operation. He took over the substitute fuel in bulk against immediate payment, provided special storage, and then blended, shipped, and dispersed it through his own outlets and collected payment from the ultimate consumer.

Foreign-exchange Restrictions.—In the interwar period exchange restrictions [1] were used by a number of countries, as a general rule, in order to balance their international payments, although other objectives have, at least ultimately, been sought. In Germany, for example, exchange control became an important part of their program to prepare for war. In other countries exchange restrictions were employed to promote national industry, to raise revenue, or to achieve other objectives.

The American petroleum industry's foreign-exchange experience as both an exporter from and an importer into foreign countries has had substantially the same net result: a considerable increase in costs. Because exchange restrictions prevented dollar remittances, it was necessary, in certain South American countries, to accept notes, varying in maturity from 2 to 15 years, in order ultimately to transfer funds accumulated. So far, none of these notes has come into default, although, subsequent to their issuance, they sold in the market at substantial discounts. The risk of loss is, however, always present. This situation is referred to as a source of potential cost increase and, therefore, one that has "contributed to an increase in the industry's risk assumption."

Classic Example of Nationalization in Mexico.—Mexico furnishes a classic example of the nationalization trend in Latin America. In reciting it in some detail it should be pointed out that the possibility of making retroactive the nationalistic or other restrictive legislation enacted in foreign countries is a definite risk to the foreign operations of American companies. This has more than fear as its basis; it has the background of costly experience. Not alone can the possibility of retroactive legislation act as a deterrent to companies against entering foreign countries, but it definitely can adversely affect operations after investments have been made. Mexico furnishes such a double example. But, first, some interesting history.

[1] J. E. Crane in testimony before the Special Senate Committee Investigating Petroleum Resources on June 28, 1945.

CHAPTER III

EXPROPRIATION AND SEIZURE

It follows naturally that American oil operators who were opening up new areas in the United States in the early days also should have gone into contiguous countries in their search for oil. A Boston ship captain, having purchased at Tuxpam, Mexico, a quantity of *chapopote*, or tar, for use on board ship, took some of it to Boston in 1876. A company was formed, and when he returned to Tuxpam he acquired a lease on Chapopote Nunez and Cerro Viejo, drilled two or three wells, found oil in small quantities, and built a little refinery on an island in the Tuxpam River. He brought the oil to the refinery at great expense and treated it, producing kerosene that he marketed in small quantities to the natives thereabouts. His associates in the business refused to furnish the funds for further exploitation. The old captain became discouraged and committed suicide. His bones lie buried at Tuxpam.

Later, a Londoner named Burke told Cecil Rhodes of the oil possibilities of the country south of the Tuxpam River. They formed a syndicate, called the London Oil Trust, in which Rhodes became a participant. After spending about £90,000 without result, they abandoned their direct efforts and sublet their holdings to a company called the Mexican Oil Corporation, which also spent £70,000 in an unsuccessful effort to develop the property profitably.

Before the turn of the century, the Waters-Pierce Oil Company (American) was operating a refinery in Mexico, importing oil from the United States.

Edward L. Doheny, an American who had prospected for gold in Mexico in the seventies and in the early nineties had drilled the first oil well within the city limits of Los Angeles, went back to Mexico in 1900 hunting oil. With him were C. A. Canfield, his California oil-prospector partner, and A. P. Maginnis, of the Santa Fe railway, some of whose locomotives were starting to burn oil. They made the trip at the suggestion of A. A. Robinson, president of the Mexican Central Railway Company, who had hopes of seeing oil developed somewhere near the line of his railroad.

At this time the law of Mexico for many years had specifically recognized the ownership of petroleum deposits by the surface-fee owner. Doheny and his associates invested $600,000 U. S. currency in the fee purchase of land in this district. In 1900 after the registration of the Mexican Petroleum Company (of California), drilling commenced near Ebano station in 1901, and in May of that year a small well was brought in. In 1904 the company removed its operations to Cerro de la Pez, a few miles south, where in that year it brought in its No. 1 well, which flowed for at least nine years, during which time it yielded approximately 3½ million barrels.

In September, 1910, the Huasteca Petroleum Company (a subsidiary of the Mexican Petroleum Company) brought in its Juan Casiano No. 7, first of Mexico's famous gushers to be successfully produced. Until the end of November, 1919, when it turned to salt water, it yielded 80 million barrels. In February, 1916, it brought in its Cerro Azul No. 4 well, which was certified by Dr. I. C. White, geologist, as producing 300,000 bbl. daily when it was opened.

Mexico's "Golden Lane."—The British Pearson (Cowdray) interests in 1906 began to acquire properties in the Tuxpam-Tampico region by the acquisition of the Pennsylvania Oil Company, and in April, 1908, the San Diego field, 52 miles south of Tampico, was discovered; but before the year was out, the entire field was destroyed when a well known as Dos Bocas "drilled itself in," caught fire, and burned and destroyed itself for some forty days. Dos Bocas was actually the first great gusher brought in in Mexico.

In 1910 the Portrero del Llano field was discovered by Aguila Company (Cowdray) when, in December, the famous Portrero del Llano No. 4 was brought in, making 100,000 bbl. daily. Over 100 million barrels were obtained from this well to December, 1918, when it went to salt water.

By 1911 Mexican oil production being marketed had reached 34,000 bbl. daily, of which more than half was American-owned, and proved reserves were estimated between 600 and 700 million barrels.

Mexico's Major Producing Areas.—There were two major oil-producing areas in Mexico—the "heavy-oil" fields in the Tampico, or Panuco River, area and the "light-oil" fields in the Tuxpam area, nearly all of which lay north of the Tuxpam River.

Mr. Doheny and his associates pioneered in the development of the heavy-oil fields, the first to be developed. The oil was of fuel-oil grade, ranging from 8 to 12° Bé. with practically no gasoline content. In the early years of this field's development the industries of the world thought of fuel in terms of coal—and decidedly not in terms of fuel oil; hence one can readily understand some of the obstacles that confronted the opening of the Mexican oil fields. The problem was essentially one of finding a market for oil of inferior quality.

Market Had to Be Created for Mexican Oil.—To complicate Doheny's problem, the great Spindletop gusher had just come in in the United States, and America had all the heavy oil it knew what to do with. Failing to make a fuel contract with the Mexican Central, Doheny organized a paving company in the City of Mexico.

"We finally paved about 50 per cent of that part of the City of Mexico that is now paved and also did all the paving done in the cities of Guadalajara, Morelia, Tampico, Durango, Puebla, and Chihuahua," Mr. Doheny said in 1922. "Thus failure to have a railway contract with the Mexican Central Railroad gave Mexico the best pavement on terms probably cheaper than any other country. These cities soon ranked among the best paved in the world."

Doheny also pioneered in creating a market in ships and locomotives and in factories for fuel oil burned under boilers.

"The markets were slow to absorb our product," he said, "although our first large customer, the Standard Oil Company, took from us 2 million barrels a year for a period of five years, paying for a large part of it in advance, much to our relief. We found it necessary to build up a market. This we did with success in the New England states and other North Atlantic ports."

Part Americans Played in Mexico's Great Oil Era.—The increased use of oil-burning ships for both commercial and military purposes created a tremendous demand during the First World War for the heavier grades of crude oil such as those produced in Mexico. The country, therefore, underwent its greatest expansion during and immediately following the First World War, with Americans leading the way. American-owned production amounted to 79.5 per cent in 1922.

The development of Mexican production between the period 1912–1922 and the part American companies played in it are shown graphically in Table 6.

Standard Oil and Independents in Mexico.—Standard Oil and many independent American oil interests went into Mexico, in both the light- and heavy-oil fields during and immediately after the First World War.

"With the Doheny and Standard interests they have made the so-called Tampico area, which is the center of the most important oil-production section of the republic, a small cross section of Yankeeland," Isaac Marcosson wrote in 1924. "During the periodic Mexican revolutions—and they are almost as regular as civil wars in China—Tampico invariably becomes a storm center. More than once American warships have been sent there to awe the rebels and protect the American properties whose value runs into many millions of dollars."

TABLE 6.—AMERICAN SHARE OF MEXICAN OIL PRODUCTION

(In barrels daily)

Year	Production	American-owned production	% American-owned
1912	45,200	25,900	57.3
1913	70,400	40,300	57.2
1914	71,900	41,200	57.3
1915	90,200	51,600	57.2
1916	102,300	58,600	57.3
1917	151,700	99,500	65.6
1918	175,900	124,800	70.9
1919	253,300	187,900	74.2
1920	445,500	320,800	72.0
1921	549,500	401,900	73.1
1922	508,500	404,200	79.5

During the period of greatest development more than 25 American concerns were active in producing Mexican oil, including Mexican Petroleum Company of California (Doheny), Huasteca Petroleum Company (Doheny), Texas Company of Mexico, Island Oil & Transport Company, East Coast Oil Company (Southern Pacific), Mexican Gulf Oil Company, Southern Oil & Transport Company, Freeport & Mexican Fuel Oil Corporation (Sinclair Gulf), Cia Mex. de Combustible (Pierce Oil), Panuco Boston Oil Company (Atlantic Refining Company), International Petroleum Company (John Hays Hammond), Transcontinental Oil Company (Standard Oil Company of New Jersey), and Penn Mex. Fuel Company (South Penn Oil Company).

United States Has Brief Experience as Net Importer of Oil.—A substantial part of Mexico's great post–First World War output was imported into the United States to offset the deficiencies in United States supplies. In the three years 1920, 1921, and 1922 total imports into the United States were greater than its exports—the only time in the history of the industry in the United States, prior to the Second World War, that this country was a net importer.

Decline of Mexican Output.—The producing fields in the "Golden Lane" started to show water in 1920. However, new areas were discovered, not only helping to retard the decline but expanding output to an all-time peak of 550,000 bbl. daily in 1921. The discovery of new areas did not continue at a rate sufficient to offset the decline of the older fields, however, and during the next five years the output of the country was reduced by over 50 per cent. Output declined further in the ensuing years, never again to reach the early levels.

Political Developments Retarded Mexican Operations.—Shortly after the pioneers found oil in that country, Mexico was torn by civil strife and revolution. On May 1, 1917, the Carranza Constitution vesting ownership of the subsoil in the state was adopted. The effect of this was almost as restrictive as a geological or physical limitation of the pay territory. It definitely held operations largely to so-called "old territory," *i.e.*, to the lands that had been legally acquired by the companies largely in fee from old owners, since fear that its provisions would be made retroactive stifled the incentive to extend operations to new areas.

Through the next 10 years producing operations were limited to lands owned or leased from individuals before May 1, 1917, and all in the two districts—the northern or Panuco district, known as the "heavy-oil district," and the southern or Tampico district, containing in all about 30,000 hectares.

In 1926, practically all of the wells finishing in the pay were being drilled in old territory—in territory well drilled at a previous time and consequently subjected to heavy drains or in territory being rapidly drilled up and heavily drawn upon. At that time it was pointed out that there was not a really genuine wildcat among the list of pay completions.

This restriction of operations largely to old territory in Mexico reflected the legal uncertainties surrounding the acquirement and development of new areas after the adoption of the Carranza Constitution. Eight years elapsed before a petroleum law was passed interpreting the terms of the constitution, making it practically impossible in the meantime for the oil companies to conduct normal operations. In the matter of acquiring new lands doubt existed as to how and with whom to deal for properties.

irst shipment of oil in May, 1911, from Huasteca fields of Mexico by S.S. "Captain . F. Lucas."

Doheny also pioneered in creating a market in ships and locomotives for fuel oil burned nder boilers." See page 26.

hotographs by courtesy of Standard Oil Company (Indiana) from "Mexican Petroleum," Pan American Petroleum d Transport Company, 1922.

3unkering of S.S. "Aquitania" from S.S. "Edward L. Doheny, Junior," New York, July, 920.

"More Than 25 American Concerns Were Active in Producing Mexican Oil" Before Nationalization.   See Page 27.

Photograph by courtesy of Standard Oil Company (Indiana)

Mexican Petroleum Company's refinery No. 1 at Tampico, 1922.

Incomplete returns of "losses sustained by American companies as a direct result of expropriation in Mexico" total over $100,000,000.   See page 32.

Gulf Oil Company of Mexico building road in Mexico.

Photographs from Oil Trade Journal, July, 1918

Tanker and tug installing The Texas Company's loading line in Mexico, 1918.

Mexico's "Golden Lane" Gushers Finally Went to Salt Water

"Potrero del Llano No. 4 well of the British Pearson interests 1909–1919 was located by American geologist, E. L. de Golyer. Over 100 million barrels were obtained from this well to December, 1918, when it went to salt water." See page 25.

Potrero del Llano No. 4 well, world's greatest producer of oil.

Photographs on this and next page from Oil Trade Journal, January, 1919.

Camp house at Potrero del Llano in 1909 before field was developed where Mr. de Golyer lived.

Potrero No. 4 immediately after it w capped in March, 1911.

Potrero del Llano No. 4 came in Dec. 27, 1910.   Picture on preceding page was taken by Mr. de Golyer when it was 10 days old.

Concrete structure erected over Potrero No. 4 in 1911 and completely sealed in 1913 when political disturbances forced American and British oil men to leave the country. L. F. Russ (standing) and Mr. de Golyer (1911).

Four different petroleum codes were introduced in the Mexican Congress at different times after 1917 and passed by one or the other branch of the legislature, without becoming law. In 1925 a petroleum law was finally passed.

President Carranza in 1918 did attempt to carry the change of ownership resulting from the constitution into effect and issued decrees that required the companies to recognize the nation's title and to pay rentals and royalties to the government, but the companies instituted *amparos*, or injunctions, on the ground that if the constitution were applied retroactively according to its terms, confiscation of their property would result.

Certain other *amparo* suits were decided by the Supreme Court that stated that properties owned prior to May, 1917, upon which it could be shown that some "positive act" had been performed showing the intention of the owner to devote that particular land to petroleum exploitation, retained for the surface owners subsoil ownership. The question as to what constituted a positive act was the subject of discussion between oil executives and Mexican officials and figured in the diplomatic phases of the matter.

Diplomatic Notes Stressed Retroactive Feature.—All during the intervening years conferences were held between Americans and other foreign oil interests and the Mexican government. The Mexican government stood behind the petroleum law signed by the president on Dec. 26, 1925, and the regulations of that law published on Apr. 8, 1926. The crisis was reached at the end of the latter year, which was the limit prescribed for oil companies owning land or leases acquired prior to May 1, 1917, to make application for "confirmatory concessions."

Correspondence between the American and Mexican governments released by Secretary of State Kellogg revealed that the American State Department strongly backed the contention made by the oil companies, that the new law was in effect retroactive. The "final" communication of Secretary Kellogg had as its chief point that the Mexican government had agreed during the conferences of the Mixed Commission in Mexico City in 1923 that the land and petroleum laws would not be made retroactive with regard to American properties acquired before these laws went into effect. With the rejection of this point in the response of Foreign Minister Saenz, dated Nov. 17, 1926, the strained diplomatic relationship was precipitated.

Under the contention of the United States, these laws were confiscatory of properties held by foreigners and, if made retroactive, would mean that the oil fields, mines, and ranches purchased by American citizens would become the property of the Mexican government in accordance with provisions of the Mexican Constitution of 1917, which the law that became effective on Jan. 1, 1927, was intended to carry out.

In his correspondence Secretary Kellogg pointed out that under the Mexican oil law owners who acquired titles prior to the enforcement of the Constitution of May 1, 1917, were required, under penalty of forfeiture, to apply within one year for "confirmation" of their titles and to accept concessions for not more than 50 years from the time exploitation work began.

"In these circumstances," the American note said, "American nationals who have made investments in Mexico in reliance upon unqualified titles would be obliged to file applications virtually surrendering these vested rights and to accept in lieu thereof concessions of manifestly lesser scope and value.

"That a statute so construed and enforced is retroactive and confiscatory because it converts exclusive ownership under positive Mexican law into a mere authorization to exercise rights for a limited period of time is, in the opinion of my government, not open to any doubt whatever."

The American note further objected to the Mexican contention that the owner of the surface land who acquired title prior to May 1, 1917, acquired only an optional right to the subsoil, and that, consequently, he held no vested right until he performed an act looking to appropriation of the oil deposits.

"It has been and is the position of my government," Mr. Kellogg stated in this respect, "that the surface owner in these cases is the owner of certain subsoil deposits, including petroleum, that under proper application of the doctrine of positive acts the rights of American nationals claiming petroleum deposits under titles acquired prior to May 1, 1917, must in most, if not all, instances be effectively conceded.

"My government does not feel that it is just to require in any case that the deed or lease of lands, or the lease of subsoil rights, shall have set forth the purpose for which the property was to be used. It is unreasonable to expect that the seller should have included in the instrument of transfer the statement of the purposes for which the purchaser was acquiring the property or right."

The attitude of the Mexican government in backing the petroleum law may be summed up in the following from its reply of Oct. 7, 1926: "The mere retroactive character of a law, taken by itself and until it does produce confiscatory effects or is harmful in any way when applied, cannot give rise to any objection whatsoever, nor be the cause of diplomatic representation."

That the foreign oil interests were amply justified in their fear of retroactive application of the Constitution of 1917 was eventually borne out. The support of American companies by our government was ineffectual in the thirties as agitation against foreign oil interests by communistic labor elements in Mexico gathered momentum, culminating in seizure of properties.

Unconscionable awards to labor were made. Management was stripped of many of its normal administrative functions. Companies felt that justice was denied them in the Mexican courts. Finally, as the result of their inability to carry out a labor award beyond their economic capacity, the Mexican government, on Mar. 18, 1938, expropriated properties of the American and British oil companies with few exceptions. This action substantially culminated the retroactive application so long feared by the operators, since the Mexican government, in applying the decree of expropriation, and the courts, in interpreting it, did so on the basis that the subsoil had belonged to the government.

American oil companies unsuccessfully litigated in the Mexican courts. Having exhausted remedial steps open to them in Mexico, there was nothing further the companies could do. The matter then became one for the two interested governments to handle. While recognizing the right of the Mexican government to expropriate the properties, the Department of State insisted that the companies were entitled to prompt, adequate, and effective compensation.

Certain American companies made monetary settlements by direct negotiations with the Mexican government. With respect to other American companies, the Secretary of State and the Mexican ambassador in 1941 agreed upon a general plan of settlement under which a commission, known as the Cooke-Zevada Commission, consisting of two experts, one for each government, would fix compensation for nationals of the United States whose properties and rights in the petroleum industry in Mexico were affected by the acts of expropriation or seizure of the Mexican government subsequent to Mar. 18, 1938. While the companies affected by the plan did not approve this plan of settlement, data were submitted to assist the experts appointed by the two governments in the performance of their duties. Under this plan the valuation placed by the experts on the properties appraised was approximately 24 million dollars plus interest of approximately 5 million dollars, although the properties were valued by the owners at several times that amount.

Losses from Expropriation in Mexico.—An attempt to ascertain losses sustained by American companies as a direct result of expropriation in Mexico has been made by a questionnaire sent to the companies. Incomplete returns from only four American companies show the following:

(In U. S. dollars)

	Estimated gross loss	Compensation received [1]	Estimated net loss
Total for four companies. . .	104,363,000	23,710,000	80,653,000

[1] Exclusive of interest.

These total figures are neither complete nor representative as showing the actual loss incurred in the Mexican expropriation but are given simply as actual for the four companies reporting.

Properties of British companies in Mexico were also expropriated, following which England embargoed all oil from this source, an embargo still in effect. On Feb. 7, 1946, through an exchange of notes by the Mexican government with the Dutch and British diplomatic representatives, an agreement was reached for negotiating a settlement for the expropriated oil properties of Dutch and British nationals.

Experience Costly to Mexico Itself.—To the end of 1943 the fields in Mexico had produced 2,125 million barrels and at the end of 1943 had a proved reserve remaining of over 680 million barrels, all of which were in fields discovered by the expelled private operators. The Mexican government so far has been unable to develop any new reserves.

"It seems to me that in the long run the Mexican experience is an unfortunate one not only for this country but also for Mexico itself," Edward F. Johnson concluded in his testimony.[1]

"Mexico contains large deposits of oil. It is the nearest substantial source of oil supply outside this country. It would seem that oil reserves closest to home would be the most important because of their ready accessibility in time of need. If the action taken by Mexico has

[1] Before the Special Senate Committee Investing Petroleum Resources June 28–29, 1945.

any validity or influence as a precedent on other oil-producing countries, its influence could be far-reaching and harmful to the national interests of the United States. With the American oil industry operating in Mexico during the First World War, Mexican oil badly needed was then available in abundance. In contrast, during the Second World War, with the American oil industry ousted from Mexico, no important quantity of oil was available from that country for war purposes. Fortunately, Venezuela with its open-door policy averted what might have been serious oil trouble."

As noted by Mr. Johnson, important oil fields had been discovered in Venezuela where operating conditions were favorable and the policy of the government was to encourage development by foreign capital. The companies turned their attention to these new and more promising fields as the period of liquidation and of abandonment of Mexican investments began.

It was only natural that threatened seizure of American oil, land, and other properties in Mexico should have aroused concern in oil circles here. Mexico is our next-door neighbor. The value of the holdings ran to substantial amounts—considerably beyond the capacity of that country to pay if confiscated. And there was the fear that if Mexico succeeded in the expropriation, radical elements in other governments might follow suit.

Seizure of American Properties in Bolivia.—The seizure of the properties of the Standard Oil Company of Bolivia by the Bolivian government on Mar. 15, 1937, raised similar fears.

After the First World War, when concern over a possible shortage spurred a world-wide search for oil, the Standard Oil Company (New Jersey) acquired in 1921 from the Richmond Levering Company, an American corporation, the latter's rights to a concession in Bolivia. The government approved the transfer in July, 1922, by a formal resolution that included certain mutually agreed-upon modifications in the original agreement with Richmond Levering.

The company's concession was in the heart of a tropical jungle, isolated from all transportation facilities. Geologists had to explore this wild country on foot. Roads had to be cut through the tangled underbrush and over mountains, and drilling machinery, shipped from the United States, had to be hauled to well locations by horsedrawn vehicles. Up to 1937 the company spent 17 million dollars in exploration, in drilling 28 wells, and in the construction of two small refineries, camps, roads, and sanitation facilities.

Falling crude prices during the middle twenties made it impossible for Bolivian oil to compete with imports at consuming centers. Domestic oil consumption was comparatively small. Bolivia has no seacoast, and since the wells were located in the southern part of the country, Argentina would normally have been the most logical foreign market. But high Argentine import duties and the lack of transportation facilities discouraged exports in that direction.

So while there was oil in Bolivia, the absence of sufficient markets, either domestic or foreign, made intensive development economically unsound. Nor did the company's contract with the government, which was to run for 55 years, require it. Prior to 1928 the Bolivian government raised the question as to the proper date when "production" began under the contract and the correspondingly higher surface rentals applied. In July of that year it was agreed that, irrespective of production, higher rentals should begin Jan. 1, 1930, and thereafter the company paid the graduated scale of taxes, reaching the maximum some time prior to the seizure of its properties.

In July, 1931, the succeeding administration suddenly revoked this agreement and ordered the company to pay surface rentals as though production had begun in 1924 instead of in 1930. Court action followed. In November, 1936, the president and cabinet signed a decree authorizing the return to the company of a bond that had been posted as a guarantee, stating in the preamble that the company had fully complied with obligations for which the money had been deposited.

At this point a radical change of the government's oil policy became apparent. The first step came in December, 1936, when the Yacimientos Petroliferos Fiscales Bolivianos, a government-sponsored oil enterprise, was created.

On Mar. 15, 1937, a government representative, accompanied by agents of the Y.P.F.B., appeared without warning at the La Paz office of the Standard Oil Company of Bolivia with notice of a decree issued secretly two days before, declaring forfeit the company's entire possessions in Bolivia. Wells, refineries, equipment, records, and office furniture were seized.

The confiscation decree was signed by the same president and cabinet that only five months before had authorized return of the company's bond on the ground that it had complied in every way with the terms of its contract.

The confiscation was based on the charge that the Standard Oil Company (Argentina) was secretly importing crude oil from Bolivia by a "clandestine" pipe line. The Argentine government previously had appointed a commission to investigate, which visited the region and in December, 1935, reported that the accusations were without foundation.

The government claimed the right to confiscate the properties of the Standard Oil Company of Bolivia in case of fraud under a clause in the old contract with the Richmond Levering Company in 1920.

During several years beginning in 1935 there was a violent campaign against the company in Bolivia. On Mar. 8, 1939, came a ruling of the Bolivian Supreme Court dismissing the company's appeal. The company's last possible legal remedy in Bolivia was therefore exhausted.

Up to the time of the seizure of its properties the Standard Oil Company of Bolivia had recovered neither interest nor amortization on its 17-million-dollar investment in that country. The company petitioned the U. S. State Department formally to intervene with the Bolivian government, seeking either a return of the properties or the submission of the case to international arbitration.

"The concern of Standard Oil Company (New Jersey) over the arbitrary seizure of its subsidiaries' holdings in Mexico and Bolivia extends far beyond the actual value of the properties involved," the company said. "For if the action of these nations in confiscating without warning, recompense, or the slightest shred of legal basis the rightful possessions of American citizens who have made heavy investments in the best of faith and spent long years in developing the natural resources of the countries is permitted to go unchallenged, it inevitably will lead to the deterioration of economic and political relations on the American continents."

Bolivian Settlement Represents Large Loss.—A settlement was made, dated Jan. 27, 1943, between the government of Bolivia and the company. Under this agreement the government of Bolivia paid to the Standard Oil Company (New Jersey) a total of $1,500,000 U. S. currency for the sale of all its rights, interests, and properties in Bolivia and those of its subsidiary, Standard Oil Company of Bolivia, as they existed immediately prior to Mar. 13, 1937. This represented a net loss of $15,500,000 to the company.

Restrictive Governmental Policies in Other Latin American Countries.—The great percentage of oil operations of Colombia and Peru is conducted by foreign oil companies in which American interests have a large investment, and each country has developed fairly substantial production, most of which is exported. Ecuador has also been the scene of nominal oil developments for foreign capital.

In his previously mentioned memorandum, Mr. Rayner refers to the "diplomatic aid consisting of the extension of our good offices looking to the expeditious and equitable handling of operating problems" in the cases of Venezuela and Colombia and states where "satisfactory results have been achieved."

This statement is not concurred in by the American foreign petroleum group, which points to the record as being far from satisfactory because "of lack of strong diplomatic support." For example, Mr. Rayner paints the situation in Colombia as quite favorable. That American participation in the development of oil in Latin American countries has been increasingly difficult and complicated is evident. Colombia's oil laws have long contained various restrictive provisions that have hindered expensive exploratory work, and as a result the country has not had the same intensive development as occurred in Venezuela, for instance.

Summary of Political Problems.—American oil interests have been ousted from Bolivia through confiscation and from Mexico through expropriation. Their activities in Argentina, Chile, and Uruguay have been substantially curtailed by government action. In Brazil they are not permitted to participate in the search for oil. In Venezuela serious problems have arisen but thus far have been satisfactorily dealt with.

In the Middle East the American position seems to be established favorably. In the Dutch East Indies prior to their occupation by the Japanese during the Second World War, Americans engaged in the oil industry there fared acceptably.

On the other hand, there are some countries—among them India, Burma, China, and the Philippines—with oil-producing possibilities from which American oil interests are either barred outright or are faced with inhospitable laws.

CHAPTER IV

TIME LAGS THAT MEAN MILLIONS

As if political risks were not enough to contend with in foreign petroleum investment, there is always high venture in the form of economic risks. Of course, as previously stated, the oil companies have to expect and take these risks on their own responsibility, but that they have so wholeheartedly accepted them is a tribute to the daring of American enterprise.

However, it is a "big-company" field largely; it has to be because the hazards and financial cost are far too great for small companies to assume as a general rule. In fact, even the larger companies find that the factors of risk and cost have increased to the point of taxing their individual facilities and have sought to join their efforts in many cases, especially in the field of exploration and production and to a lesser degree in refining and marketing. These joint ventures are usually in the form of jointly owned companies operating in a particular area.

American Companies with Foreign Investments.—Only 22 American companies with foreign investments are listed, of which six engage in all branches of activity abroad directly or through subsidiaries and affiliates. There are many others that make and sell American petroleum products for export without having any direct investment abroad on their part.

A list of some of the American oil companies that have foreign investments is given on page 38. These companies, representing probably 93 to 95 per cent of the total American oil investment abroad, have several hundred subsidiaries and affiliates. While, as indicated, six companies are in all branches of activity abroad, it will be noted, all but two engage in exploration or production.

Joint Venture to Share Cost and Risk.—Although joint ventures are for the most part concluded between American companies, some also are with foreign companies. The Iraq Petroleum Company represents one of the first ventures of this kind. Originally organized in 1911 by British, Dutch, and German interests and an individual foreign entrepreneur, it became the subject of considerable negotiation after the

37

First World War (see p. 91). With the urging and support of our State Department five American companies acquired a combined 23¾ per cent interest. Later three of these American companies ceded their

AMERICAN OIL COMPANIES WITH INVESTMENTS IN FOREIGN COUNTRIES [1]

Company	Exploration and/or production	Refining	Transportation	Marketing
Amerada Petroleum Co.	Yes			
American Maracaibo Co.	Yes			
The Atlantic Refining Co.	Yes			Yes
Barnsdall Oil Co.	Yes			
James B. Berry Sons' Co.				Yes
Cities Service Co.	Yes			Yes
Compania de Petroleo Ganso Azul Ltda.	Yes	Yes		Yes
Continental Oil Co.	Yes			
Gulf Oil Corp.	Yes	Yes	Yes	Yes
Maracaibo Oil Exploration Co.	Yes			
Pantepec Petroleum Co.	Yes			
Phillips Petroleum Co.	Yes			
Pure Oil Co.	Yes	Yes		
Seaboard Oil Co. of Delaware	Yes			
Sinclair Oil Corp.	Yes	Yes	Yes	Yes
Socony-Vacuum Oil Co.	Yes	Yes	Yes	Yes
Standard Oil Co. of California	Yes	Yes	Yes	Yes
Standard Oil Co. (New Jersey)	Yes	Yes	Yes	Yes
Sun Oil Co.	Yes			Yes
The Texas Co.	Yes	Yes	Yes	Yes
Tide Water Associated Oil Co.		Yes		Yes
Union Oil Co. of California	Yes	Yes		

[1] Subsidiaries or affiliated companies are not included in this list.

share to the remaining two. As a result the Iraq Petroleum Company today is jointly owned by British, Dutch, French, and American interests. The American interests are Standard Oil Company (New Jersey) and Socony-Vacuum Oil Company, together owning 23¾ per cent of the company.

There also is the fifty-fifty partnership in the Kuwait Oil Company formed in 1934 by the D'Arcy Exploration Company (subsidiary of Anglo-Iranian Oil Company, Limited) and the Gulf Exploration Company (subsidiary of Gulf Oil Corporation), which is developing oil in Kuwait on the Persian Gulf.

Development of concessions in the Middle East on the island of Bahrein in the Persian Gulf and on the mainland of Saudi Arabia, as well as in the Dutch East Indies and elsewhere in the Middle and Far East, is a joint venture of the Standard Oil Company of California and The Texas Company.

Another illustration is the joint venture of Cities Service Company and Socony-Vacuum Oil Company to drill on a possible oil structure in the waters off Prince Edward Island.

Exploration and Production "Teams" in South America.—Joint venture in foreign exploration and production, particularly in South America, has been on an increased scale by American oil companies in the last few years.

Formation of Tri-Pet Corporation, jointly owned by Sinclair Oil Corporation, Cities Service Company (Pennsylvania), and the Richfield Oil Corporation of California, was recently announced. Tri-Pet Corporation has formed a company to operate in Colombia under the name of Compania Unidas de Petroleo.

In 1939, on completion of the Sagoc pipe line jointly owned by Socony-Vacuum and The Texas Company, an agreement was reached to explore and develop jointly extensive areas in the province of Bolivar, Colombia, adjacent to the pipe line.

Two minor cooperative ventures in Colombia for the purpose of exploration, each covering only a single concession, were undertaken in 1941 by Socony-Vacuum Oil Company, The Texas Company, and Richmond Petroleum Company (Standard Oil Company of California) and in 1944 by Socony-Vacuum and Shell Oil Company.

Many types of joint-interest operation exist in Venezuela, the details of which are not generally available.

Other Types of Joint Venture.—Another type of joint venture is the integration of enterprises when the facilities or supplies of one company complement those of another company. An example is the integration of the Far Eastern production and refining of Standard Oil Company (New Jersey) and the marketing facilities of Socony-Vacuum Oil Company through the formation of the Standard-Vacuum Oil Company.

The Bahrein Petroleum Company, Limited, formed by joining the Bahrein Island production of Standard Oil Company of California with the distribution and marketing facilities of The Texas Company in the East, is another example

Of the same general type, though differing in form and character in some respects, is the Intava arrangement between Standard Oil Company (New Jersey) and Socony-Vacuum for the distribution in all areas outside the United States of petroleum products for aviation purposes. In this joint venture the distribution facilities of Socony-Vacuum in those areas in which it operates complement those of the Standard Oil Company (New Jersey) in those different areas where it has such facilities. This joint venture made possible the servicing by American nationals of international air lines at important points throughout the world outside the United States.

Usually Local Subsidiaries with Local Minority Shareholders.—In many if not in most instances foreign refining and marketing operations in which American companies are interested are carried out through locally incorporated subsidiaries in which there are frequently local minority interests in the form of individual shareholders. For example, Standard Oil Company (New Jersey) operations in Denmark, Norway, Finland, Holland, Belgium, France, and Italy are conducted through local subsidiary companies in which there are local minority shareholders.

France is a market in which the Standard Oil Company (New Jersey), Gulf Oil Corporation, and Atlantic Refining Company interests in refining and marketing operations are shared through an American holding company. This in turn controls French operating companies in which as minority shareholders are a French bank and numerous private individuals.

It is also true that British and Dutch interests in Continental European and Mediterranean markets are comprised of locally incorporated subsidiary companies in which there are frequently quite extensive minority holdings in the hands of local and private shareholders.

Heavy Initial Investment.—Foreign oil operations are much more difficult as a rule than those in this country. They involve not only extraordinary expenditures for exploration work but also usually the creation of all necessary plant facilities for storing and transporting of material to and in the producing field and the handling and storage of oil therefrom to and on board ocean tankers.

In other words, there is a heavy initial investment.

"Long Time No See" Money Return.—Moreover, there is a considerable time lag between initial investment and initial returns, if any—and that is where high-water costs sometimes go to flood levels.

Except possibly in Europe and parts of Canada, American oil companies in foreign operations have found it necessary to construct their own highways, to transport their own materials and supplies, to build houses and industrial buildings in addition to drilling their own wells. In fact, often they have had to construct completely integrated communities. All the activities and services incidental to the exploration, production, and handling of crude oil must be created at oil-company cost and with oil-company labor.

Unlike a domestic manufacturing undertaking, for instance, an oil company in foreign operations has to exist through an indefinite period of exploration before any income is obtained. Experience has taught that, when oil production eventually is found and established, the proportion of cost of production represented by the amortization of the deferred charges of exploration and development is a very considerable proportion of cost of production. It also has shown that, while costs of production are appreciable when compared with domestic cost, they are nevertheless a minor part of the total cost of production in foreign operations.

Often heavy initial expenditures have to be made in foreign countries far out of proportion to those necessary for starting work in the relatively accessible fields of the United States. The mere embarking on the undertaking by investing in a concession or lease usually involves commitments far in excess of the first expenditure. These commitments are made in connection with the development program to be undertaken within a time specified either by the local law or company program or both. Almost invariably, large amounts of capital are required to meet these initial-investment costs.

Initial Cost and Time Lag, and Concessions That Don't Pan Out.— Some idea of the magnitude of these "deferred charges" is given in the many typical examples listed in the Report of the Group on American Petroleum Interests in Foreign Countries.

Furthermore, many leases and concessions upon which considerable money is expended for exploration and development do not pay out at all. Examples are given involving losses from about $100,000 to nearly 9 million dollars.

Many American oil companies lost heavily on their investments in Mexico during the First World War and in the early twenties when Mexican producing fields went to salt water. Some pioneer companies, however, on the whole, were on the right side of the ledger and made substantial profits in the venture.

Refineries were built in Mexico costing millions of dollars, and some were never operated or were closed six months after completion. Pipe

lines were laid that did not transport enough oil to lubricate them properly. One oil company purchased a railroad for both freight and passenger traffic, running from Tampico to Panuco. It was forced to sell the
road for scrap because of lack of traffic.

Struggle to Develop Barco Concession.—A classic example of time
lag in monetary return is the development by American interests of the
Barco concession in Colombia originally held by the Carib Syndicate,
Limited, an American company. Graphic testimony to the inaccessibil-
ity of this tract later to become producing only after the most arduous
experiences of several American oil companies is an account of an expedition made to it in 1917 by W. E. Griffiths, C. K. MacFadden, J. E.
Burnett, A. J. Fyfe, V. Barco, Jose Murillo, George Dubois, and other
Carib Syndicate officials. A large party of woodsmen and rivermen
accompanied the party.

The Barco concession, though located in Colombia, was scarcely accessible except through Venezuela, for it is situated on the eastern slope
of the Andes adjoining the Venezuelan boundary line. It consisted of
a solid body of land containing about 800,000 acres on which numerous
seepages were known.

The party left New York early in March on one of the steamers that
called at Puerto Rico and Curaçao, en route to Maracaibo, Venezuela.
Arriving at the latter place, it took a shallow-draught river steamer to
the mouth of the Catatumbo River on the west side of Lake Maracaibo
and proceeded up this river to Encontrados, Venezuela, a distance of
about 200 miles.

Evinrude Motors on Canoes.—Here, because of the extreme low water
in the river, the party transferred to boats of shallower draught and
followed the course of the Catatumbo to the Zulia River and up this
stream about 100 miles to Villamizar, Colombia. To assist the polemen,
who under these unusual conditions would have had to pole the boats
against a rather rapid current, four Evinrude motors with 4 hp. each
were attached to a dugout canoe of native construction and, with a
larger barge in tow containing the baggage and passengers and a heter-
ogeneous assortment of freight and mail, a record trip was made.

At Villamizar a stop of a few days was necessary to complete the out-
fitting of the expedition, during which time the city of Cúcuta, capital
of the state of North Santander, was visited. Then the real explorative
work started.

The land contained no white inhabitants. It was covered with un-
broken virgin forests, traversed by numerous clear streams, many of

which are navigable throughout the year. The forests were full of game, which supplemented the commissary of the expedition. The party visited many of the oil seepages. Often a way had to be cleared. The advance trail makers of the party had a lively skirmish with a wandering band of Motilone Indians, who were evidently on a hunting expedition and some 75 miles away from their usual stamping ground in the higher mountain land to the north in Venezuela. A description of this adventure follows.

Indians Kill Trail Cutter with Arrows.—"These savages are stated to be perhaps the most uncivilized in South America and although armed only with bow and arrow are not to be despised as warriors. In the initial brush with the savages, one of the natives employed by the expedition in cutting a trail to an important seepage was struck by two large wooden arrows. The first entered the shoulder, breaking the collar-bone; the second entered the back and went almost entirely through the body of the victim, passing through the lung and causing the death of the man. The two arrows were removed from the body, and they, with eight or ten others found in the forest at the point of attack, form a rather gruesome exhibit of this feature of the trip.

"The Colombian government at once provided the party with a company of sharpshooters for protection and no further evidence of Indians was found, nor does the party anticipate any difficulty in future operations on the property; for former experience with this tribe by the Colon Development Company, an English company operating in Venezuelan territory near by, points to the Indians keeping a safe distance from the white settlers and their camps and habitations."

Over the Andes and down the Magdalena.—The party then explored access to the Barco concession keeping within the confines of Colombia. After returning to Cúcuta, a 200-mile trip across the Andes was commenced. A pack train of about 20 mules was used, and after some interesting experiences in trying to keep warm at an elevation of 8,000 to 10,000 ft. the warm and humid valley of the Magdalena was reached where a steamer was taken to Cartagena, and from there another to the United States.

Many Vicissitudes before Oil Developed.—The Barco concession underwent many vicissitudes before its oil began to travel over the mountains and down to the sea. It was originally granted in 1905 to General Don Vergilio Barco, who had discovered seepages that suggested the probability of large deposits in the area. For several years General

Barco tried unsuccessfully to enlist capital in the development of the concession.

In 1918 the concession was transferred to Compania Colombiana de Petroleo. Three quarters of the company's shares were owned by Henry L. Doherty & Company and one quarter by the Carib Syndicate. In 1925 the Doherty interest was taken over by the South American Gulf Oil Company, a wholly owned subsidiary of the Gulf Oil Corporation. The following year the concession was canceled by the Colombian government on the claim that the required amount of development work had not been performed. Attempts to obtain its reinstatement resulted, in 1931, in an undertaking known as the Chaux-Folsom agreement, which was ratified by the Colombian Congress. It granted to the Colombian Petroleum Company a contract for exploration and development of the Barco concession and to the South American Gulf Oil Company authority to construct a pipe line to tidewater with the specific provision that the line must extend wholly through Colombian territory.

During the next few years much preliminary work was done and several wells were drilled. Then, in 1936, the entire holdings of the Gulf Company were purchased by The Texas Company and Socony-Vacuum Oil Company. Later they acquired the interest of the Carib Syndicate. Except for a few shares the Colombian Petroleum Company, capitalized at 10 million dollars, is owned in equal parts by Texas and Socony while the South American Gulf Oil Company is wholly owned on the same basis.

Pipe-line and Refinery Stipulations.—The present concession, which runs for 50 years from Aug. 24, 1931, covers approximately 1 million acres lying between the Perija Mountains and the Colombia-Venezuela boundary line in the upper Catatumbo basin. Under the terms of the contract the concession holders were required to select at specified times blocks of acreage to total about one-half million acres. The remainder of the concession, except for necessary rights of way would then revert to the government.

Other provisions stipulated that within three years after production reached a specified daily rate, a pipe line should be laid and that on arrival at another specified daily rate, a refinery should be built on the concession. In accordance with these requirements the pipe line has been built and a refinery has been constructed at Petrolea.

Four fields have been located on the Barco concession. Of these the one most fully developed is the Petrolea field. A second Tibu field is now in the process of exploration and development. Some small produc-

"Up to 1937, the company (Standard Oil Company of Bolivia) spent 17 million dollars in exploration, drilling 28 wells, in the construction of two small refineries, camps, roads, and sanitation facilities."   See page 33.

Courtesy of "The Lamp," October, 1928.

The Sanandita well No. 2, Bolivia, drilling in.

Improvised motor dugout. Wilson E. Griffiths of Colombian Petroleum Company (foreground). *Right:* Alfred D. Lenz of Carib Syndicate, Limited, on trusty burro, 1919.

"A classic example of time lag in monetary return is the development by American interests of the Barco concession in Colombia originally held by the Carib Syndicate, Limited, an American company." See page 46.

Photographs from Oil Trade Journal, March, 1919, and June, 1917.

Carl K. MacFadden of Carib Syndicate, Limited (*left*) and W. E. Griffiths with Colombian jungle "game." 1917.

Original Campo Barco at Petrolea on the Barco Concession, Colombia, 1919.

Photographs from Oil Trade Journal, March, 1919.

One of first drilling camps on Rio del Oro, Barco concession. 1919.

Americans Pioneered Development of the De Mares Concession,

Clearing road on De Mares concession.

Tractor and trailer on concession.

Since the first investment in 1916 to first oil commercially marketed in 1926, $48,600,000 were invested in the concession. See page 47.

Photographs from Oil Trade Journal, June, October, 1920.

Tropical Oil Company's No. 1 well.

Casing at Cartagena waiting shipment to De Mares Concession.

Carrying supplies up Colorado River.

buis Restrepo greets burro at Port Colombia; Link Bowden (*center*).

Left to right: F. M. Martin, R. D. Burnham, Leon F. Russ, John W. Leonard, Ernest Wiltsee, Edwin B. Hopkins, A. L. Bowden, Don Roberto De Mares, and F. M. Fenn.

merican oil men inspect Tropical Oil Company's properties in Colombia in 1920.

arranca Bermeja in 1920 was a few houses n Magdalena River.

Don De Mares (*right*) at site of oil.

Photographs from Oil Trade Journal, August, 1920.

Venezuelan Operations Took Time and Money

Forty-four million dollars were spent on Eastern Venezuelan concessions in 15 years from first exploration to first marketing of oil. See page 48.

Photograph by Vachon, courtesy of Standard Oil Company (New Jersey).

Wildcat well near Jusepin field, Eastern Venezuela.

tion has been found in the Carbonera field south of Petrolea. The northern end of the concession, the Rio de Oro field, has several completed wells but is not now connected to a pipe line.

Great Difficulties Overcome.—Development work in these fields presented many difficulties since the whole area was virgin jungle that had to be cleared away for roads, camps, and drilling sites. The thousands of tons of machinery and supplies required for the operations were brought in by way of Lake Maracaibo and moved up the Catatumbo on barges. Material for Petrolea went up the Tarra and Sardinata rivers to Puerto Reyes or by railroad to Puerto Leon and thence by road to Petrolea.

Equipment for Rio de Oro was moved up the river of that name to the camp. From the Colombian side a road was built connecting the camp with Cúcuta. Airplanes were relied upon largely for communication and the movement of personnel. Airports have been built at both Petrolea and Rio de Oro. Within the concession itself a light railway and several kilometers of surfaced highway connect important points.

Pipe-line Material Flown In.—After extensive surveys the route for the pipe line was decided upon and construction authorized in 1937. Actual work on the line was begun in February, 1938. Because of the requirement that the line must lie wholly within Colombian territory it was necessary to carry it over one of the Andean ranges, and the whole eastern section of the route traversed jungle territory without towns, roads, or transport facilities. A large part of the cost of the line has been incurred in building a modern highway that parallels the pipe throughout the eastern portion of its course.

To meet the immediate problem of transporting the pipe-line material, however, the airplane was called into play, and the Barco pipe line has the distinction of being the first ever constructed in which a great part of the equipment was conveyed by air. Ten freight planes were employed and moved a total of 11 million lb. of materials. Suspension bridges 350 ft. in length and weighing 176,000 lb. each were especially designed to be transported by plane. For one bridge alone 240 separate trips were made, carrying 8,000 bags of cement, bridge steel, concrete mixers, and other machinery. The total distance flown in the course of construction work was over 1 million kilometers.

How Long It Took and What It Cost to Get Any Return.—It took an investment of over 21 million dollars and an elapsed time of 17 years from the date of first investment to the first discovery well on the Barco concession. Another 39 million dollars had to be spent, with a lapse of

another six and a half years, before the first oil from the Barco concession could be commercially marketed.[1]

Colombia's Largest Producing Area Entailed Heavy Initial Cost.—
The development of the Barco concession may be an extreme example.
However, there are other striking ones listed in the report, for instance,
the De Mares concession in Colombia from which most of the country's
production has come to date.

Early American Pioneering on De Mares Concession.—As early as
1918 John W. Leonard of Pittsburgh and American drillers and native
workers were developing the De Mares concession in Colombia, then
held by the Tropical Oil Company, and clearing the well sites of tropical
vegetation and boa constrictors. By 1924 the headquarters of the Tropical Oil Company was established at the river port of Barranca Bermeja
400 miles up the Magdalena River from the Caribbean coast and at the
outlet of the Colorado River. Here the company built houses for quarters and offices, a machine shop, and storehouse. Launches were operated on the Colorado River during the wet season to the oil wells, which
were located at the junction of the Oponcito River with the Colorado,
30 miles southeast of Barranca Bermeja. The known oil fields lay between the Colorado River and the Sogamoso River, in the department
of Santander.

Dense Tropical Jungle.—The land was level for 4 or 5 miles back from
the river and then "is very broken and covered with a dense tropical
jungle and hardwood timber. The country becomes more difficult farther to the east and south toward the high mountains of the Eastern
Cordillera."

The Colorado River was so low in the dry season, seven months, that
it could not be navigated, even by canoes, so the company was constructing a good wagon road from Barranca Bermeja to the oil wells, over
which a pipe line also was being laid to bring the crude oil down from
the wells to a small refinery being erected at the river at Barranca Bermeja, a distance of 35 miles. The camp at the wells was to be headquarters of the new prospecting work being done farther to the north-
east in lands of the concession.

The small refinery that Tropical Oil Company installed at Barranca
Bermeja in 1924 was figured to have a sufficient capacity to supply the
entire country with its needs of gasoline, kerosene, and lubricants. Bogotá, Colombia's capital and first city, was distant about 300 miles up
the Magdalena River. A large center of consumption—the second

[1] See Appendix Table 8.

largest, if not the largest in the country—was Medellín, the ᴄ Antioquia. To reach this market from the site of the refinery 77-mile trip by river to Puerto Berrio, from which point Mede gained by a 109-mile rail haul over the Antioquia railway. The in greatest demand in Colombia was figured to be residual fuel oil for the river steamers, of which there were about 140 plying on the Magdalena and its tributaries. Fuel oil would take the place of the wood then used for fuel and "will greatly facilitate the operation of river transportation."

Colombian Oil Enters World Market.—In 1924 there were only three producing wells on the Tropical Oil Company's De Mares concession, in Colombia. Later, after International Petroleum Company (Standard Oil Company, New Jersey) acquired the concession, the refinery was greatly increased as more production was brought in and a pipe line was laid to the coast 300 miles away.

Owing to the lack of means of transportation, production of oil had to be very limited at first, as shown by the following figures: 1921, 182 bbl. daily; 1922, 887; 1923, 1,164. But in 1927 Colombia was producing 41,000 bbl. daily from this operation, and Colombian oil had entered the world markets.

Since the first investment in the De Mares concession, the record of initial investment and time lag follows: date of first investment, approximately January, 1916; date of first discovery, Apr. 29, 1918; total investment between these periods, $800,000 (estimated); date of first oil commercially marketed, July 3, 1926; total investment between date of first investment and first commercial marketing, $48,600,000 (estimated).

Large Initial Costs and Time Lag in Venezuelan Operations.—As an example of the cost and time lag in operations in Venezuela, the case of two American companies that acquired substantial blocks of private concessions and free zones of national lands in the state of Anzoátegui, Venezuela, in 1925 is interesting. In order to locate these properties it was necessary for the companies at their own expense to survey the entire boundaries of the state (area, 16,718 square miles) and all district and municipal lines therein, and also many of the private properties within the state; thousands of miles of transit lines were run. The companies built, at their own expense, many first- and second-class public roads (including about 150 miles of asphalt-surfaced highways) and permanent bridges across waterways. In the area selected for prospecting there were no towns and only few houses; consequently, the companies built entire communities to house their workmen and their families, together with recreational facilities, hospitals, schools, and churches.

The exploration work consisting of surface geology and various forms of geophysical survey covered the entire state. Because there were no oil-well supply stores in the country, the companies imported and maintained on hand something like 30,000 different material and equipment items—everything conceivable from toothpicks to a drilling boiler—and most of such material had to be ordered from abroad at least six months prior to the time when it might be needed on the job.

The discovery well was started in 1933 but was not completed and tested for several years later. When it was ascertained that oil in commercial quantities had been found, plans were then made to build a 16-in. pipe line from the field 100 miles distant to deep water on the Caribbean, where a complete crude-oil handling terminal was constructed. Thus it was that in December, 1939, nearly 15 years after the initial investment had been made by these American companies in eastern Venezuela, there was delivered on board tanker the first barrel of crude at an over-all cost to that date of 44 million dollars.[1]

There are numerous examples of heavy initial concession and development commitments by American companies operating in Venezuela.[2]

Investment in Iraq Involved Time Lag.—The 75-year oil concession of the Iraq Petroleum Company was originally acquired in 1925. The discovery well was completed two years later, and in 1933 a pipe-line system was completed across the vast deserts and rugged mountains from the producing fields near Kirkuk to the ports of Tripoli in Syria and Haifa in Palestine where crude-oil handling terminals were built.

The operating company found it necessary to house completely its staff and workmen in the oil fields, as well as at the intermediate pipeline pump stations, to provide for their educational, recreational, and medical care, to build roads, and to create all those services commonly found available in areas of oil development in the United States or in Europe. On Aug. 1, 1934, the first cargo of Iraq crude was loaded on board an ocean tanker in the Mediterranean. It is estimated that the Iraq international group expended for all purposes in the period 1925–1934 approximately 62 million dollars, of which the American share was 14.7 million.[3]

---

[1] See Appendix Table 9; see also Table 10.
[2] See Appendix Tables 11, 12, and 13.
[3] See Appendix Table 14.

Experiences in Dutch East Indies.—Nederlandsche Koloniale Petroleum Maatschappij (N.K.P.M.), a subsidiary of an American company (now the Standard-Vacuum Oil Company) was formed in 1912 for the express purpose of developing oil production in the Dutch East Indies. Commercial production by this company was not established until 1922.

During the 11-year period, 105 wells were drilled, of which only 13 proved productive, and of these only two resulted in the discovery of what can be considered worth-while commercial production. The remaining 11 discovery wells were divided among three very small noncommercial and nonprofitable fields.

Between 1912 and 1922, the company expended $12,584,000. During this time a total of 235,000 barrels of crude oil was produced. Practically all this oil was utilized as fuel in carrying on exploration drilling.

In 1926 the field was put on commercial production as a result of constructing a pipe-line outlet to seaboard and completing a small refinery. Up to that time a total of $21,422,000 had been expended.[1]

The company also acquired operating rights on certain mining concessions in the Dutch East Indies, and these operating contracts required a sustained geological and exploration drilling program. To meet these contractual obligations, the company expended an amount of $5,648,000 over a period of 11 years, which was over and above the cost of acreage in the indicated amount of $3,642,000, making a total of $9,290,000 expended before establishing commercial production.

Another American company in the Dutch East Indies reported that between the date of first investment in 1931, and the date of first discovery in June, 1939, it had invested $5,619,000 in an operation in that country.

Many Leases and Concessions Do Not Pan Out.—Examples are given, as stated, involving losses from about $100,000 to nearly 9 million dollars on leases and concessions that did not pan out at all.

In the early twenties there was considerable activity in leasing and exploration in Cuba in which large and many small American companies participated without developing commercial production and took uncounted losses. Again in the thirties there was a revival of interest in Cuban oil development. The Atlantic Refining Company, among other American companies, was represented. Between 1929 and 1941, it had spent over $3,396,000 in the country without getting any oil. Another American company reports it has expended in Cuban oil ex-

[1] See Appendix Table 15.

ploration and development since 1937 to date a total of $1,625,000 with no oil discovery up to this time.

Losses from Operations in Mexico in Early Twenties.—It already has been stated that many American oil companies lost heavily on their investments in Mexico during the First World War and in the early twenties when Mexican producing fields went to salt water, whereas the earlier companies, on the whole, were on the right side of the ledger and made substantial profits in the venture.

Indeed, a new version is given of the derivation of the appellation "Golden Lane" for a strip of land about 25 miles long and 1 mile wide in Mexico, which in the First World War and shortly thereafter produced many million barrels of oil chiefly from large gusher wells. Familiarly, "Golden Lane" connoted the yielding of fabulous wealth in black gold. Actually, the phrase is said to have been first used to illustrate an entirely opposed situation. The coiner of it was protesting against the tremendous expenditures in the area then known as the South fields by many of these "late-comer" American companies. "The money being spent in that area would cover the entire producing structure from the Juan Casiano field in the north to the Toteco field in the south with 20-dollar gold pieces, and this golden lane will never return the amount of money being spent in it," he said.

At any rate, these words proved prophetic. Among American companies that took large losses in Mexico in the twenties were the Atlantic Lobos Oil Company and Panuco Boston Oil Company. At this time the Standard Oil Company (New Jersey) and Cia. Mexicana Holandesa "La Corona" (Royal Dutch) had made heavy investments, and it was only after further acquisitions and after many years that their investments began to return a profit.

Some refineries and pipe lines, after being built, were never operated, as previously stated, and some companies never even completed the laying of their pipe lines before their producing wells were practically exhausted.

Little Wildcatting for New Reserves in Mexico.—"The seriousness of the Mexican producing situation is not that some of the old pools are playing out so much as that there has been no adequate wildcatting work in Mexico," the *Oil Trade Journal* of March, 1920, reported. "The Mexican pools have been probably the most prolific in the world, and wells have made records in production that may never be equaled again. Experienced operators have always understood that these pools would not continue producing forever. However, the political situation in Mexico, bandit depredations, and latterly the promulgation of nationalization decrees have operated against a widespread and systematic wildcat campaign in the republic. Investment and operation have been centered in the fields easy of access and more or less proven.

"Geologists are agreed that there are immense fields in Mexico yet to be found and developed.

"The greater part of the likely oil fields in Mexico have long been under lease or outright ownership, but the wildcatting has been desultory, *i.e.*, largely confined to territory outlying known production. In all Mexico since the beginning of the industry in 1901 to the present time there have been completed only 1,100 wells. One authority estimates that out of this number probably no more than two or three hundred could be classed as real wildcat wells, less than the number that is drilled in proving up small areas in the United States. Because salt water has invaded the proven fields and reduced and imperiled present production, Mexico as a whole cannot be condemned as to future production in the light of the inadequate wildcatting work that has been done."

Before the close of 1921, salt water had invaded the Amatlan and was spreading into the Toteco district, newest producing area. Within another two years *finis* was written under Mexico's "Golden Lane" so far as large new flush production was concerned.

After 1921 Mexican production began to decline.[1] Not every company had paid out by any means as shown above, and those still in Mexico had heavy commitments. They had to operate henceforth, if they remained in the country, on an old declining-field rather than a new flush-field production basis.

$2 out of Every $3 Received for Oil Stayed in Mexico.—It was estimated in 1926 that out of every $3 received for Mexican oil, $2 stayed

[1] Further to complicate the Mexican situation, Mexican oil taxes precipitated a crisis in 1921, when Mexican production reached its peak. In that year President Obregon increased the tax rates to such a point that they were considered confiscatory. This resulted in the companies' discontinuing exports of petroleum until agreement was reached as to the amount of taxes the industry could bear. The peak oil-tax revenue was reached in 1922 (the peak year for Mexican oil exports); by 1925 they were cut in half, reflecting the decline in Mexican oil production.

Nevertheless, Mexican exports and production and export taxes, a large proportion paid by American oil companies, for the years 1921–1925 yielded the Mexican government $153,016,000 U. S. currency, the production tax aggregating $110,222,000 and the export tax $42,794,000. If bar and tonnage dues were added, the total amount paid to the Mexican federal government by the oil companies was over 200 million dollars.

in Mexico, contradicting the impression that foreign oil companies milked Mexico for its oil.

"Strictly on a financial accounting, entrance into and stay in Mexico has been profitable for that country," *The Lamp*, October, 1926,[1] says. "Far from being the rapacious adventurer swooping down upon a helpless country and making away with its treasures, the company (and its experiences have not been essentially different from that of other foreign companies) took great risks and worked hard to make a moderate profit on the capital employed and, for every dollar made, paid a like dollar into the government's treasury and another like dollar to Mexican labor. This is better evidence than the unsupported charges to the contrary that have been made by people on both sides of the Rio Grande.

"Now that the story is told, has Mexico any reason to regret the entrance of the oil companies with their hundreds of millions of dollars for developing operations and taxes? When it is realized that out of every $3 received from Mexican oil $2 stayed in the country, the talk of exploitation of a helpless nation by foreign capital can be valued at its real worth."

It might be added that out of the remaining $1, the companies had to pay expenses in the United States as well as the price for purchases of material in the United States.[2]

Production increased progressively to a peak of 193,397,500 barrels in 1921, from which point it dropped almost as precipitately as it had risen to 90,420,000 barrels in 1926. However, the total for the 10-year

---

[1] Published by the Standard Oil Company (New Jersey).

[2] There was scarcely a company of major world importance that had not invested considerable sums in the Mexican oil fields by the end of 1921. Among the most important might be mentioned Compania Mexicana de Petroleo "El Aguila" (British), Compania Mexicana Holandesa "La Corona" (Royal Dutch), and the following American companies: Standard Oil Co. (New Jersey), Pan American Petroleum and Transport Co., Sinclair Consolidated Oil Corp., Pierce Oil Co., South Penn, Gulf Oil Corp., The Texas Co., Magnolia Petroleum Co., Atlantic Refining Co., Atlantic Gulf & West Indies, Island Oil & Transport Corp., National Oil Co., English Oil Co., Marland Oil Co., Tide Water Oil Co., General Petroleum Corp., Richmond Petroleum Co. of Mexico, Standard Oil Co. of Mexico, Southern Pacific Railway Co., Cities Service Co., Warner-Quinlan & Co., Mexican Seaboard Oil Co., and a number of lesser importance. A gigantic system of pipe lines, tank farms, terminals, and refineries was installed and a fleet of ocean-going tankers constructed at war prices, predicated on conditions then obtaining and in the expectancy of constantly expanding operations. This investment in installations and in acquisition of oil properties reached well over 1 billion gold pesos (500 million dollars U. S. currency).

Oil well derricks at Pangkalan Soesoe, North Sumatra, 1923.

American interests spend over $21,000,000 in Dutch East Indies development between 1912 and 1926 before first oil was commercially marketed. **See page 49.**

Photographs on this and following page by courtesy of Fred B. Ely, taken by Mr. Ely in 1923.

Mud volcano, few miles S.E. of Wuosari, western edge of oil fields, N. Central Java.

Tremboel oil field in 1923. Well No. 2 of N.K.P.M. in distance.

American oil operations in the Dutch East Indies in the early days.

General view of N.K.P.M. refinery near Tjepoe, 1923.

Saipuru No. 1 showing landslide.

Geological party on Rio Vitiacua.

In the eight years 1921 to 1928, 35 field expeditions forced their way into the wilderness, over rocks and up well-nigh impossible cliffs to locate and drill 14 wells in Bolivia. **See page 53.**

Photographs on this and next page from "The Lamp," October, 1928.

Difficult road building.

Range where Sanandita field is located.

Above: Saipuru No. 1 well, Bolivia, with casing delivered after great transportation difficulties.

Right: Swimmer carrying theodolite strapped on his head, ready to cross Rio Grande. The light log is carried under one arm for buoyancy allowing the swimmer to transport small loads without wetting. The entire outfit for several days' survey was moved down the Rio Grande gorge in this manner.

Treacherous quicksand in Rio Cangapi.

Well location, Bolivian mountains.

period 1917–1926 attained the impressive figure of 1,137,000,000 barrels. The Mexican oil industry enjoyed an era of prosperity.

During the same decade oil pay rolls averaged close to 75 million pesos ($37,500,000 U. S. currency) per annum.[1]

As has been pointed out, production had dropped by 1926 to 90,420,000 barrels. The following year saw a still further decline to 64,121,000 barrels, or to less than one-third of the 1921 peak. This was due to causes already related (Chap. II, p. 28).

In the meantime important oil fields had been discovered in Venezuela and Colombia. In the first-mentioned country especially, operating conditions were favorable and the policy of the government was, as it still is, to encourage development. The companies turned their attention to these new and more promising fields. Then began a period of liquidation and of abandonment of Mexican investments.[2]

Money Spent in Other Central American Countries.—In other Central American countries American companies have expended large sums in exploration and some drilling without any financial return. As an example, a company cites the following experience in Nicaragua: cost of acreage, $100,000; development-program commitment, $597,000; time involved, four years.

Costly Experience in Bolivia.—In the eight years from 1921 to 1928, 35 field expeditions in charge of the geologists and engineers of the Standard Oil Company of Bolivia forced their way into the wilderness, over rocks, and up well-nigh impassable cliffs to locate and drill 14 wells in the departments of Tarija, Santa Cruz, and Chuquisaca, Bolivia.

Over 18,000 square miles had been surveyed by the field expeditions of the company in this wild, mountainous country. Nearly 350 miles

---

[1] Employment was between 30,000 and 49,000 men. Taxes for the same period reached an average of from 45 to 50 million pesos ($22,500,000 to $25,000,000 U. S. currency) in round numbers. In addition, substantial sums were paid to Mexican landowners in rentals and royalties; and large disbursements by way of supplies and materials purchased and other operating expenses made up an enormous outlay in Mexico that benefited those directly dependent on the industry as well as every small merchant throughout the region.

[2] Of the 22 major entities enumerated previously, seven definitely retired from business in this country. These were The Texas Co., The Atlantic Refining Co., Island Oil Transport Corp., National Petroleum Co., English Oil Co., Tide Water Oil Co., and General Petroleum Corp. With perhaps one exception, these companies sustained severe losses.

The Mexican holdings of nine others were absorbed by purchase by other companies. No new companies of importance ventured into the field during this period except the semiofficial Petroleos de Mexico.

of new roads had to be blasted and cut into the sides of rocky hills, and over 1,000 miles of the roadway from Yaicuba to Santa Cruz were maintained by the company in order to get in the truckloads of drilling material and camping equipment. Besides furnishing employment to large numbers of Bolivians, this necessary side activity opened up hitherto undeveloped regions for the use of the Bolivian public.

On their expeditions into Bolivia the geologists and engineers of the Standard Oil Company of Bolivia, when they arrived at the end of the railroad line in northern Argentina, found mules, tents, canned foods, transit, pots, pans, quinine, notebooks assembled for a prolonged journey in the forest-covered ranges where they could study the rocks and "dope out the structure."

They took up the trail into Bolivia through hills ranging from 2,000 to 5,000 ft. The ridges were long and narrow, with steep sides and narrow valleys in between, occurring in fairly orderly parallel arrangement, like huge corrugations.

By following narrow gorges and canyons, which cut cross sections through the ranges, the dip or inclination of the rock could be studied and the geological structure observed.

The geologists had to determine whether oil might be present in sufficient quantities to encourage transport of 300 tons of machinery and equipment more than 7,500 miles for the drilling of a test well.[1]

Indeed, facing an almost impossible series of natural obstacles—trackless forests, frowning cliffs, racing streams, rock-strewn gorges, snakes, wild animals, and countless insects—the job that confronted the transportation man and his engineer assistant was well-nigh superhuman.

---

[1] Buenos Aires, the nearest industrial center to the oil lands in southeastern Bolivia, lay over 1,000 miles away, or 48 hours by train from the most accessible point of the area being prospected. La Paz, the capital of Bolivia, was four days to the northwest by the quickest possible route other than airplane, and the closest large Bolivian city to the concession was Santa Cruz, with a population of 22,000. The distances of the various wells from the nearest rail point ran from 30 to 275 miles.

Drilling equipment and supplies shipped from New York and landed at Buenos Aires therefore traveled 6,000 miles by water, 1,100 miles by rail, and 30 miles by motor transport and mule carts to the most accessible location, just 7,130 miles from their starting point. A piece of casing had to cover 8,725 miles from the time it is floated on a barge alongside the freighter at New York until it was lowered into the hole of the most remote well in the Bolivian hills. When it is considered that the weight of the tools, boilers, derrick, and casing required for a single 3,000-ft. well is approximately 300 tons, to say nothing of camp equipment, machine shops, foodstuffs, and rolling stock, it will be seen that the landing of these materials on location was a man-size job.

Of the 14 wells drilled, only three showed any real promise, although some excellent production has been encountered in eight of them. Still others were dry holes, while others failed on account of mechanical difficulties. The problem of establishing production still remained to be solved after eight years, although results had offered some encouragement.

Altogether, as stated, the company spent 17 million dollars from which there was no income yield up to the time of expropriation in 1937 (see Chap. II, p. 33).

Foreign Operations Can Be Profitable.—Despite time lags that mean millions, the persistence with which American interests have pursued their foreign activity and the tenacity with which they have clung to their foothold abroad have had their rewards. In citing the costs and the political and economic risks encountered, it is not intended to convey the idea that all foreign oil enterprise by the American petroleum industry has been necessarily unprofitable.

Against the large initial investment and the long time lag before any returns on production operations may be expected, there can happen the ultimate favorable development of a major producing operation that may extend over a long period of years.

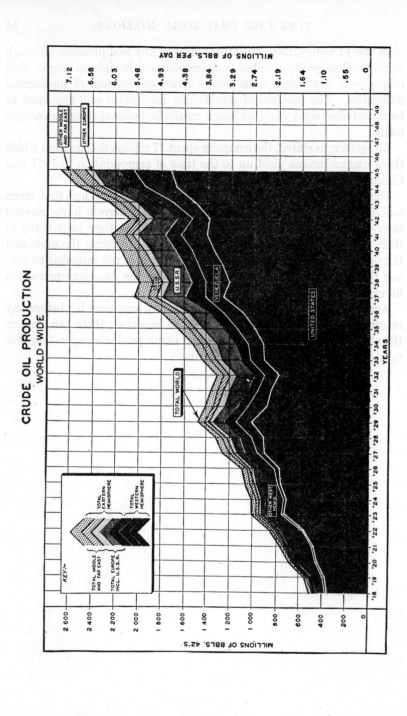

CRUDE OIL PRODUCTION
WORLD-WIDE

CHAPTER V

STRUGGLE FOR SHARE OF WORLD OIL

When, after the First World War, our government became concerned because of the belief that we should have to go increasingly abroad for our oil supplies in order to meet our domestic requirements, the activities and scope of foreign oil combines with which American companies had to compete in the struggle for a share of world oil received serious attention. At the present time, when the same concern is felt, it is important to see how American interests have fared in the struggle, and to observe that they have gained footholds, sometimes against almost insuperable odds, in most (although by no means all) of the great strategic oil-reserve areas of the earth.

The two great foreign groups comprise the British-Dutch group and Soviet Russia. The largest elements in the first are the Royal Dutch–Shell Company (British-Dutch), the world's biggest oil combine, and the Anglo-Iranian Oil Company, Limited (British). Russia's is a state monopoly with production and reserves up to this time wholly within the Soviet Union, but Soviet Russia's expanding sphere of influence and interest embraces rich oil territory outside the boundaries of the country itself in Europe and in the Middle East.

Remarkable Growth of Foreign Combines.—Support of the U. S. State Department has been a factor in the American gains. For instance, there is no question but that, without the diplomatic support of the government, American oil companies could never have obtained rights along with the Anglo-Iranian Oil Company, Limited, in Iraq and along with the Royal Dutch–Shell in Netherlands India (see Chap. I).

In the early twenties the expansion and ramifications of the Anglo-Persian Oil Company (later Anglo-Iranian Oil Company, Limited), in which the British government itself owned shares, came into prominence as our State Department fought against the San Remo Agreement. Anglo-Iranian was found not only to be dominant in the Near and Middle East but also to be pushing an expansion program into Europe, the Far East, Oceania, and the Western Hemisphere. The exchange of diplomatic correspondence between the Netherlands and our government in connection with the Djambi controversy also brought into the open the remarkable growth of the Royal Dutch Company and its absorption of the British Shell interests (see Chap. I).

Royal Dutch Company Born in Indies.—As the twentieth century dawned, development of the rich oil lands of the Dutch East Indies came into prominence. J. B. August Kessler, a director at Batavia of a Dutch firm trading in East Indian products, had organized in 1890 the Koninklijke Nederlandsche Maatschappij Tot Exploatatie Van Petroleumbronnen in Nederlandsch-Indie (Royal Dutch Company for the Working of Petroleum Wells in Dutch East Indies). It was formed to deal with oil-bearing properties in the Dutch East Indies.

After securing a strong, exclusive position in oil concessions and production in Sumatra, Borneo, and Java, he enlarged its operations. Then under the leadership of Henri Deterding, who became managing director in 1901, the company extended its operations into many other parts of the world by constant absorption of and merger with other companies.

Deterding had proved his capacity as a salesman with headquarters at Singapore, expanding the company's markets into China and other countries where Standard Oil had pioneered. In doing so, he entered into an arrangement with the Shell Transport & Trading Company (British) to carry his oil from the Dutch East Indies to China and elsewhere. From this came the merger with Shell.

Combined with British Shell Interests.—Toward the close of the eighties Marcus Samuel (later Lord Breasted) of the firm of M. Samuel & Company (British) had formed the Dutch Indies Industrial & Trading Company under a Dutch charter to take over an oil and coal concession in Borneo, having the support of the Rothschilds, who henceforth were identified with its constantly expanding operations. In 1897 the Shell Transport & Trading Company was formed by M. Samuel & Company. It carried on a business of transporting illuminating oils to India, China, Japan, and other countries. It concentrated more and more on the carrying of oil and the development of the tanker. The vast Shell tanker fleet by the early 1900's was operating on every sea. All the while the Samuel organization was acquiring and absorbing subsidiary oil concerns much like the Royal Dutch Company.

In 1907 Deterding and Samuel brought about the affiliation of Royal Dutch and Shell, one which grew into the world's greatest oil combine. Deterding later was knighted by the British government but remained a citizen of the Netherlands.

Briefly, two companies were formed, the Anglo-Saxon Petroleum Company, Limited, registered in England, and the N. V. de Bataafsche Petroleum Maatschappij, incorporated in Holland. The shares in these companies were apportioned 40 per cent to the Shell and 60 per cent to the Royal Dutch. Approximately the same relative interest was retained by each group in a third company, the Asiatic Petroleum Company, Limited. These three companies are the principal operating companies of the group, the Bataafsche and the Asiatic being chiefly responsible for producing and refining operations and the Anglo-Saxon for other phases of the business.

The shares in the Anglo-Saxon and the Bataafsche are all held by the Shell and Royal Dutch, respectively, whereas the shares of the latter companies, as well as some of the stock of the Asiatic Petroleum Company, are on the market and owned by the general public.

During the First World War the holdings of British nationals in Royal Dutch–Shell as well as in other foreign corporations were impounded to help stabilize exchange, which tended to substantiate a report that the British government had acquired a controlling interest in the Royal Dutch–Shell combine.

While British government participation in Royal Dutch was not substantiated, the opposite was the case in respect to Anglo-Persian Oil Company. In 1921 the Chancellor of the Exchequer stated in the House of Commons that the British government held 5 million ordinary shares and £199,000 debentures (controlling interest), and that the government had no intention of disposing of its holdings.[1]

Anglo-Iranian Oil Company, Limited, Beginnings.—Indeed, from almost the beginning the development of oil in Persia (Iran) had the blessing of the British government.

In the 1910's, Winston Churchill, then First Lord of the Admiralty, took up the fight of Admiral Lord Fisher for a naval oil supply. We have some notes on an exhaustive statement by Churchill in the House of Commons on July 17, 1913, in which he pointed out the immediate need of an Admiralty policy that would ensure oil supplies at reasonable cost. Four years before, the first flotilla of ocean-going destroyers wholly dependent on oil had been completed. Each successive year another flotilla of "oil only" destroyers had been built. At the time he spoke, there were built or being built over 100 British destroyers solely dependent on oil fuel. Furthermore, oil was being employed in coal-

[1] Federal Trade Information Service, Apr. 5, 1921.

burning battleships and cruisers to enable them to utilize fuller powers when exceptional speed was required.

Churchill said that the Admiralty's ultimate policy should be to become the independent owner and producer of its own supplies of liquid fuel and the owner or at least the controller at the source of at least a proportion of the supply of natural oil that it would require. He said, "We are moving toward that position of independence outside the oil market which it is our ultimate policy to secure."

He referred to Persia.

The eyes of the British government had followed the fortunes of William Knox D'Arcy, a British gold miner, who in 1901 secured from the shah of Persia an exclusive concession for the exploitation of natural gas, petroleum, and asphalt for the whole of Persia except the five northern provinces, to run for 60 years.

"He [D'Arcy] organized the First Exploitation Company, with a capital of £600,000, which he largely subscribed himself," Isaac Marcosson wrote in 1924. "He began operations about 100 miles north of Bagdad and brought in two fairly good wells. The country was primitive, supplies had to be hauled on the backs of donkeys and camels, and there was no adequate port. To commercialize Persian oil it was necessary to have an outlet on the Persian Gulf, and this was an expensive business, for it meant a pipe line over the mountains.

"D'Arcy found that running a sort of personal oil show was a costly luxury. By the end of 1903 he had expended more than £300,000—$1,500,000—out of his own pocket, and he had only two moderate oil wells to show for it.

"In the course of time, the British Admiralty, thanks to the pounding of Lord Fisher, woke to the value of oil as fuel for the navy.

"The Admiralty asked if he [D'Arcy] would defer taking on any outsiders until some independent British interest could negotiate with him to keep Persia under the Union Jack so far as oil was concerned. He agreed, and the Burma Oil Company, Limited, (British, with a monopoly in British India) came forward and formed the Concessions Syndicate to develop that part of the D'Arcy concession not being operated by the First Exploitation Company.

"Meanwhile D'Arcy was plugging away in Persia. In 1907, and in the section locally known as Maiden-i-Naftun, which means Fields of Oil, and adjoining the ruins of an ancient fire temple, the first gusher (F7) was struck with such force that it wrecked the derrick. This well

may be said to have christened the British oil conquest of Persia because it is the center of what is now a great producing region.

"More than this, it led to the imposing merger of interests which soon
became incorporated as the Anglo-Persian Oil Company (Anglo-Iranian
Oil Company, Limited)."

While Persian oil became available in time to aid Britain slightly
during the First World War, it was not until after that war that the
Anglo-Persian interests and operations were intensified and expanded.
Meantime, the British navy had become 90 per cent oil-burning. Large
additions were made to the company's Abadan refinery on the Persian
Gulf; a great new refinery was constructed in Llandarcy, Wales, to
operate chiefly on Persian crude oil.

Sir Charles Greenway, chairman, in 1922, could tell the shareholders
of Anglo-Persian as reported in the English press: [1]

"It is particularly satisfactory to learn that output from that quarter
[Persia] is exceeding all expectations. To quote only one example, well
F7 has produced during the past 10 years no less than 4 million tons of
oil and is still giving yield of 2,000 tons per day, which is considerably
more than average for the past decade. No other well of equal capacity
and continuity has ever been known in any field producing light-gravity
crude, and the area in question is believed to possess even better wells.
Equally remarkable is rapid progress being made (by the company) in
other parts of the world. Important concessions have been obtained in
Argentine Republic, Egypt, and Canada, while a refinery is in course of
erection in Australia. In France a huge organization has been built
up through Société Générale des Huiles de Pétrole, which now has capital of 220 million francs, and extensions are foreshadowed in Belgium,
Denmark, and Norway. Negotiations are also proceeding for acquiring
similar interests in other countries."

However, except for limited activity in the Western Hemisphere, the
policy of the Anglo-Iranian Oil Company, Limited, has been to restrict
its producing efforts to the Near East and those countries lying within
the sphere of the British Empire, its dominions and protectorates, and
its refining and marketing operations to the markets within easy transport of these areas.

Vast Ramification of British-Dutch Group.—In 1923 the Federal
Trade Commission broadcast the gains made by the Royal Dutch–
Shell and Anglo-Persian Oil, calling attention to the "extraordinary
ramifications of the Royal Dutch–Shell group as shown by a list of sub-

[1] *Financial Times, London Times, Manchester Guardian,* Dec. 22, 1922.

sidiary companies," which covered five pages of fine type in the Appendix of the report.[1]

"At the present time," the report stated, "the Royal Dutch–Shell group, in addition to its possessions in the Dutch East Indies, owns exclusive or important petroleum properties in Sarawak (British Borneo), Rumania, Egypt, Venezuela, Trinidad, Mexico, and the United States; and it controls five refineries in the United States with a daily capacity of 65,000 barrels, four in Mexico with a daily capacity of 155,000 barrels, one in Venezuela, one in Trinidad, one in Curaçao, one in Suez, and others in Europe and the Orient, together with compression plants, storage facilities, and other equipment in different parts of the world. It has 752 miles of trunk pipe lines in the United States and about 240 miles of pipe in Mexico. It also owns or controls about 1,144,000 tons of tankers, barges, and tugboats.

"In 1921 the Royal Dutch–Shell group controlled about 2 per cent of the petroleum production of the United States, which was increased to nearly 3½ per cent in the first six months of 1922. From its present holdings it produced 9,043,000 barrels of crude petroleum (about 50,000 bbl. daily) during the first half of 1922, and in October, 1922, it was producing at the rate of 80,000 bbl. daily. . . .

Restrictive Policies in Favor of Foreign Combines.—"Although it is not uncommon for foreign governments to place some restrictions upon the exploitation of the petroleum resources within their domains by aliens, prominent cases of exclusion of citizens of the United States which have been brought to the attention of the commission were in British India and the Dutch East Indies," the report continued.

"In the case of British India a single company, the Burma Oil Company, Limited, has had a monopoly of the crude-petroleum-producing business in the oil fields of Burma. The Burma Oil Company, Limited, is partly owned by the Anglo-Persian Oil Company, in which the British government is interested. [This probably should be reversed. Today, next to the British government, the Burma Oil Company, Limited, is the largest shareholder in the Anglo-Iranian Oil Company, Limited.]

"American interests have repeatedly, but unsuccessfully, attempted to obtain oil concessions in British India. . . .

"The foregoing shows the attitude of the British government during the early history of the petroleum industry," the report went on. "Subsequent events have indicated a continuance on the part of Great Britain

[1] Report of the Federal Trade Commission on Foreign Ownership in the Petroleum Industry, Feb. 12, 1923. Summary, p. xii, pp. 39, 40; Appendix, pp. 64–69.

and British colonies of policies of restriction upon foreigners in respect to the development and exploitation of some of their most promising oil areas. Such restrictive policies are followed not only by the British Empire but by the Netherlands, France, and other countries. These restrictions in nearly all, if not all, cases apply ostensibly to all foreigners; and so far as the United States is concerned, they amount to discriminations only in the sense that citizens of this country are not accorded the same rights in these foreign countries as are accorded the citizens of such foreign countries in the United States."

The restrictive policies were further exemplified and publicized by the attempt within the San Remo Agreement to keep mandated territory in the Near and Middle East exclusively for the British and French (see Chap. I).

Struggle for Share in Foreign Countries.—This briefly was the situation insofar as foreign combines and restrictive national policies were concerned at the time American oil interests were given the mandate from their government to participate vigorously in foreign oil development.

Eloquent evidence in the ensuing years of the struggle for oil between the British-Dutch group on the one hand and the American companies on the other is given in Table 7 showing the percentage of oil controlled by each in foreign countries in 1910–1926.

The British-Dutch group (Royal Dutch–Shell) and the Anglo-Iranian Oil Company, Limited, increased their controlled production in foreign countries (other than Russia and the United States) from 44.3 per cent of the total in 1910 to 55 per cent in 1912 and to a peak of 59.1 per cent in 1915. When the First World War ended in 1918, its percentage was reduced to 47.9 even though it developed large production in Mexico. This was mainly because American interests were even more successful in that country.

The American share of the total was only 6.6 per cent in 1910, but, in large part because of participation in Mexico, it increased to 16 per cent in 1912, 24.5 per cent in 1915, and 38.2 per cent in 1918.

Then, with the State Department squarely behind them, American interests forged ahead of the British-Dutch interests in the next four years, reaching a peak participation of 57 per cent in 1922.

By the end of that period Americans had begun producing operations in Peru, Dutch East Indies, Venezuela, Colombia, Canada, and Poland and in the rehabilitated Rumanian fields and had raised Mexican output to peak levels. British-Dutch nationals owned oil production in

Mexico, Venezuela, Ecuador, Trinidad, Canada, Argentina, Peru, Rumania, Egypt, India, Burma, Dutch East Indies, British Borneo, and Iran. (Their Russian properties were confiscated in 1919.)

TABLE 7.—OIL PRODUCTION CONTROLLED IN FOREIGN COUNTRIES BY BRITISH-DUTCH AND AMERICAN GROUPS, 1910–1926 [1]

(In thousand barrels daily)

Year	British-Dutch			American		
	Production	% total foreign	% foreign excluding Russia	Production	% total foreign	% foreign excluding Russia
1910	60.0	18.5	44.3	9.0	2.8	6.6
1912	103.8	29.2	55.5	29.9	8.4	16.0
1915	151.8	36.5	59.1	63.1	15.1	24.5
1918	163.2	40.4	47.9	129.9	32.1	38.2
1921	278.2	33.7	37.2	415.2	50.2	55.6
1922	263.3	31.4	35.6	421.9	50.4	57.0
1923	312.9	39.8	46.1	311.4	39.6	45.8
1924	306.6	37.1	43.7	328.6	39.8	46.8
1925	316.6	37.6	45.4	304.9	36.2	43.7
1926	352.9	39.4	49.0	276.4	30.9	38.3

[1] Table covers foreign countries only and thus excludes the United States.

For a number of succeeding years—until 1926—Americans were able to keep neck and neck percentage-wise with the British-Dutch interests reflecting the results of the U. S. government command to American oil companies, "Go abroad and find oil!" Then came the overproduction of oil in the United States prompting many American companies to withdraw from foreign activities with resultant decline in the American foreign oil percentage.

Nevertheless, the struggle for an American share in the world's principal producing areas was carried on by the American companies remaining in the field and new ones joining them. This is best described by relating what happened subsequently in the important oil areas of the Western Hemisphere and the Eastern Hemisphere (see Chaps. VI and VII).

Big Three in Foreign Oil Production Share Almost Equally.— Percentage-wise the fluctuating struggle between British-Dutch interests and American interests insofar as foreign oil production (exclusive

TABLE 8.—OIL PRODUCTION CONTROLLED IN FOREIGN COUNTRIES BY BRITISH-DUTCH AND AMERICAN GROUPS, 1927–1944 [1]

(In thousand barrels daily)

Year	British-Dutch			American			Russian	
	Production	% total foreign	% foreign excluding Russia	Production	% total foreign	% foreign excluding Russia	Production	% total foreign
1927	391.6	39.7	50.4	293.0	29.7	37.7	208.9	21.2
1928	470.5	40.5	51.0	354.1	30.5	38.4	239.5	20.6
1929	541.2	41.0	52.2	392.1	29.7	37.8	282.1	21.4
1930	573.6	40.1	54.2	368.1	25.7	34.8	372.5	26.0
1931	522.5	36.5	53.1	332.5	23.2	33.8	449.1	31.3
1932	550.1	38.4	54.6	328.3	23.0	32.6	425.2	29.6
1933	567.4	38.6	54.3	340.1	23.2	32.6	424.2	28.9
1934	632.9	38.0	53.3	417.0	25.1	35.1	475.4	28.6
1935	665.5	37.1	51.5	461.9	25.8	35.8	502.7	28.0
1936	707.5	37.1	51.6	484.2	25.4	35.3	538.1	28.2
1937	810.8	38.7	52.8	562.8	26.8	36.7	562.0	26.8
1938	810.0	38.1	52.5	506.9	23.8	32.9	585.9	27.5
1939	795.3	35.7	49.1	554.8	24.9	34.3	609.6	27.4
1940	710.5	32.7	46.4	527.8	24.3	34.5	638.6	29.4
1941	661.9	29.6	42.0	610.2	27.3	38.8	659.4	29.5
1942	560.3	29.3	43.8	357.9	18.7	28.0	633.6	33.1
1943	596.5	27.0	39.2	438.4	19.9	28.8	683.6	31.0
1944	707.3	28.8	40.6	653.2	26.6	37.5	709.7	29.0

[1] Table covers foreign countries only and thus excludes the United States.

of Russia) is concerned is shown in the third column under each of the two headings in Table 8. The Russian interest as one of the Big Three in foreign oil also is shown in this table, as well as the percentage of total foreign production of all three groups. It will be noted that in 1944 the share was 28.8 per cent British-Dutch, 26.6 per cent American, and 29.0 per cent Russian. The balance of roughly 15 per cent in foreign

SHARE OF CRUDE OIL PRODUCTION BY MAJOR GROUPS
TOTAL FOREIGN

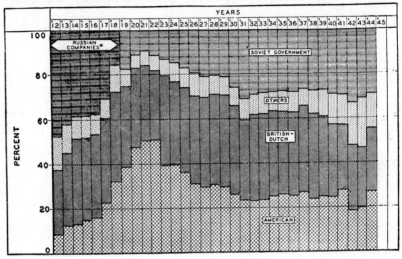

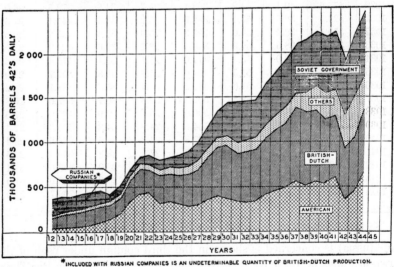

*INCLUDED WITH RUSSIAN COMPANIES IS AN UNDETERMINABLE QUANTITY OF BRITISH-DUTCH PRODUCTION.

production is held by other nationals—largely by government or nationally incorporated companies in the various producing countries.

The American group's interest has held fairly steady through the years at around 25 per cent of the total, except for 1942 and 1943 when the percentage dropped below 20. Russia's standing reflects the continued increases in that country's own production, matching increases in foreign production elsewhere.

TABLE 9.—ESTIMATED FOREIGN OIL RESERVES AS OF JAN. 1, 1945 [1]

(In million barrels)

	American	British-Dutch	Other foreign	Total
Total foreign excluding Russia..	17,371.7	17,277.9	2,905.2	37,554.8
Per cent....................	46.3	46.0	7.7	
Total foreign including Russia..	17,371.7	17,277.9	8,670.2	43,319.8
Per cent....................	40.1	39.9	20.2	

[1] Table covers foreign countries only and thus excludes the United States.

British-Dutch interests that controlled 29 per cent of the foreign production in 1912, 40 per cent in 1918, and 31 per cent in 1922 rebounded to 41 per cent in 1929 mainly because of increases in Iran, Venezuela, Dutch East Indies, and Mexico. The British-Dutch percentage declined again (36 per cent at the outbreak of the Second World War in 1939) principally because of the loss of properties in Mexico. Wartime shutting in of Iran and Iraq and the loss of East Indies and Rumanian properties to the Axis further lowered the group's position to 27 per cent in 1943. But reopening of Middle East wells to record levels in 1944 raised the group's position to nearly 29 per cent in 1944, practically the equivalent of the Russian position and two points higher than the 27 per cent owned by American nationals.

The three national groups, then, shared almost equally in foreign crude-oil production during 1944. From the First World War their aggregate ownership of foreign production was more than 90 per cent until 1938 when the Mexican government expropriated British-Dutch and American properties. The seizure of oil fields by Axis armies during the recent conflict further reduced the aggregate participation to an estimated 78 per cent in 1943, but in 1944 it rose again to nearly 85 per cent—also partially estimated.

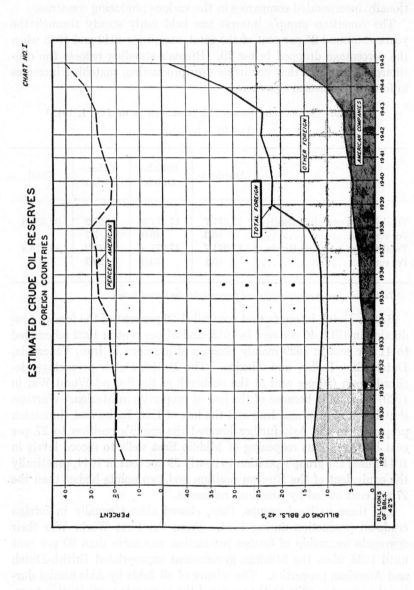

CHART NO. I

ESTIMATED CRUDE OIL RESERVES
FOREIGN COUNTRIES

It should be noted again, however, that for about a decade Russian oil has played only a minor role in international trade. Foreign consumers outside of Russia have depended primarily on British-Dutch-and American-controlled sources for the bulk of their oil supplies.

Americans Hold 40 Per Cent of Foreign Oil Reserves.—Of equal if not greater importance than foreign-oil-production participation, in that it has to do with future as well as present oil production, is the American share of estimated foreign oil reserves, which as of Jan. 1, 1945, was 40 per cent of total foreign reserves. This is matched almost to the percentage point (39.9) by the British-Dutch interests (see Table 9).

Of the total foreign reserve estimated at 43.3 billion barrels, American companies accounted for 17.4 billion barrels. The reserves of the British-Dutch interests totaled 17.3 billion barrels. If Russia is included, the position of the American and British-Dutch interests is, as stated, about 40 per cent each. The remaining 20 per cent or 8.7 billion barrels is owned by all other foreign interests. Again significant is the fact that included in this group are government-company–operated reserves in Argentina, Bolivia, Mexico, and Russia, amounting to 6.5 billion barrels, or nearly 75 per cent of the "others" classification. Of the 6.5 billion, the Russian proved reserve is 5.7 billion barrels.

Americans have developed major foreign oil reserves in the Caribbean area contiguous to the United States and in the Middle East—formerly almost exclusive stronghold of the British-Dutch. Details by major areas will be given and discussed in Chaps. VI and VII.

A combination of the estimates of reserves from various sources, with estimated American ownership, is given in Table 10.

No Exclusion in the United States.—It should be pointed out that foreign combines and companies are free to produce oil and develop reserves in the United States. A subsidiary of the Royal Dutch–Shell group, for instance, is one of the large producers, refiners, and marketers in this country. The activities of this or other foreign companies in the United States are not discussed in this book or included in percentages and comparisons given in this and other chapters, nor are the domestic activities of the American companies themselves included, for this is a study of "foreign oil."

Russia, while not sharing in United States production, is not excluded from doing so, as are American and other foreign interests from operating in Soviet Russia.

Now let us see how it has happened that American interests have gained and held a foothold in certain major oil-producing areas abroad.

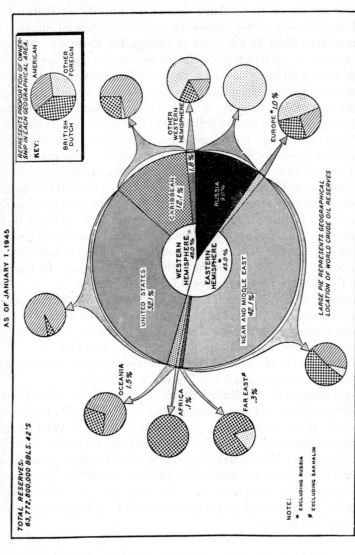

DISTRIBUTION OF OWNERSHIP OF WORLD OIL RESERVES INCL. U.S.

AS OF JANUARY 1, 1945

TOTAL RESERVES:
63,772,800,000 BBLS. 42°S

KEY:
REPRESENTS PROPORTION OF OWNER-
SHIP IN EACH GEOGRAPHICAL AREA.

AMERICAN
OTHER FOREIGN
BRITISH DUTCH

WESTERN HEMISPHERE *
46.0%

EASTERN HEMISPHERE *
45.0%

UNITED STATES
32.1%

CARIBBEAN *
12.1%

RUSSIA
9.0%

OTHER WESTERN HEMISPHERE
1.8%

EUROPE *
1.0%

NEAR AND MIDDLE EAST
42.1%

OCEANIA
1.5%

AFRICA *
.1%

FAR EAST #
.3%

LARGE PIE REPRESENTS GEOGRAPHICAL
LOCATION OF WORLD CRUDE OIL RESERVES

NOTE:
* EXCLUDING RUSSIA
# EXCLUDING SAKHALIN

TABLE 10.—FOREIGN OIL-RESERVE ESTIMATES, WITH AMERICAN SHARE [1]

(In thousand barrels)

As of Jan. 1	Total foreign	American companies	% American total foreign	Total foreign (excluding Russia)	% American total foreign (excluding Russia)
1928	12,597,189	2,080,216	16.5	9,175,179	22.7
1929	13,036,445	2,592,961	19.9	9,702,118	26.7
1930	12,664,932	2,519,227	19.9	9,433,606	26.7
1931	12,190,353	2,423,225	19.9	9,094,362	26.6
1932	11,709,744	2,505,456	21.4	8,776,793	28.5
1933	11,284,668	2,497,868	22.1	8,506,002	29.4
1934	11,003,560	2,477,836	22.5	8,177,978	30.3
1935	11,203,574	3,054,363	27.3	8,796,160	34.7
1936	11,428,860	3,180,649	27.8	9,692,972	32.8
1937	11,727,218	3,290,692	28.1	9,968,757	33.0
1938	14,278,582	4,329,367	30.3	12,375,308	35.0
1939	21,822,424	4,820,785	22.1	19,698,999	24.5
1940	21,801,986	4,727,819	21.7	19,684,160	24.0
1941	22,440,983	5,637,909	25.1	20,299,757	27.8
1942	24,058,823	6,572,646	27.3	21,553,752	30.5
1943	23,920,743	6,690,608	28.0	21,528,797	31.1
1944	31,431,522	10,233,468	32.6	25,769,924	39.7
1945	43,319,800	17,371,700	40.1	37,554,800	46.3

[1] Table covers foreign countries only and thus excludes the United States.

Data are from private sources. The information for 1944 is a combination of private information, PAW information, and the estimates submitted by E. DeGolyer after the visit of his mission to the Near and Middle East. For 1945 the data were taken from the paper presented by J. T. Duce at the hearings held before the Special Senate Committee Investigating Petroleum Resources. The latter estimate contains some reserves in the Near and Middle East that were classified by the DeGolyer mission as "indicated." The estimates from 1928 to 1943, therefore, are not comparable with those of 1944 and 1945. The figures for the earlier period are on a conservative basis because of the lack of complete data and, furthermore, do not include any "indicated" reserves. The principal differences in the estimates for 1943 and 1945 occur in Russia and the Near and Middle East as shown below (in million barrels:

Year	Russia	Near and Middle East	Others	Total foreign
1943	2,392	12,503	9,026	23,921
1945	5,735	26,800	10,785	43,320

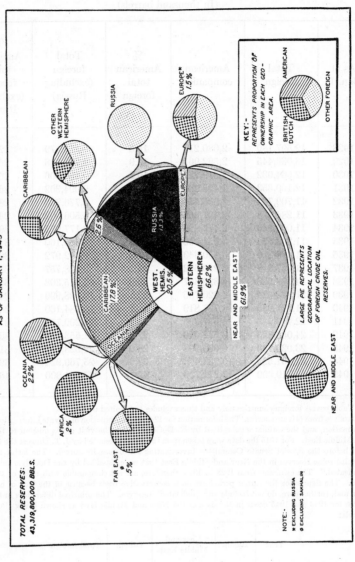

OWNERSHIP OF FOREIGN CRUDE OIL RESERVES
AS OF JANUARY 1, 1945

TOTAL RESERVES:
43,319,800,000 BBLS.

NOTE:-
* EXCLUDING RUSSIA
@ EXCLUDING SAKHALIN

KEY:-
REPRESENTS PROPORTION OF
OWNERSHIP IN EACH GEO-
GRAPHIC AREA.

AMERICAN
BRITISH
DUTCH

OTHER FOREIGN

LARGE PIE REPRESENTS
GEOGRAPHICAL LOCATION
OF FOREIGN CRUDE OIL
RESERVES.

EASTERN
HEMISPHERE*
66.2%

NEAR AND MIDDLE EAST
61.9%

WEST.
HEMIS.
20.5%

CARIBBEAN
17.8%

RUSSIA
13.3%

OCEANIA

EUROPE*

RUSSIA

EUROPE*
1.5%

OTHER
WESTERN
HEMISPHERE

CARIBBEAN

OCEANIA
2.2%

AFRICA
.2%

FAR EAST
.5%

NEAR AND MIDDLE EAST

CHAPTER VI

WESTERN HEMISPHERE—CARIBBEAN OIL

If our domestic oil supplies must be bolstered from abroad, our first reliance would be on the indigenous oil sources of the Western Hemisphere. It is, therefore, comforting to note that American interests rank first in foreign production in this hemisphere, with 56.3 per cent

TABLE 11.—SHARE OF OIL PRODUCTION OF WESTERN HEMISPHERE FOREIGN COUNTRIES [1]

(In thousand barrels daily)

Year	British-Dutch		American		Others		Western Hemisphere
	Production	% area	Production	% area	Production	% area	% total foreign production
1900	3.3	100.0	....	...	....	...	1.4
1912	25.3	48.5	25.9	49.8	.8	1.7	14.6
1921	145.7	25.2	409.8	71.1	21.3	3.7	69.8
1930	266.6	42.3	345.8	54.8	18.3	2.9	44.1
1939	328.8	36.0	441.6	48.3	143.7	15.7	41.0
1941	327.0	32.9	512.5	51.5	154.8	15.6	44.5
1943	284.3	34.4	399.4	48.4	142.1	17.2	37.4
1944	316.6	29.6	601.5	56.3	150.2	14.1	43.5

[1] Table covers foreign countries only and thus excludes the United States.

as against 29.6 per cent for the British-Dutch interests. Again, significantly, the Mexican and Argentine governments with state-owned companies account for practically all the remaining 14.1 per cent (as shown in Table 11).

Moreover, with the United States itself producing 63 per cent of the total world oil output, it is further reassuring that foreign countries in

SHARE OF CRUDE OIL PRODUCTION BY MAJOR GROUPS
WESTERN HEMISPHERE

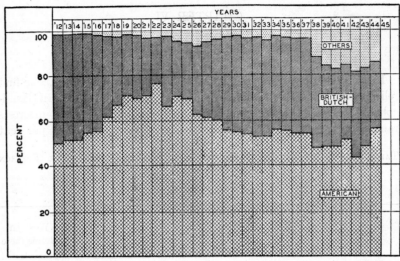

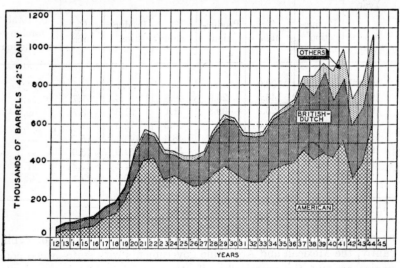

this hemisphere account for 43.5 per cent of total foreign output. In 1912 the foreign countries of the Western Hemisphere produced but 14.6 per cent, with American and British-Dutch companies sharing about equally.

Oil Reserves in Western Hemisphere.—Great as is this hemispheric production, however, and substantial as is the American share, Western Hemisphere production including the United States proceeds at a rate three and one-half times the Eastern Hemisphere largely because of the tremendous consumption of oil products within the United States. Furthermore, it is noteworthy that the Western Hemisphere has proved oil reserves smaller by over 5 billion barrels than those of the Eastern Hemisphere (see Table 12).

TABLE 12.—ESTIMATED WESTERN HEMISPHERE OIL RESERVES AS OF JAN. 1, 1945

(In million barrels)

Western Hemisphere	
United States	20,000.0
Outside United States	8,885.5
Total	28,885.5
Eastern Hemisphere	34,434.3
World total	63,319.8

Geologists say the most likely potential oil areas are in what are termed "sedimentary basins." The continental United States has only 10 to 15 per cent of the world's land area thus favorable to oil accumulation. Outside the United States the Western Hemisphere with present proved reserves of nearly 9 billion barrels has a total sedimentary-basin area of 2 billion acres from which future fields could be discovered. This favorable area is located principally in the Caribbean countries of Venezuela, Colombia, and Trinidad where discoveries may be expected to be large in comparison with the United States.

It is consequently believed that the Western Hemisphere, outside the United States, has sufficient proved and potential reserves of oil to supply the future estimated demand for these countries and, in addition, "any reasonable amounts of petroleum that may be required to supplement the United States' own crude-oil production in the future."

By contrast with the Western Hemisphere, the Eastern Hemisphere, with present proved reserves of 28.6 billion barrels, has an aggregate sedimentary-basin area of 3.6 billion acres—these figures not including Russia, which is self-contained as to present production and future reserves (see Chap. VII). It is obvious, therefore, that the Eastern Hemisphere could be self-contained insofar as oil supply is concerned and that exports of petroleum products from the United States to that hemisphere might ultimately decline to a relatively small volume as compared with the prewar trade.

American Position in Western Hemisphere.—How have Americans been able to gain their predominant foreign position in the Western Hemisphere? How they led in the development of oil in Mexico only eventually to have their properties expropriated has already been told (Chap. II). The costly experience of American interests in Bolivia and Argentina also has been related (Chaps. II and III).

In reality, the struggle for oil in the foreign countries of the Western Hemisphere has been a complicated affair between the British-Dutch and American interests on the one hand and governmental nationalist companies on the other, with the latter in full control in the three countries mentioned.

In other Western Hemisphere countries, in Venezuela, Colombia, and Peru, on the other hand, Americans have kept or gained extensive holdings. In Trinidad, which is becoming an important producing country, the American share is negligible. In Canada, where there is a relatively small production, the American share is estimated at 29 per cent.

How Peru Became an Important Producer.—The first among the countries just mentioned to have a sizable American interest aid its oil development was Peru, although originally opened up by the British. Apart from some sporadic drilling along the coast between 1867–1874, no real attempt at oil development was made until the securing of the hacienda La Brea and Parinas by Dr. H. W. C. Tweddle from the Helguero family in 1888. This led in 1896 to the formation of the London & Pacific Petroleum Company, Limited, (British), which along with the Lagunitos Oil Company and the West Coast Oil Fuel Company took its place in 1915 under the banner of the International Petroleum Company (Standard Oil Company, New Jersey) (see Chap. II).

International materially increased the production and in prewar years maintained it at a level of from 20,000 to 40,000 bbl. daily. There has been some other small production by British interests, but Americans have had control of some 80 per cent of the total for the last 20 years. As of the end of 1943 the American-owned reserves represented 81 per cent of the country's total.

All commercial production to date has been in the extreme north of the country along the seacoast, but an American operator made the

American Interests Rank First in Foreign Production in Western Hemisphere

Photograph courtesy of Imperial Oil Review.

Talara, Peru. American control 80 per cent of present Peruvian production and reserves.

"If our domestic oil supplies cannot be bolstered from abroad, our first reliance would be on the indigenous oil sources of the Western Hemisphere." **See page 73.**

Photograph by Collier, courtesy of Standard Oil Company (New Jersey).

Barranca Bermeja, Colombia. Two of eight all-steel river boats owned and operated by Tropical Oil Company to deliver petroleum products up and down the Magdalena River. Royal Dutch-Shell has ended 100 per cent American control of Colombian oil.

Western Venezuela. Americans developed over-water drilling on Lake Maracaibo, an engineering accomplishment unmatched elsewhere and one that opened vast oil reserves that otherwise would have remained untapped.

"Venezuela, largely through the efforts of American private capital, has become the second largest oil-producing country in the world." See page 80.

Photographs on this and following page by Vachon, courtesy of Standard Oil Company (New Jersey).

Drilling-barge workers on lake.   Wells against lake horizon.

"American Controlled Output Accounted for Nearly Two-thirds of the Total in 1943." See Page 80.

Eastern Venezuela—Oil well in Quiriquire field. Banana patch in foreground.

Eastern Venezuela—Venezuelan soldier serving as guard at the Caripito refinery during Second World War.

American Interests Rank First in Oil Reserves in Western Hemisphere.
See page 75.

Andean National Pipeline, near Barranca Bermeja, Colombia. Section of the pipe line
which has been moved to save it from being washed away by the Magdalena River

*"The American position in foreign oil production and reserves in this hemisphere has
increased with the years."*   *See page 82.*

Upper photo by Collier, lower by Vachon, courtesy of Standard Oil Company (New Jersey).

Eastern Venezuela—Boilers being set up for new well in jungle country—Quiriquire field.

first discovery of oil in the relatively inaccessible trans-Andean section of Peru several years ago, and this region will undoubtedly be developed as demand arises.

The adoption of a new petroleum law in 1922 led to the denouncement of large tracts for oil-exploration purposes, but, as in the case of Colombia, Peru's oil laws have been regarded by operators as acting to retard intensive exploratory effort.

Laws Have Hampered Development in Colombia.—One of the Big Three in Caribbean oil is Colombia, where petroleum exploration began along the north coastal plain in 1908. Records mention that a Colombian company, financed by American and Colombian capital, found a small amount of oil but obtained no commercial production. In 1909 this company opened a refinery at Cartagena with a capacity of 400 bbl. daily but had to operate it on crude imported from the United States.

Prior to 1900, Roberto de Mares, a Colombian, secured a concession on some 2½ million acres in the province of Santander, jungle country of the upper Magdalena River Valley some 300 miles from the coast. The first efforts to interest American capital in the property met with failure because of the revolution of 1898–1904. The concession was renewed in 1905 and again in 1916, when the Tropical Oil Company, of Pittsburgh, became interested in the project. This resulted in active prospecting of the property during 1917, 1918, and 1919 and the bringing in of three flowing wells.

Later the Tropical Oil Company was taken over by the International Petroleum Company, subsidiary of the Imperial Oil Company (Standard Oil Company, New Jersey), which made great progress in development work (see Chap. III). A refinery was erected adjacent to the fields in 1922 to supply local markets. In 1926 a 335-mile pipe line to the seacoast, an outstanding engineering achievement, was completed, and Colombian crude reached the world market. Another early concession obtained in Colombia was the Barco concession across the Andes on the Venezuelan border, in which Americans held a minority interest for some time. Later, American companies developed this remote concession, overcoming great physical handicaps (see Chap. III).

Because of legal entanglements exploration work on the Barco concession did not start until early in 1930. The first producing well was completed in 1933, following which development proceeded slowly until a pipe line, another great construction achievement, was completed in 1939 over a near-by mile-high range of the Andes to the coast.

Since completion of the first pipe line in 1926, Colombia's production has ranged between 40,000 and 69,000 bbl. daily, fluctuating with export market and shipping conditions. All production to 1943 was under American control, but the Royal Dutch–Shell has had favorable results in developing commercial production, thus ending the 100 per cent American phase of Colombia's oil history.

At the end of 1943, 310,900,000 barrels of oil had been produced in Colombia. Reserves are estimated at over 200 million barrels, of which about 90 per cent is American-owned.

Colombia's oil laws have long had various restrictive provisions that have hindered intensive exploratory work, but during the past quarter of a century many American companies, both large and small, have held acreage in Colombia and drilled exploratory wells. Several companies of other nationalities also have been interested at one time or another. However, the country has not had the same intensive development apparent in Venezuela's history, largely because of the less attractive terms of its oil laws.

Historically, it should be noted that, as Mexico's restrictions became more onerous, the oil operators began to look elsewhere in Latin America for new oil fields. At first they explored the possibilities in Colombia and Venezuela. When their investigating parties began to arrive in Colombia, the reaction was to pass legislation to "safeguard the sovereign interests" and "protect" the "richest oil deposits in the world." The result was that aside from the development of the De Mares and Barco concessions governed by previous laws no development of consequence took place in Colombia. Venezuela, in contrast to the policy then adopted by Colombia, modified its oil legislation to make the conditions more workable and fair to invested capital with the result that capital flowed into development of the country's oil. In due course Venezuela rose to second place in the world as a producer of oil. It paid off its foreign debts and operated for years without a deficit, largely because of its revenues from the oil industry.

Venezuela Holds Stellar Place in Caribbean Oil.—Indeed, Venezuela holds the stellar place in Caribbean oil production and reserves. What is known as the Maracaibo basin, the district around Lake Maracaibo, has proved to be one of the richest petroleum areas in South America.

The first commercial oil well was drilled there in 1913 by the Caribbean Petroleum Company, then a subsidiary of the General Asphalt Company, an American company. A short time afterward, control went to the Royal Dutch–Shell group, and the wells on this concession were shut down for a number of years.

In 1915 the Royal Dutch–Shell groups also acquired control of the Venezuelan Oil Concessions, Limited, holding 3,000 square miles in the districts of Maracaibo and Bolivar. Thus British-Dutch interests for a time had much more extensive concession holdings than did Americans, whose interest did not take the form of active search until the early twenties, coincident with the decline of Mexican producing areas.

New Petroleum Law Starts Large-scale Development.—The Venezuelan government in 1920 passed a petroleum law that was widely regarded as providing a base for oil development, mutually equitable for the nation and the foreign operating companies. By this time it was quite evident that Venezuela had vast oil resources, and the government's encouragement of foreign capital gave a great stimulus to exploration activity.

Commercial Development Dates from 1923 with Americans in the Fore.—By 1920, 29 wells had been drilled in Venezuela, resulting in four discoveries with an estimated reserve of around 400 million barrels. Production amounted to about 1,000 bbl. daily. Nevertheless, development work on the whole was disappointing in the Maracaibo basin until the Barroso No. 2 of the Venezuelan Oil Concessions, Limited (Royal Dutch), drilled itself in on Dec. 14, 1922, in the La Rosa field. It flowed wild more than 100,000 barrels a day for nine days before sanding up. Later the Venezuelan Oil Concessions made the important discoveries west of the lake at La Paz and Concepcion in the district of Maracaibo.

Actual commercial development of Venezuelan oil fields can be said to date from Jan. 1, 1923. By the end of 1924 several American oil companies had acquired concessions and were in the production column. These included Standard Oil Company (New Jersey) through purchase of the Creole Petroleum Corporation and also Gulf Oil Corporation.

American-owned Production Rises Rapidly.—Some 35 American companies, many then still active in Mexico, started to acquire petroleum exploratory concessions in Venezuela and carried out exploratory work to such good effect that by 1925 the estimated proved reserves of the country were increased to around 900 million barrels. The Creole Petroleum Corporation developed unique over-water oil operations in Lake Maracaibo. It conducted drilling and producing activities in water over 100 ft. deep. This engineering accomplishment, unmatched elsewhere, is one that opened vast oil reserves that would otherwise have remained untapped.

After 1925 American-owned production in Venezuela rose rapidly in both amount and percentage of the total to over 50 per cent in 1928.

Efforts of American companies also were responsible for important fields being developed in eastern Venezuela in the 1930's and 1940's, until American-controlled output accounted for nearly two-thirds of the total in 1943.

The course and the American-owned share of production in Venezuela from 1921 are shown in Table 13.

TABLE 13.—AMERICAN SHARE OF VENEZUELA PRODUCTION

(In barrels daily)

Year	Industry production	American-owned production	% American-owned
1921	4,100	0	0
1922	6,600	36	.5
1923	13,000	200	1.5
1924	25,000	1,200	4.8
1925	55,900	17,600	31.5
1926	101,200	37,400	37.0
1927	175,100	83,400	47.6
1929	376,800	206,300	54.8
1932	322,700	171,600	53.2
1936	426,000	256,300	60.2
1939	562,800	335,100	59.5
1940	508,600	312,200	61.4
1941	625,000	403,500	64.6
1942	405,500	247,000	60.9
1943	491,500	317,500	64.6

Up to the end of 1943 Venezuela produced 2,600 million barrels of oil. Proved crude-oil reserves at the end of 1943 have been estimated at close to 5,900 million barrels, of which Americans held rights to nearly 74 per cent.

Venezuela Secures Greater Share of Oil Returns.—"Venezuela, largely through the efforts of American private capital, has become the second largest oil-producing country in the world. A stable and friendly government forms a solid base on which has been built a great industry," Mr. Rayner states in his State Department Memorandum.[1] "In the early stages of the industry's development and before the producing possibilities of the country were clear, it is fully understandable that

[1] See Chap. I.

the companies exploring for petroleum required very favorable contracts before they could risk the hundreds of millions of dollars involved in exploratory and development work. Mutually agreeable contracts were negotiated by the companies with the Venezuelan government or the Venezuelan private interests concerned, and the operation over a period of years was eminently successful.

"As time passed and as the base of the industry became broader, the element of risk decreased progressively. The government of Venezuela came to the conclusion (which was shared by the petroleum companies) that the government and people of Venezuela should be given a greater share in the returns from petroleum operations. In the spirit of the utmost frankness and respect for one another's rights and obligations and with the clear recognition of Venezuela's legitimate interests, representatives of the government of Venezuela and of the foreign operating companies held extensive discussions which contributed in a most important way to the passage by the Venezuelan Congress in February, 1943, of new petroleum legislation which should form the basis for the highly efficient operation of the petroleum industry in the world's second largest producing country for many years to come. It is to be strongly underlined that, throughout, each and every determination was one taken by the sovereign will of the government and people of Venezuela. Nevertheless, that government and people fully recognized the legitimate interest of the companies concerned.

"Here is a classic case where cooperation in an atmosphere of mutual respect and confidence has borne fine fruit. Throughout, there was the closest collaboration among the government of Venezuela and private interests involved and the accredited representatives of the United States."

Trinidad Oil Mostly British.—The American interest (General Asphalt Company) that pioneered in Venezuela, was in Trinidad, a British possession, even earlier—but developing natural asphalt rather than petroleum.

Country of the famed "pitch lake" and now second ranking country of the Big Three in Caribbean oil, Trinidad entered the oil-producing column as early as 1909. It was in the neighborhood of the pitch lake that the earliest important progress in developing oil was made. There, through the enterprise of the American concessionaires of the lake and their associates, the Trinidad Lake Petroleum Company, Limited, a number of wells were drilled, a refinery was built, and the first shipment of oil was made in May, 1911.

In 1911 the Trinidad Oil Fields, Limited (British), obtained a very prolific well estimated to have produced 25,000 barrels in three and a half hours before it became choked.

The companies controlling the largest areas in 1918 were the Trinidad Central Oilfields, Limited, Trinidad Leaseholds, Limited, and the United British West Indies Petroleum Syndicate, Limited, all British.

Only in comparatively recent years has Trinidad's oil production become impressive, reaching 65,000 bbl. daily in 1942 as against 32,000 bbl. daily and less than 6,000 bbl. daily in 1935 and 1920, respectively.

This development has been kept largely British by restricting the issuance of leases on Crown lands to British companies. The American share, almost insignificant, amounts to 89 bbl. daily, or 0.1 per cent of the total.

Anglo-Iranian Oil Interests Not Large in Western Hemisphere.—The expansion program of the Anglo-Persian Oil Company in the Western Hemisphere in the early twenties never assumed large proportions.

In about 1922 the Anglo-Persian acquired some small concessions for drilling in the Comodoro Rivadavia fields in Argentina and acquired an interest in a small refinery there. Both of these projects were abandoned a few years later.

The Anglo-Persian, through a subsidiary, D'Arcy Exploration Company, has a third interest in an area in northern Trinidad held by the Trinidad Northern Areas, Limited. The balance of the stock of this company is divided equally between the Shell and the Trinidad Leaseholds, Limited. Exploratory work and test drilling are at present in abeyance on these properties, according to Skinner's "Oil and Petroleum Year Book."

Some years ago Anglo-Iranian did some exploratory drilling in the province of New Brunswick, Canada, but this venture was abandoned. In 1937 Anglo-Iranian secured some concessions in the Bahamas, and it is understood exploratory drilling recently commenced in this area.

The foregoing comprises the total effort that the Anglo-Iranian has put forth in the Western Hemisphere over a period of approximately 25 years.

American Position Improves in Western Hemisphere.—In summary, the American position in foreign oil production and reserves in this hemisphere has improved with the years. Venezuela's emergence as the second major producer of the Western Hemisphere—only exceeded by the United States—was crowned in 1939 when it exceeded Mexico's record production of 1921. As previously mentioned, American interests at first had to be satisfied with second place in Venezuela, and as a result America's share of foreign production in the Western Hemisphere dropped from 76 per cent in 1922 to 53 per cent in 1933. The British-Dutch position, on the other hand, rose from 20 per cent in 1922 to 43 per cent in 1933.

From then until Mar. 18, 1938, when Mexico expropriated foreign oil holdings, the relative position of the two groups remained about the same. The British-Dutch suffered a larger production loss in Mexico,

TABLE 14.—SHARE OF FOREIGN OIL RESERVES OF WESTERN HEMISPHERE [1]

(In million barrels)

Area	American	British-Dutch	Other foreign	Total	% American	% British-Dutch	% Foreign
Caribbean............	5,596.5	1,958.2	184.9	7,739.6	72.3	25.3	2.4
Other Western Hemisphere......	195.6	173.8	776.5	1,145.9	17.1	15.2	67.7
Total Western Hemisphere....	5,792.1	2,132.0	961.4	8,885.5	65.2	24.0	10.8

[1] Table covers foreign countries only and thus excludes the United States.

but this was partially offset by gains in Venezuela, Trinidad, and Canada. However, in the great Venezuelan developments, the American share rose, as we have seen, to more than 60 per cent, and when that country reached a peak in 1944, the American position in the hemisphere as a whole increased to 56.3 per cent (see Table 11).

Caribbean Countries Have Most of Hemisphere Foreign Reserves.— It is estimated that oil reserves on Jan. 1, 1945, in the Western Hemisphere (excluding the United States) totaled 8.9 billion barrels, or about 21 per cent of the total foreign reserve including Russia and about 24 per cent of the total foreign excluding Russia. The American share was 65.2, the British-Dutch 24, and the balance was accounted for almost entirely by government-owned and -operated reserves, 10.8 per cent (as shown in Table 14).

It is to be noted that the major position of American companies in the foreign Western Hemisphere reserves is brought about by the ownership of 5.6 billion barrels by the American companies in the Caribbean area (Venezuela, Colombia, and Trinidad), or 72 per cent of the total reserves in that sector. The British and Dutch companies own a little over 2 billion barrels of reserves in the Western Hemisphere, or 24 per cent of the total. The reserves of the British-Dutch companies are also concentrated in the Caribbean area although their position in that region amounts to but 25 per cent.

Most important is the American interest in foreign production and reserves in the indigenous countries of the Caribbean in that such developments have a direct bearing on ensuring readily available supplies to meet the great and increasing consumption of petroleum products in the United States. But it is a matter of more than secondary interest that American companies also have gained reserves in the Eastern Hemisphere almost double the amount of the total they control in the Western Hemisphere—the respective totals being 11.6 billion barrels and 5.8 billion barrels.

Caribbean oil potentialities as estimated to date have to play second fiddle to the Middle East.

CHAPTER VII

EASTERN HEMISPHERE—OIL SPOTLIGHT ON MIDDLE EAST

Having seen what has transpired in the struggle,for oil in the Western Hemisphere, now let us turn for a similar review to the major oil areas of the Eastern Hemisphere—(1) Europe and Africa, (2) the Near and Middle East, and (3) the Far East. Backward in consumption as it is as compared with the Western Hemisphere yet rich with oil reserves and with tremendous potentialities, the Eastern Hemisphere rates closest attention.

As already pointed out, the rise of the British-Dutch interests into a dominating world position was largely an early-twentieth-century phenomenon dictated by the necessities of nations dependent on colonial or foreign sources for petroleum inasmuch as they had little or no home sources. It had its inception in the Eastern Hemisphere in the Far East, spread to the Middle East, and then expanded to the Western Hemisphere.

Russia, considered here as the second of three major groupings, owed her strong position in oil to her large home production and reserves in both the European and Asiatic regions of the Eastern Hemisphere.

The Americans, the third group, while marketing in all countries of the Hemisphere, however remote, were represented in the producing column of only one Eastern Hemisphere country—Rumania—prior to the First World War.

Americans Persistent in Europe and Africa.—Since that time, in addition to Rumania, Americans have participated in the development of oil in the European countries of Poland, Italy, Germany, Austria, Hungary, and England and have explored for oil in other European countries. They have sought oil in Egypt, Portuguese East Africa, and Ethiopia. Percentage-wise the results of their activity in the Europe-Africa area stood at only 2.1 per cent in 1919, 2.9 per cent in 1935, and 2.6 per cent in 1939. Nevertheless, American companies have persisted in their participation and just prior to the Second World War made important discoveries in Hungary and Austria, as well as in Germany proper, only to have the fields seized by the Axis when they were in the early stages of development.

85

SHARE OF CRUDE OIL PRODUCTION BY MAJOR GROUPS
EUROPE AND AFRICA

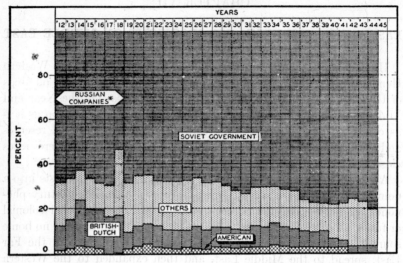

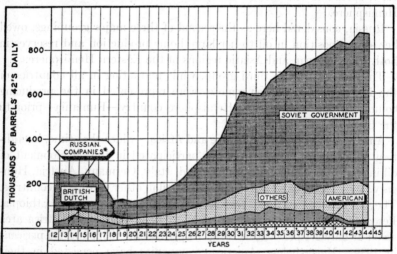

*INCLUDED WITH RUSSIAN COMPANIES IS AN UNDETERMINABLE QUANTITY OF BRITISH-DUTCH PRODUCTION.

The British-Dutch interests, after having their properties in Russia confiscated in 1919, controlled about 7.4 per cent of the area's production, having a sizable stake in Rumania and all the production in Egypt. Their position remained between 8 and 9 per cent until 1937 when it dropped to 7 per cent, staying at the level until their properties in Rumania were taken over by the Nazis in 1940. However, discovery of

TABLE 15.—SHARE OF OIL PRODUCTION IN EUROPE AND AFRICA [1]

(In thousand barrels daily)

| Year | British-Dutch | | American | | Russian | | Area % of total foreign production |
	Production	% of area	Production	% of area	Production	% of area	
1914	48.3	20.5	8.3	3.5	148.1	62.8	61.3
1919	9.6	7.4	2.5	2.1	88.2	68.1	25.7
1926	26.1	10.0	5.3	2.0	174.9	66.5	29.4
1930	43.1	8.4	10.4	2.0	370.7	72.2	35.9
1935	59.3	8.6	19.7	2.9	497.5	71.8	38.6
1940	30.1	3.8	21.1	2.6	630.0	78.2	37.1
1944	27.7	3.2	...	..	700.0	80.4	35.5

[1] Table covers foreign countries only and thus excludes the United States.

the Rhas Gharib field in Egypt and development of a small commercial production in Great Britain itself during the Second World War tended to strengthen the British-Dutch position in the area.

But it is Russia that dominates this area, having since 1919 produced from 65 per cent to 80 per cent of the total, as shown in Table 15.

American Producers in Rumania since 1903.—Rumania had a very small oil "industry" based on shallow hand-dug wells two years before the drilling of the Drake well in the United States in 1859. Production developed but slowly, however, until after 1900. Romana Americana (Standard Oil Company, New Jersey) first entered Rumania in 1903. By 1914 the American share was 24 per cent of the total production. It declined after the First World War, however, and by 1939 was down to 11.4 per cent.

Rumanian Oil Nationalization Hampers.—In 1924 Rumania adopted a new mining law that provided a form of nationalization of producing companies, state monopolization of pipe lines, and the ultimate monopolization of the internal marketing of petroleum products. The provisions of this law were the subject of protest by the principal foreign interests, including American, operating in Rumania, who asserted that they were, in effect, confiscatory.

Over most of Rumania's oil history, government policy has restricted operators to leasing of small tracts, a situation generally unfavorable to broad exploration programs involving large expenditures on preliminary work. Largely as a result, much of the country's potential oil area remained untested at the outbreak of the Second World War, despite the long history of the industry.

The Second World War again brought devastation to the oil fields of Rumania as had the First World War, with American interests much more heavily involved because of the considerable expansion of investment during the interwar period (see Chap. XIII).

Americans Hold Small Interest in Poland.—The Polish oil industry, which began as early as 1874, also was severely stricken by both world wars. Americans were interested in a small way in Poland as early as 1920 when the Standard Oil Company (New Jersey) acquired a fourth interest in a company called Nobel Brothers, in which the Nobel interests and the Posner Bank held, respectively, 25 and 50 per cent. This company had originally been formed by the union of the former Nobel properties in Poland and working capital supplied by the Posner Bank, the respective interests being then fifty-fifty.

The Standard Oil Company (New Jersey) eventually put into this combination the plant and equipment formerly belonging to its German subsidiary but located within Polish territory after the First World War and thus acquired a 25 per cent interest. Nobel Brothers in Poland had some producing properties and subsequently secured others. The Vacuum Oil Company also had an operating subsidiary in Poland with some production.

The latest reported American production in Poland was 2.7 per cent of the total production.

American Share in Other European Producing Countries.—First American production and latest reported daily output in other European countries in which Americans have interests are shown as follows: Italy, 1927, latest reported American percentage of total, 62.8 per cent; Germany, 1933, 13.5 per cent; Austria, 1938, 4.2 per cent; Hungary, 1937, when Americans first opened up Hungarian oil fields, 99.3 per cent; and England, 1939, 0.2 per cent.

Inasmuch as in these countries special political and economic conditions had developed before the Second World War and in many the postwar conditions today are similar or obscure because of military occupation, the experience in these countries of American oil companies in endeavoring to develop oil resources and to carry on a business in the borders of such countries is treated further in Chap. XII (see also Chap. II).

Russia Leading Foreign Producer Prior to the First World War.— Along about the time of the First World War, Russia held first place in foreign oil production, with Rumania third just behind Mexico, and Poland fifth just behind the Dutch East Indies. While American oil drillers worked in the Russian oil fields, American interests were never active producers. The oil pioneers in that country were the Swedish Alfred and Robert Nobel, sons of Emmanuel Nobel, the perfector of the torpedo. Robert was the first person to build a successful pipe line after the American fashion in the Baku field and was the real father of modern oil development in that one-time land of the Romanovs. His firm became a factor in the industrial life of the empire.

Because of Russia's vast oil potentialities foreign capital sought participation. In 1910 the Royal Dutch–Shell began to acquire these Russian interests. They also obtained producing properties at Grozny.

Oil Industry Nationalized by the Soviet.—With the overthrow of the century-old Czarist and brief Kerenski regimes in 1917, the Bolshevists seized all property, including the oil fields. In June, 1918, the Russian petroleum industry was nationalized by a decree of the Soviet of People's Commissars. All petroleum properties were declared state property, and trade in petroleum and its products was made a state monopoly. Administration of the industry was confided to the Chief Naphtha Committee attached to the Fuel Department of the Supreme Soviet of People's Economy.

The Standard Oil Company (New Jersey) had an agreement with the Nobels for joint operation at Baku after the Soviet government took over if private ownership were reestablished. It sustained a loss of approximately 9 million dollars—the amount paid the Nobel family—for these holdings were never recovered from the Soviet government, nor was private enterprise permitted.

From an output of 170,000 to 190,000 bbl. daily before the First World War, oil production soon shrank to considerably less than half in the next few years. A decree of the All-Russian Central Executive Committee, promulgated in June, 1922, placed the administration of petroleum stores in the hands of the Chief Fuel Administration, which had complete charge of the sale of all products and stores.

It was not until 1926 that state operation restored Russian production to prewar levels. After that, Russian production increased steadily, reaching 200,000 bbl. daily in 1927, 300,000 and 400,000 bbl. daily in 1930 and 1931, and 600,000 bbl. daily in 1939.

Soviet Interests until the Second World War Lay within Own Territory.—Despite her great home production, Russia may be considered less a factor in world oil competition than the British-Dutch interests and American interests, for her activity has been confined to her own borders and her preoccupation has been to develop her own rich resources and to make Russia self-sustaining. Nevertheless, the very fact that Russia's reserves are so large places the country among the Big Three of the world's principal oil groups. With an estimated proved reserve of 5.7 billion barrels and a sedimentary-basin area in Europe and Asia of about 2.8 billion acres, Russia would seem to be in a self-sufficient position for a long time to come.

Now within Soviet Russia's expanding military and political sphere are Rumania, Austria, Hungary, and Poland in Europe and, toward the Middle East, the indigenous and fabulous reserves of Iran, Iraq, and Arabia.

Americans Improve Position in Near and Middle East.—Indeed, the spotlight today is on the Near and Middle East. While knowledge and use of petroleum in the Near East go back beyond the dawn of history when seepage oils and tar were utilized for many purposes, little or no modern drilling had been done up to the First World War. With the breaking up of the Turkish Empire at that time, British, Dutch, and French interests took up rights to explore in various of the newly established mandates and protectorates, and it was only after vigorous diplomatic action by our government after the First World War that American interests succeeded in getting representation in the Middle East (see Chap. I).

It was in the middle thirties that American companies succeeded in securing a foothold in other potentially important oil lands in the Persian Gulf area. Standard Oil Company of California and The Texas Company, through jointly owned Bahrein Petroleum Company, Limited, acquired the oil rights on 300 square miles in Bahrein Island. This company developed substantial production and built a refinery, with an original capacity of 25,000 bbl. daily. The capacity has since been increased to 65,000 bbl. daily.

The Arabian American Oil Company (previously the California Arabian Standard Oil Company), jointly owned by Standard Oil Company of California and The Texas Company, having obtained 160 million acres under concession in Saudi Arabia on the Arabian mainland, has four fields in which production has been encountered in Saudi Arabia. A new refinery, completed in 1945, is now processing in the neighborhood of 80,000 bbl. daily.

Sole rights to the development of the sheikdom of Kuwait have been acquired by the Kuwait Oil Company, Limited, in which a subsidiary of Gulf Oil Corporation has a 50 per cent interest and a subsidiary of Anglo-Iranian Oil Company, Limited, the remaining 50 per cent interest. Here nine wells have been completed, each one having a large production, and further drilling developments are now in process.

Struggle in Near and Middle East.—These interests were obtained by Americans only through perseverance against great odds. As previously related (Chap. I), after the First World War the British government took, in effect, the position that, since the American government had never ratified the Versailles Treaty and had not become a member of the League of Nations, it was not entitled to participate in the development of the mandated territories such as those in this area. To this position the State Department took strong exception and specifically with respect to Mesopotamia (Iraq).

After prolonged negotiations agreement was finally secured in 1927, and an American company (the Near East Development Corporation) secured a 23¾ per cent interest in the Iraq Petroleum Company, as a result of the insistence of the State Department that American firms be given equal opportunity in obtaining concessions.

The field that has been developed by the Iraq Petroleum Company at Kirkuk is one of the largest proved fields in the world. Furthermore, as the Iraq Petroleum Company, itself or through subsidiaries, has spread its operations in other areas of Iraq and around the Persian Gulf, American participation in these new areas has been ensured by the terms of the original agreement.

Even after the Iraq oil agreement the position of American oil companies in the Near and Middle East remained tenuous, however, because of treaty provisions in various countries that their foreign affairs should be conducted by the British. For instance, American companies desiring to obtain concessions in Bahrein were confronted with the initial difficulty that they were entering into an area in which the British had long been paramount.

The concession now American-held at Bahrein was originally obtained on Dec. 2, 1925, by a British group, the Eastern & General Syndicate. On Nov. 30, 1927, the Eastern Gulf Oil Company, an American corpora-tion, secured two option contracts from the British syndicate, which covered the existing concession at Bahrein, and a concession as yet un-signed for the Kuwait area. On Dec. 21, 1928, the Bahrein contract was transferred to the Standard Oil Company of California, which organized a wholly owned subsidiary, The Bahrein Petroleum Company, Limited, registered as a British corporation under the laws of Canada, to receive the assignments of the concessions.

By this time the British government had become aware of the fact that American oil interests were seeking to enter the Persian Gulf terri-tory and not only raised obstructions that threatened to annul the en-tire transaction but also raised a question of policy that engaged the immediate attention of the United States State Department. Our Em-bassy in London was instructed in March, 1929, to request a statement of policy from the British government with regard to the granting of concessions, such as the one in Bahrein, in the semi-independent Arab states of the Persian Gulf. At the same time our Embassy was instructed to point out the liberality of our own laws in this connection.

In a note dated May 30, 1929, the British Foreign Office replied that it was prepared in principle to admit the participation of "United States interests" in the Bahrein concession, provided that it would be satisfied as to the certain conditions including those under which American capi-tal would take part. At the suggestion of the British Foreign Office negotiations were then initiated between the American company and the British Colonial Office, which were carried to a successful conclusion. In May, 1930, the first representatives of the Standard Oil Company of California arrived in Bahrein, and the field has since been developed very successfully and refining facilities installed that have played an important part in the Allied war effort.

"Here again the prompt and positive action by the State Department had secured results favorable to an American-owned company," Mr. Rayner in his State Department Memorandum [1] says. "By securing the entry of American oil interests into Bahrein, the way was paved for some American interests to obtain concessions in near-by Arabia."

The sheikdom of Kuwait also has long been under British influence. On Nov. 27, 1931, the Eastern Gulf Oil Company, formally called the department's attention to the fact that the British Colonial Office was

[1] See Chap. I.

Spotlight Today Is on the Near and Middle East. It Was in the Mid-thirties That American Companies Succeeded in Securing a Foothold in Other Potentially Important Oil Lands in the Persian Gulf Area—Bahrein Island, Saudi Arabia—Kuwait. *See Page 85.*

An ancient desert traveler surveys the Ras Tanura refinery of the Arabian American Oil Company, Saudi Arabia.

Photographs on this and next five pages by Robert Yarnall Richie, courtesy of Arabian American Oil Company.

Abqaiq field, Saudi Arabia.

Bringing in a well—Damman field, Saudi Arabia.

Camp at Dhahran airport.

Pipe lines from Ras Tanura refinery to Marine Terminal.

Pipe line—Abqaiq to Dhahran.

Arab worker reading meter of Stabilizer at Dhahran.

Company airplane en route from Dhahran to Riyadh.

Arab pay line—Ras Tanura.

Arab worker at Ras Tanura refinery.

These Interests Were Obtained by Americans Only through Perse-erance against Great Odds." See page 91.

Training Arab worker—Ras Tanura.

"It was in the middle thirties that American oil companies succeeded in gaining a foothold in other potentially important oil lands in the Persian Gulf area." See page 90.

Arab working on well.

Arab refinery worker.

Arab foundry worker.

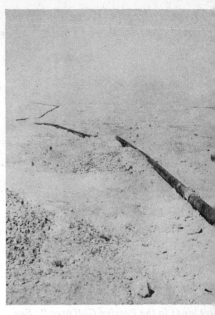

The Bahrein Island Petroleum Company, Limited. Setting foundations forms for crude distillation unit.

Bahrein pipe line.

Photographs by courtesy of The Bahrein Petroleum Company, Limited.

Mooring of S.S. "William M. Meredith" near Sitra Wharf, Bahrein Island.

Submarine loading lines elevated for removal of marine deposits, Bahrein Island.

Installing of Sea Oil-loading Line for Handling Kuwait Oil

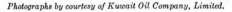

Today the Near and Middle East with vast oil reserves are the scene of continued ruggle for position between American, British-Dutch, Russian, and other nationals."

Photographs by courtesy of Kuwait Oil Company, Limited.

Laying pipe for the Abqaiq-Damman pipe line, Saudi Arabia.

Photograph by courtesy of The Bahrein Petroleum Company, Limite

Building wharf, Bahrein.

insisting on the so-called "nationality clause" in the Kuwait concession. This clause in effect prevented anyone except a British subject or firm from obtaining a concession in Kuwait. On Dec. 3, 1931, our Embassy in London was instructed to make representations with a view to securing equal treatment for American firms.

These lengthy negotiations were complicated at a late date by the fact that the British-controlled Anglo-Persian Oil Company (now the Anglo-Iranian Oil Company, Limited), which had previously expressed its disinterest in Kuwait, suddenly endeavored to secure a concession from the sheik of Kuwait. Again, our State Department insisted on the open-door policy, and finally agreement was reached; on Dec. 23, 1934, a concession was granted to the Kuwait Oil Company, 50 per cent British (Anglo-Persian Oil Company) and 50 per cent American (Gulf Oil Corporation).

In Saudi Arabia, concession was obtained in 1933 by the company now known as the Arabian American Oil Company (a subsidiary of the Standard Oil Company of California and The Texas Company). While no intervention by our State Department was necessary, the department's earlier efforts that had resulted in the Bahrein concession were doubtless helpful in favorable negotiations with the Arabian government. In fact, when extended concessions were negotiated in 1939, Ibn Saud awarded the concession to the Arabian American Oil Company, even though this private company offered less than government-controlled Japanese and German companies, whose diplomats at Jidda were extremely pressing with their offers. This concession is believed to contain some of the largest oil fields in the world.

British-Dutch Hold 87 Per Cent of Production.—While a foothold in this rich oil territory has been gained by American companies, they are yet to be represented in the production column of Iran, which before the Second World War became the third largest foreign oil-producing country in the world. All Iran production remains British (Anglo-Iranian Oil Company, Limited). Considering this and the fact that the British-Dutch interests also hold a preponderant share in the Iraq Petroleum Company (53.75 per cent against 23¾ per cent held by Americans), it is not to be wondered at that this group's share of Near and Middle East oil production is over 87 per cent as against less than 13 per cent for American companies (see Table 16).

It will be noted that the area's share of total foreign production, only 1.3 per cent in 1913, rose to 14.2 per cent in 1939 with Kirkuk (Iraq) and Bahrein added to Iran as producing countries. Wartime

SHARE OF CRUDE OIL PRODUCTION BY MAJOR GROUPS
NEAR AND MIDDLE EAST

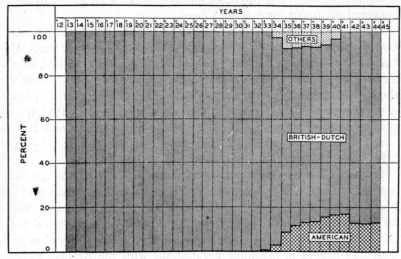

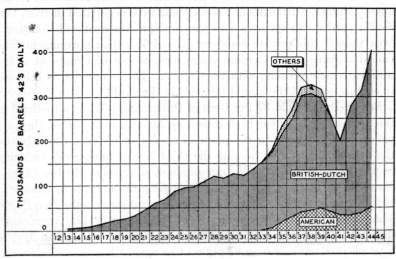

shut-backs in Iran and Iraq reduced the share to 9 per cent in 1941 despite new production from Saudi Arabia. The reopening of Iraq and Iranian wells, however, coupled with increased production in Arabia, sent crude-oil production up in 1944 until it was equal to 16.5 per cent of the foreign total in that year.

TABLE 16.—SHARE OF OIL PRODUCTION OF NEAR AND MIDDLE EAST COUNTRIES [1]

(In thousand barrels daily)

Year	British-Dutch		American		Others		Area % of total foreign production
	Production	% of area	Production	% of area	Production	% of area	
1912							
1913	5.1	100.0	...	...	...	..	1.3
1921	45.7	100.0	...	...	...	..	5.5
1933	150.6	99.9	0.1	0.1	...	..	10.2
1939	247.5	78.3	49.8	15.7	19.0	6.0	14.2
1941	167.1	83.2	33.7	16.8	...	..	9.0
1943	278.4	87.7	39.0	12.3	...	..	14.4
1944	353.4	87.2	51.8	12.8	...	..	16.5

[1] Table covers foreign countries only and thus excludes the United States.

Today the Near and Middle East with vast oil reserves is the scene of continued struggle for position between American, British-Dutch, Russian, and other nationals.

Struggle in the Far East.—British-Dutch nationals control most of the oil production in the Far East, chiefly in India and the Dutch East Indies. American companies in the Far East gained production for the first time in 1921, but output was negligible for a number of years. In 1926 the American position still was only 1 per cent, but it rose to 3.1 per cent in 1927, reached 7.5 per cent in 1930, and jumped to 23 per cent in 1936. Thereafter, it fluctuated between 18.5 and 21 per cent until the Japanese invaded and captured the Dutch East Indies. All the American production was drawn from the Dutch East Indies and was in excess of 40,000 bbl. daily when lost to the Japanese.

The first oil production in the East Indies was developed by Dutch interests in 1893, and for many years thereafter all operations were

SHARE OF CRUDE OIL PRODUCTION BY MAJOR GROUPS
FAR EAST

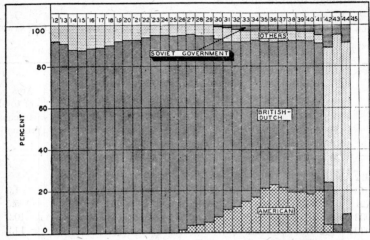

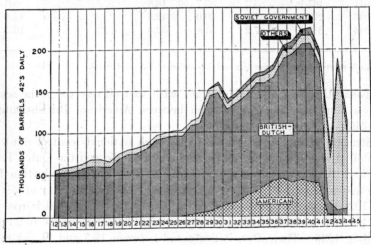

confined to nationals, who had preference on state land. The N.K.P.M., (N.V. Nederlandsche Koloniale Petroleum Maatschappij) controlled by Standard Oil Company (New Jersey), had production concessions in the Dutch East Indies before the First World War, as did the Royal Dutch–Shell and certain German interests. After the war the problem of the disposal of the German concessions arose. The American consul in Batavia at the time learned and reported to our State Department that the Netherlands government was planning to turn over to Royal Dutch–Shell all of these concessions as well as concessions in other areas where petroleum was thought to exist. On the basis of this report, the department immediately instructed the American Legation at The Hague to make representations to the Netherlands government with a view to obtaining for American companies equal opportunity to acquire additional concessions in Netherlands India, in accordance with international obligations of the Netherlands government to follow an open-door policy with respect to the exploitation of the Indies.

The Netherlands government at first did not accede to our representations, and negotiations continued through the early twenties. With a view to exerting further pressure on the Netherlands government the American government took steps to block the issuance of further concessions to the Royal Dutch–Shell in public lands in the United States (see Chap. I). The final result was that the N.K.P.M. was given additional producing concessions in the Indies that turned out to be some of the richest in the islands. These were principally in Sumatra.

In the twenties the Standard Oil Company of California and the Gulf Oil Corporation began their efforts to obtain concessions in the Dutch East Indies. They first obtained exploration concessions, which they worked without success. The Gulf Oil Corporation withdrew from the field. In 1930 the Nederlandsche Pacific Petroleum Mij. was formed with Standard Oil Company of California in control. This company has continued its explorations in the Indies since that time and is now owned by the Standard Oil Company of California and The Texas Company. Throughout this period the State Department, through the American consul in Batavia, was keeping constant pressure on the Dutch authorities to abide by the open-door policy. Netherlands New Guinea had never been explored thoroughly, and it was unknown whether the reports were true that very rich oil territory existed there. The Nederlandsche–New Guinea Petroleum Mij., owned by subsidiaries of the Royal Dutch–Shell, Standard-Vacuum, Standard Oil of California, and The Texas Company, was formed to explore and develop any petroleum deposits that might be found in New Guinea as a combined operation.

"There seems to be little question that, without the diplomatic support of the American government, American oil companies could never have obtained equal facilities with Netherlands companies for the development of petroleum deposits in Netherlands India," Mr. Rayner states in his State Department Memorandum.

In 1939 the share held by American interests in the Dutch East Indies was 27 per cent of production and 35 per cent of the oil reserves.

Relatively Small Production in Far East Area.—The Far East area as a whole averaged only 10 and 12 per cent of foreign output from 1921 to the outbreak of the Second World War. Very little was known about operations in the Dutch East Indies, British Borneo, Burma, and Japan during the Second World War, although it is believed that 1943 was the best year under Japanese dominance, when it is estimated that output represented about 8.5 per cent of all foreign production.

EASTERN HEMISPHERE OIL RESERVES

In the Eastern Hemisphere, exclusive of Russia, the American companies owned reserves totaling 11.6 billion barrels, a 40 per cent share,

TABLE 17.—SHARE OF FOREIGN OIL RESERVES OF EASTERN HEMISPHERE [1]

Area	Million barrels				Per cent		
	American	British-Dutch	Other foreign	Total	American	British-Dutch	Other foreign
Europe excluding Russia....	168.1	171.0	290.8	629.9	26.7	27.1	46.2
Africa....................	....	86.0	......	86.0	....	100.0	
Near and Middle East......	11,136.0	14,047.0	1,617.0	26,800.0	41.6	52.4	6.0
Far East (excluding Sakhalin).................	....	167.4	36.0	203.4	....	82.3	17.7
Oceania.................	275.5	674.5	......	950.0	29.0	71.0	
Total Eastern Hemisphere excluding Russia.......	11,579.6	15,145.9	1,943.8	28,669.3	40.4	52.8	6.8
Russia in Europe and Asia..	....	....	5,765.0	5,765.0	....	....	100.0
Total Eastern Hemisphere including Russia.......	11,579.6	15,145.9	7,708.8	34,434.3	33.6	44.0	22.4

[1] Table covers foreign countries only and thus excludes the United States.

according to estimates as of Jan. 1, 1945. The British-Dutch group owned 15 billion barrels, or nearly 53 per cent of the total reserves in the Eastern Hemisphere, and all other companies owned about 2 billion barrels, or 7 per cent of the total reserve (see Table 17).

The comparative magnitude of the estimated reserves of the Near and Middle East is apparent. They dwarf reserves in all other areas of the Eastern Hemisphere and, for that matter, all other areas of the world except the United States.

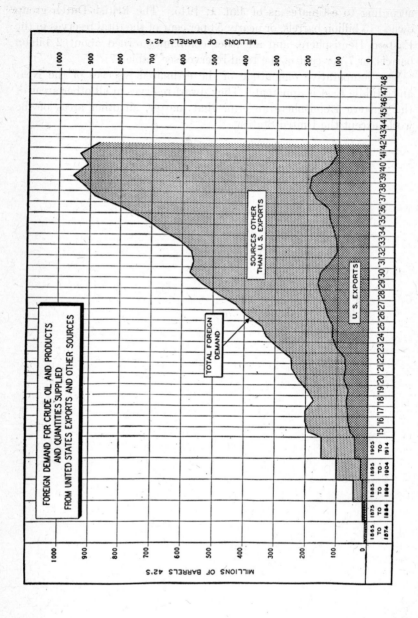

CHAPTER VIII

AMERICAN POSITION DECLINES IN FOREIGN MARKETS

Certainly during the early years of steady industry growth and until the world depression in the 1930's, American oil companies profitably shared in many foreign markets. In fact, they lost little time before entering this trade.

Within a few short years of the drilling of the Drake well in Pennsylvania in 1859—the event that changed the production of oil from a primitive to a modern industry—energetic Americans in this new industry were opening up new markets abroad for their kerosene. Symbolic of the progress made is the epic story of the pioneering of the Standard Oil Company of New York in Far Eastern markets and the bringing of the oil lamp to backward peoples. In Europe, in the Near East, in remotest Africa, American oil companies built up before the First World War a great export market for the products of their refineries, chiefly kerosene and lubricating oils. Standard Oil Company, Tide Water Oil Company, Pure Oil Company, and scores of other companies with refineries in the Pennsylvania oil region and along the Atlantic seaboard marketed their products abroad.

American Participation in Foreign Markets Necessary.—The fact is that today and in the future the continued participation in this foreign trade by American petroleum companies is vital from the standpoint of their retaining their hold as foreign producers. Such participation essentially aids their chances of developing reserves in strategic foreign oil areas that our State, War, and Navy Departments consider of paramount concern to our own national defense and to world peace; for, obviously, American-owned oil production and reserves cannot be developed unless there is at the same time American sharing of the natural outlets for such production in the foreign oil markets.

Furthermore, directly involved is the protection of an investment by American oil companies in foreign marketing and refining of over a billion dollars and of an export business in petroleum products valued at 385 million dollars in the year 1939.

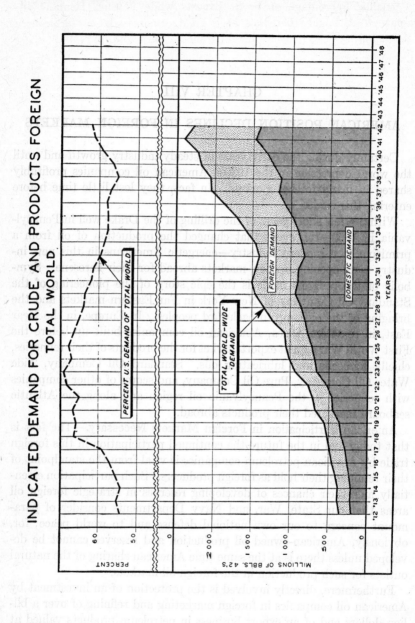

INDICATED DEMAND FOR CRUDE AND PRODUCTS FOREIGN
TOTAL WORLD

PERCENT U.S. DEMAND OF TOTAL WORLD

TOTAL WORLD-WIDE DEMAND

FOREIGN DEMAND

DOMESTIC DEMAND

PERCENT

MILLIONS OF BBLS. 42.5

YEARS

'12 '13 '14 '15 '16 '17 '18 '19 '20 '21 '22 '23 '24 '25 '26 '27 '28 '29 '30 '31 '32 '33 '34 '35 '36 '37 '38 '39 '40 '41 '42 '43 '44 '45 '46 '47 '48

Smaller Percentage of U. S. Exports while Foreign Demand Increases.—Although there has been greatly increased consumption of petroleum and products in foreign countries and total exports of these products from the United States have mounted, the percentage relationship of American exports to total indicated foreign demand has declined in the last 20 years as shown in Table 18.

TABLE 18.—TOTAL FOREIGN PETROLEUM DEMAND VERSUS U. S. EXPORTS [1]

(In thousand barrels of 42 U. S. Gal.)

Period, years	Years	Average annual total foreign demand	Average annual U. S. exports	Per cent total demand
10	1865–1874	3,417	2,887	84.5
10	1875–1884	14,125	9,706	68.7
10	1885–1894	45,684	16,289	35.7
10	1895–1904	101,413	23,319	23.0
10	1905–1914	150,142	40,555	27.0
5	1915–1919 (First World War)	192,640	63,054	32.7
10	1920–1929	352,706	115,021	32.6
10	1930–1939	726,901	142,190	19.6
3	1940–1942 (Second World War)	903,520	118,734	13.1

[1] Also see Appendix Table 20.

It is seen that the relative position of U. S. petroleum exports to total foreign demand fell off gradually in the last quarter of the nineteenth century—from 80 per cent in the 1870's to 19 per cent in 1903. The proportion advanced again during the First World War to nearly 39 per cent in 1918 as the United States supplied the bulk of military needs for oil of the Allied armies and navies.[1]

Since that year the trend has been downward, reaching the prewar low point of 17 per cent in 1936. Exports fell off again after 1938 because of the blockade against Axis countries and because of restricted exports for civilian requirements in neutral and Allied countries.

However, with the development of production abroad by American companies, the major proportion of which has been marketed abroad,

[1] See Appendix Table 20.

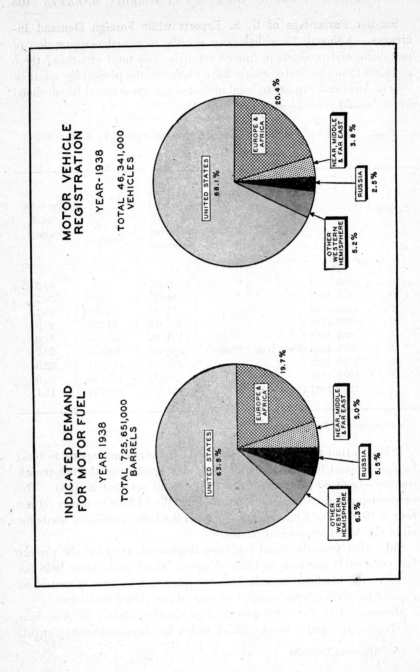

MOTOR VEHICLE
REGISTRATION

YEAR - 1938

TOTAL 46,341,000
VEHICLES

UNITED STATES
68.1 %

EUROPE &
AFRICA
20.4 %

NEAR, MIDDLE
& FAR EAST
3.8 %

RUSSIA
2.5 %

OTHER
WESTERN
HEMISPHERE
5.2 %

INDICATED DEMAND
FOR MOTOR FUEL

YEAR 1938

TOTAL 725,651,000
BARRELS

UNITED STATES
63.5 %

EUROPE &
AFRICA
19.7 %

NEAR, MIDDLE
& FAR EAST
5.0 %

RUSSIA
5.5 %

OTHER
WESTERN
HEMISPHERE
6.3 %

these companies were able to supplement U. S. exports although faced with the keenest competition. The foreign oil combines (Royal Dutch–Shell and Anglo-Iranian) extended their activities in all countries and drew on foreign oil sources in increasing amounts. Persian Gulf oil made great inroads.

TABLE 19.—FOREIGN MOTOR-FUEL DEMAND AND AUTOMOBILE REGISTRATION, 1938

Area	Indicated demand for motor fuel		Motor-vehicle registration		Indicated per-vehicle consumption annually, barrels
	Thousand barrels	% total foreign	Thousand units	% total foreign	
Western Hemisphere..	45,539	17.2	2,412	16.3	18.9
Europe and Africa.....	143,069	54.1	9,459	64.1	15.1
Near, Middle, and Far East.............	36,055	13.6	1,746	11.8	20.7
Total foreign (excluding Russia)...	224,663	84.9	13,617	92.2	16.5
Russia..............	40,051	15.1	1,156	7.8	34.6
Total foreign (including Russia)...	264,714	100.0	14,773	100.0	17.9
Per cent total world.	36.5		31.9		
United States........	460,937		31,568		14.6
Per cent total world.	63.5		68.1		
Total world......	725,651		46,341		15.6
Per cent.......	100.0		100.0		

An index to the marketing position of U. S. companies just prior to the Second World War indicates that in the year 1938 American-owned oil entering foreign markets, from foreign and domestic sources combined, amounted to 44 per cent of total foreign requirements, excluding Russia.

Foreign Motor-fuel Demand Not Comparable to Demand in United States.—In considering foreign markets, it is to be noted that the United States far exceeds foreign countries combined in consumption of petroleum products. In considerable part this is due to the fact that abroad there has been no such mass adoption of the automobile as has occurred in the United States.[1]

For example, the United States, with 68.1 per cent of world motor-vehicle registration in 1938, accounted for 63.5 per cent of the indicated total world demand for motor fuel. Incidentally, Europe and Africa account for 64 per cent of the total foreign car registration and 54 per cent of the foreign motor-fuel demand (see Table 19).

It will be seen that although the United States has a motor-vehicle registration totaling 31½ million as compared with total foreign of 14¾ million, or 68 per cent of the world total, foreign registration was increasing markedly in the interwar period.[2] In 1919 it was only 14 per cent of the total world. It rose to 32 per cent in 1938, from 1¼ million to 14¾ million vehicles. Russia showed the greatest rate of growth but had only a little over 1 million vehicles, or 2½ per cent of the world total, virtually all commercial.

Restrictions Affecting Foreign Marketing.—Despite accelerated foreign demand for crude oil and refined petroleum products, the percentage of foreign demand to total world demand had dropped from 46 per cent in 1912 to 38 per cent in 1942.

Generally speaking, this is explained by the fact that the foreign demand was retarded owing to the effects of two wars, high duties, and taxes and other restrictive factors (see Chap. II).

Not unrelated factors are the measures taken by many countries, some of which were actually designed to increase their self-sufficiency with respect to oil, but which have operated to keep the automobile in the luxury class and to stifle any semblance of such universality of use of petroleum products as is seen in the United States.

American oil companies have made and maintained great investment in distribution and marketing facilities abroad in recent years despite the many recognized political and financial hazards over and above normal economic risks. Examples of restrictions and discriminatory measures by some foreign governments, of nationalization, government-controlled cartel systems, trade barriers and agreements, and of nations' virtually compelling the building of refineries as the price of staying in the marketing business are given elsewhere. Therefore, it is sufficient to add here only briefly an interesting statement relating to taxes.

In most countries abroad oil can be landed at the port of importation just as cheaply as in New York, but a great many countries have im-

[1] See Appendix Tables 17 and 19 through 23.
[2] See Appendix Table 17.

posed very heavy taxes. For example, the average of taxes of all the countries of Europe amounts to about 23 cents per gallon on gasoline as compared with 5½ cents in the United States. This caused selling prices for Europe to average during 1939 about 43 cents per gallon compared with 19 cents in the United States.[1]

That lower taxes might substantially increase consumption abroad may be concretely illustrated in the case of Turkey where a 47 per cent reduction in import duty on gasoline resulted in a 92 per cent increase in consumption within two and a half years.

Foreign Distribution Methods Attaining U. S. Level.—Meantime, American companies have been at the forefront in modernizing foreign oil-distribution methods. Today, it is a far cry from the time when the delivery of the product was always in cans and drums. European and other countries now have service stations on a fairly large scale.

In order to supply these stations, it was necessary for the American companies to make large investments in interior bulk plants and also in tank trucks and distributing equipment. Modern distribution methods, especially for bulk distribution of gasoline through pumps and service stations, were entirely the result of American missionary effort. Not only were American companies at the forefront in modernizing foreign distribution methods, but they had to do it almost over the dead bodies of their competitors and often in the face of determined resistance on the part of local authority.

The conservatism of Continental Europe proved no mean obstacle to overcome, and it was almost entirely due to American incentive and American industry that just prior to the Second World War distribution in many countries throughout the world had reached almost the same degree of efficiency as in the United States. This was particularly true in such countries as England, France, Holland, Belgium, Sweden, Germany, Italy, Brazil, and Argentina.

The philosophy of service to the customer, so highly developed at the service stations in the United States, has been introduced abroad by American oil companies. In the industrial field American petroleum engineers have brought modern, efficient lubrication to the manufacturers in foreign countries.

World Servicing for Ships and Planes.—The development of oil-burning ships created a large demand for bunker fuel oil in many countries throughout the world. To meet this, American oil interests erected storage tanks and maintained bunkering facilities at all important fuel

[1] See Appendix Table 18.

stations throughout the world so that a steamship company could negotiate a contract with the assurance that bunker fuel oil would be available at ports of call. American oil companies also made available to
steamship lines uniform marine lubricants at all the principal ports.

In 1914 the petroleum-powered vessel registrations of the world totaled 1½ million gross tons, representing but 1.7 per cent of the total
merchant-marine tonnage, and by 1929, 26 million gross tons, or 39 per
cent; in 1939 the figure rose to 37½ million gross tons, or nearly 55 per
cent.

World-wide organizations have been formed by American interests to
supply fuel and lubricants to international airways as well as to local
airways.

The availability of petroleum products throughout the world can be
attributed in large part to the foresight and large-scale investment of
American oil companies accomplished in spite of severe competition
and political policies often restrictive to foreign operations.

British and Americans Build Early Tank Ships.—Transportation of
oil by tank ship has played its important part in foreign marketing.
British and American marine architects designed what were the precur-
sors of the modern tanker, but bulk shipments of oil began in the sailing
ships.

Bulk oil transportation by water started in the early 1860's when
Captain Vandergrift first built his Allegheny River oil barges for hauling
oil from the Pennsylvania fields. Europe, eager to purchase kerosene
from the United States, first began to equip cargo ships with permanent
tanks. So equipped was the Belgian ship "Charles," a sailing vessel
that plied between New York and European ports between 1869 and
1872. Her capacity was 794 tons, and she was fitted with two rows of
tanks in the hold and two rows in the 'tween decks—59 tanks in all.
They were entirely unconnected; there was no automatic arrangement
for keeping them full, but salt water was run into those that were found
to leak during the voyage.

By the early 1880's "vessels for transporting liquid cargoes in bulk"
in considerable variety were being sent down the ways in all maritime
countries including the United States. A new branch of marine engineering arose to solve the problems of bulk transportation of oil.

Reflecting the dominance of the British maritime facilities, as well as
the dependence of Great Britain upon outside countries for petroleum
products, is the fact that until the First World War the tanker tonnage
under the British flag far exceeded that of all other countries. Lloyd's

Baltimore refinery. Pipes leading on to the pier at the loading docks.

American oil companies have an investment in foreign marketing and refining of close to a billion dollars and an export business valued at 385 million dollars annually. See page 101.

Photograph at top by Vachon, at bottom by Parks, courtesy of Standard Oil Company (New Jersey).

Portland, Me. Two tankers emptying their crude-oil cargo at the Portland Pipeline docks.

Aruba refinery of Creole Petroleum Corporation. Crude lines running past tanks, used for conveying crude from ships to tank farm storage.

Photograph at top by Vachon, both by courtesy of Standard Oil Company (New Jersey).

Port Jerome refinery, Rouen, France. Gasoline Recovery plant.

Register showed gross American tonnage only 150,000 tons in 1914, compared with 837,000 British and 1,441,000 tons total world.

But during the First World War American shipyards began to turn out a great tonnage of American tankers for the American oil companies' ownership and operation.

Tankers Owned and Operated Largely by Shipping Interests.—By 1926 American tank-vessel tonnage was 2,421,000 tons, compared with 1,933,000 tons British and 5,519,000 tons total world. In other words, from a little over 10 per cent of world tonnage in 1914, U. S. tanker tonnage went to almost 50 per cent.

In the 1930's many tankers that might have been built and operated by American companies were built abroad and registered under foreign flags because of conditions that made it difficult for American shipyards and shipping concerns to compete with foreign-built, -owned, and -operated vessels. The trend was one in which tankers, while an essential part of the petroleum industry, were increasingly owned and operated by shipping interests rather than directly by the oil companies, although many large oil-company tanker fleets continued to be operated and even were expanded.

As an over-all result, however, some 44 per cent of the approximately 1,600 ocean-going tank ships afloat at the outbreak of the Second World War was owned outside the petroleum industry and the majority of tankers was under foreign flags. Nevertheless, some 10 to 15 per cent of these were American-owned, and these, added to American flag tonnage amounting to around 25 per cent of the world total, make about 35 to 40 per cent of the total world tanker tonnage operated by Americans.[1]

American tanker construction was on an accelerated scale during the Second World War—a favorable factor as postwar foreign markets open up.

Early Transportation Methods in Foreign Oil-producing Countries.— In foreign producing countries, Americans have also led in establishing modern land-transportation methods. In the early days crude oil was transported in the most primitive manner. Thus, in upper Burma it was conveyed in earthenware vessels from the wells to the riverbank, where it was poured into the holds of boats. It is interesting to note that a crude pipeline of bamboo existed in 1874 at Yenangyaung for conveying the crude oil from the wells to the river but the loss by leakage was so great as to lead to its immediate abandonment.

[1] See Appendix Tables 24 and 25.

In Russia, until 1875—at a time when the American petroleum industry had already established the trunk pipe line—the crude oil was carried in barrels on Persian carts known as *arbas*. "These are carts with two wheels 8½ to 9 ft. in diameter, and they were used to a very large extent, as much as £100,000 per annum having been paid for the transport of the oil from the wells to the refineries. The body of the cart carried one barrel, and another was slung beneath the axle. In outlying districts up to quite recent years crude oil was brought to central distributing points in sheepskins carried on camels." [1]

The first pipe line following the American method was from the Baku wells to the refineries at Black Town. It was laid by Nobel Brothers in 1879, and it was found necessary to erect throughout its length of 8 or 9 miles a series of watchhouses occupied by armed men to prevent willful injury to the pipes by the owners of the *arbas*.

Construction of pipe lines in Rumania began about the same time as in Russia, first from wells to refineries in the oil regions; and in 1913 a line from Baicoi to Constanza was started, not to be finished, however, until after the First World War.

Foreign Pipe Lines Built by Americans.—The principal pipe-line systems abroad owned by American oil companies or in which these companies have an interest are: in Venezuela, the lines from Mulata-Jusepin-Quiriquire to Caripito, from Jusepin to Puerto la Cruz, from Oficina to Puerto la Cruz, and from Santa Barbara to Guanta; in Colombia, the lines from the De Mares concession to Cartagena and from the Barco concession to Covenas; in the Middle East, the line from the Kirkuk field in Iraq to Haifa and Tripoli, in which American companies have a 23¾ per cent interest; and in the Far East, the line from the Talang Akar area to Palembang in the Dutch East Indies.

The transportation of oil and gas by pipe line is a typically American development that was brought about in our country by the need for economical transportation of oil and gas from widely dispersed producing areas to the refining and marketing centers of the nation. In the United States this pipe-line transportation system has now grown into a network many thousands of miles in length, serving all parts of the country.

In foreign fields no counterpart has ever been created. The countries in which oil was developed were never called upon to provide petroleum products for a highly industrialized and motorized civilization existing within the country itself such as in the United States. Often great fields

[1] From Report of the Group on American Petroleum Interests in Foreign Countries.

were in nonindustrialized countries. Transportation needs were thus confined in many cases to transfer of crude from field to export terminal or to local refineries.

However, some of the oil reserves developed in foreign fields are destined to play an important role in the future economy of petroleum on a world scale. To be of value to the eventual consumer, these fields must be linked with world markets by pipe line and tanker. It is to be expected, therefore, that in the years to come there will be a great expansion of such transportation facilities in order to bring into the channels of world trade and industry this raw material so necessary to the modern world.

American engineering methods and American enterprise will doubtless be in the vanguard of these developments in the future as they have in the past.

Large Potential Foreign Market as Living Standards Rise.—The fact that foreign countries are behind the United States in the use of the motorcar has significance of positive rather than negative character, and it should be stressed. It suggests the great potential world market for motor fuel still untapped. In fact, as pointed out, before the Second World War there was a rapid rate of growth in consumption of petroleum products abroad.

Gasoline demand in foreign countries during the period 1927–1938 inclusive showed an average increase of approximately 19,000 bbl. daily annually, or 4 per cent per year, whereas in the United States gasoline demand in the same period increased an average of about 24,000 bbl. daily, or 2.1 per cent per year.

The demand for all petroleum products abroad, excluding Russia, for the same period almost doubled, whereas in the United States consumption increased approximately 50 per cent. With improvement in the standard of living and increased industrialization and foreign trade in foreign countries, growth in foreign petroleum demand is expected to be almost double the rate of growth of consumption in the United States over the next 20 years according to economic studies.

Some indication of great potential demand abroad is possible from the fact that our consumption is at the rate of 9 barrels per capita whereas the consumption of the remainder of the world is at the rate of only ½ barrel per capita. As foreign countries are rehabilitated, and as civilian restrictions on use are removed, an opportunity presents itself to American oil companies operating abroad to participate in the anticipated immense increase in foreign consumption of petroleum products in the future.

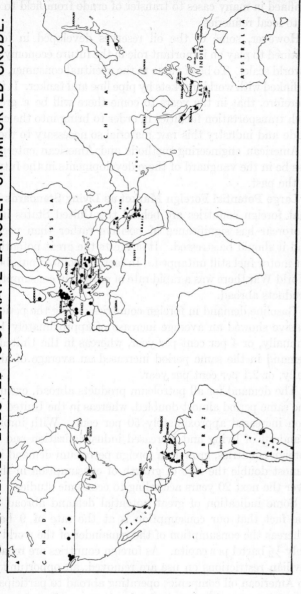

AMERICAN OWNED REFINERIES IN FOREIGN COUNTRIES

■ MAJOR CRUDE OIL PRODUCING AREAS.

▲ REFINERIES LOCATED NEAR OR AT LARGE PRODUCING FIELDS.

● REFINERIES ERECTED TO OPERATE LARGELY ON IMPORTED CRUDE.

CHAPTER IX

COMPLEX AMERICAN POSITION IN FOREIGN REFINING

Until the First World War American oil companies owned and operated refineries in only a few foreign countries, but during the interwar period the story was different. In the early twenties there was much expansion because of active search for oil abroad by American interests. Later, for this and other reasons, the increase in American refineries abroad continued.

Growth of American Participation, 1927–1939.—In fact, the business of refining crude oil increased enormously in foreign countries between the years 1927 and 1939. Estimates show that foreign refineries in 1927 ran 750,000 bbl. daily, of which American-owned plants accounted for 142,800 barrels, or approximately 19 per cent, and, if Russia was excluded, 23 per cent. By 1939, runs were averaging 2,240,000 bbl. daily, of which the American share was 23 per cent of total foreign and 31 per cent, excluding Russia (see Table 20).

Foreign Refineries Classified.—There are 66 American-owned refineries in foreign countries having an estimated capacity of 876,095 bbl. daily of crude oil. Of these, 26 with a capacity of 596,060 barrels, or 68 per cent of total capacity, are located at or near crude-oil producing areas, and 40 with a capacity of 280,035, or 32 per cent, were distant from crude production and erected to run largely on imported crude oil.[1]

American-owned foreign refinery capacity was 24.7 per cent of capacity of all foreign refineries, inclusive of Russia, during the six-year period 1937–1942 inclusive. In the same period American companies controlled 24.4 per cent of total foreign crude-oil production inclusive of Russia.

The world map (p. 112) shows the major crude-oil producing areas outside of the United States and spots American-owned refineries by two groups: (1) refineries located near or at the producing fields to serve

[1] See Appendix Tables 27 and 28.

113

many markets, and (2) refineries erected to run largely on imported crude.[1]

Early American Participation in Foreign Refining.—That Americans participated only meagerly in foreign refining in the early days is due to

TABLE 20.—ESTIMATED CRUDE RUNS BY FOREIGN REFINERIES *

(In barrels daily)

Year	Foreign	Foreign excluding Russia	American companies	American % of	
				Foreign	Foreign excluding Russia
1927	757,100	613,300	142,800	18.9	23.3
1928	871,500	682,500	141,300	16.2	20.7
1929	1,064,500	840,000	219,600	20.6	26.1
1930	1,253,700	933,200	254,000	20.5	27.2
1931	1,314,900	916,700	268,200	18.9	27.1
1932	1,335,200	931,400	242,500	18.2	26.0
1933	1,369,700	1,022,800	286,400	20.6	28.0
1934	1,580,300	1,173,600	359,400	22.7	30.6
1935	1,726,900	1,304,700	405,800	23.5	31.1
1936	1,892,900	1,400,000	446,700	23.6	31.9
1937	2,078,500	1,563,200	307,400	24.4	32.5
1938	2,165,300	1,627,900	504,300	23.3	30.9
1939	2,242,500	1,669,000	524,800	23.4	31.4

* See also Appendix Table 26.   See refineries map, p. III.

the building up of a great domestic refining industry, which made enough products to meet the bulk of the demand in the markets of the world. When American interests did go into refining in outside countries, it was usually in connection with their own development of crude oil in those countries. There were the exceptions of the American company that built a refinery in Mexico predating Mexican production, and another that established a refinery in Cuba where, despite several intensive efforts, no commercial oil production has been found.

[1] In a few countries in which it is indicated that the refineries were erected to operate largely on imported crude, indigenous production has been developed to a sufficient degree whereby eventually imported crude may no longer be necessary. For example, this is expected to be the situation in Austria and Hungary.

The first record of an American refining enterprise abroad indicates that in 1880 an independent American operator commenced running crude through a refinery he had built in Galicia (Poland), then part of Austria-Hungary, with equipment imported from the United States. From that date to the start of the First World War American participation remained minor, although American-owned refineries had been constructed prior to 1913 in Canada, Cuba, Mexico, Rumania, Austria, Russia, France, and Germany. The total capacity of all these plants was probably between 35,000 and 40,000 bbl. daily—at this combined figure only equivalent to a small-sized plant by today's standards.

The expansion of the American interest in foreign refining that came with the wave of search for and discovery of new crude supplies in the various foreign countries in the early twenties did not stop with our own oversupply, however. It continued until, by 1939, substantial expenditures had been made in Argentina, Venezuela, Peru, the Dutch West Indies (handling Venezuelan crude oil), Colombia, Mexico (refining properties expropriated in 1938), Poland, Rumania, and the Dutch East Indies, and Saudi Arabia and Bahrein Island in the Middle East.

The refineries built in these countries were for the processing of local or indigenous crude-oil production.

American oil companies also built new refineries or enlarged their refining facilities in France, Germany, Italy, and other countries that did not have sufficient home or indigenous supply to meet the country's needs.

Four Categories of Foreign Refining.—As a general rule, the cheapest source of refined products in a free economy is from modern refineries of relatively large capacity located at tidewater adjacent or accessible to large proven oil reserves. These reserves ensure a period of operation sufficient to justify the heavy investment required, making possible low unit costs. Low cost factors include the lack of necessity to ship fuel, with consequent evaporation and other losses. Also, this refinery site permits the transportation of products by water—the most economical way—to bulk terminals strategically located.

The historical experience of American oil interests in engaging in foreign refining may be divided into four different categories, as follows:

1. Where local refining was attractive on a purely economic basis exclusive of artificial regulation. This situation may obtain at points where there are local crude-oil production and either a local or immediately tributary product market that could be supplied more economically

by local refining than from any other source. For example, Rumanian and the Dutch West Indies refineries fall under this category.

2. Where local refining was not attractive on a purely economic basis but was made so by means of a tariff against imports. This situation obtains in locations where there is no local crude-oil supply but where for reasons of local labor, national defense, or currency situation the local government offers protection to local refining as against importation of products. This type of refining undertaking is precarious because tariff laws can be changed on short notice and with protection removed the local refinery becomes uneconomic. Examples in this category are refineries built in Cuba and Belgium.

3. Where local refining was not attractive on a purely economic basis but was forced by means of a high protective tariff and a system of import license. Examples are refineries built in France and Italy.

4. Where local refining was forced in countries having large crude-oil reserves either developed or potential, by making refining obligatory as a part of securing or holding concessions for exploration and development. An example is Venezuela.

Middle East Plants, Examples of "Economic" Refineries.—The refineries that have been constructed by The Bahrein Petroleum Company, Limited, and the Arabian American Oil Company in the Middle East properly fall into that class constructed principally because of the economic advantages of having them close to large indigenous foreign production.

The Bahrein refinery, located on Bahrein Island, was originally constructed in 1934 because of the economic advantages of refining Persian Gulf crude locally for market requirements east of Suez instead of supplying those markets with products shipped from the United States. As this market grew and in order to meet the heavy petroleum requirements of the United Nations during the Second World War, a number of additions were made to the plant, which now is processing more than 70,000 bbl. daily.

The construction of the 50,000-barrel Ras Tanura refinery in Saudi Arabia, completed late in 1945, was authorized primarily to help the war effort. Secondary considerations were the benefits accruing to the Saudi Arab government and increased products that would be available for commercial outlets after the Second World War.

Forced to Build Uneconomic Refineries in Nonproducing Countries. —On the other hand, there are situations where a refinery is economically sound if located in a consuming market rather than close to the oil fields, even though there might be involved a considerable haul of crude oil by pipe line or tanker. The determining factor usually is the volume that can be run through the refinery in a given market and the ability of that market to absorb, in proper ratio, the by-products that are made from the crude oil.

However, the refineries of American oil companies in most foreign countries that have little or no home crude-oil production do not fall in the category of large-volume plants by any manner of means. Forced to refine in these consuming areas by high tariffs, import licenses, and other governmental pressures, the companies have bought or built small refineries as a rule. The capacity of some such plants in Austria, Italy, and Yugoslavia, for instance, ranges from 1,000 to 5,000 bbl. daily. While in France there is one American-owned refinery with 25,000 bbl. daily capacity, there are three other American-owned plants that range from 4,200 to 7,000 bbl. daily. Thus, generally speaking, these refineries are counter to two important economic principles: first, that the enterprise be based upon sound business judgment rather than on national or political necessity, and, second, that refineries located in marketing areas but not near crude-oil sources, to be inherently economic in operation, must be sufficiently large.

France, Austria, Italy, and Yugoslavia are countries where local refining is not attractive on a purely economic basis but was forced by means of a high protective tariff and a system of import licenses.

Americans Build Refineries to Protect Investment and Market.—Indeed, in the interwar period it was the general rule that many countries not enjoying indigenous production or adequate indigenous production sought to foster refining by protective tariffs favoring import of crude oil rather than finished products (see Chap. II).

Major foreign companies marketing in these countries competed with refineries protected by the domestic tariff rather than go into what they considered the basically uneconomic field of domestic refining. Then certain governments—among them France, Italy, Austria, Yugoslavia, and Brazil—resorted to some sort of import licensing system. By virtue of import quotas favoring importers of crude oil, these governments were in a position seriously to curtail the activity of marketing dependent on products imports. They finally succeeded through this quasi-mandatory policy in forcing American companies to build refineries. France furnishes a typical example.

Experience in France.—American companies had been marketing petroleum products in France as local companies since the turn of the century. None, however, had entered the field of refining, supplying these markets by imports primarily from the United States.

Although France had little indigenous production of crude oil, French companies had begun refining even before the First World War, processing imported crude. During the First World War the French government became acutely aware of its deficient supply position in petroleum products and set out as a matter of national policy to correct the situation—first through acquisition of production in the Middle East and later by fostering, if not actually forcing, domestic refining. Immediately after the First World War it set up a national bureau with broad powers to act as executive of the government's national policy.

During the first decade after the First World War the government acted to foster domestic refining through duty protection. However, none of the large foreign companies responded to this inducement. In 1928, with the rather openly avowed aim of forcing these companies which were predominantly American to enter domestic refining or risk the decline of their share in the market, the government enacted a licensing system making all imports subject in advance to government approval. It granted a 20-year general license to crude-oil importers as compared to a three-year general license to product importers.

As a result, three large American companies confronted with a crisis decided to comply and refine. One of these whose activity had been confined to the marketing of high-grade lubricants built a new modern refinery, opened in 1934, and also acquired a necessary distribution service.

In purchasing the distribution organization, it had to take over an old refinery in the south of France that the government insisted must be kept in operation. Thus, by virtue of a sweeping government decree, this American company, which for 30 years had operated in France as a leading marketer of American products, found itself operating two refineries in France.

Only because the supply of crude oil from French overseas sources— chiefly Iraq—was limited, was the company free to choose its source of crude for its French refineries.

Hardly had the refineries begun to operate when, in 1934, a government monopoly with power of expropriation was voted. However, this was subject to a study to be made by a parliamentary committee that brought in an adverse report. In 1937 the government reduced by one-tenth the quantity of products enjoying a duty concession ex-refinery. Again in 1938 bills were introduced in the French Chamber to abolish the duty preference to domestic refiners. In other words, the basically uneconomic quasi-mandatory refining operations undertaken by the American companies enjoyed a very precarious long-run political guarantee.

The French government meantime increased its own participation in refining. In 1930 it had founded the Compagnie Française du Raffinage with two refineries and in 1936 began construction of two hydrogenation plants. Needless to say, this continued expansion of government-operated refineries ultimately encroached on the business of private companies.

Experience in Italy.—Having neither domestic crude-oil production nor refineries prior to the First World War, Italy acquired two old refineries of the Austro-Hungarian Empire with the annexation of Trieste and Fiume. The Trieste plant was purchased and operated by an American company until it was taken over by the Italian government. After the establishment of the Fascist state, the government embarked on a national petroleum policy to secure sources of production at home and abroad and to encourage domestic refining. A government-owned company, A.G.I.P. (Azienda Generale Italiana Petroli), became active in both fields, and the government imposed a duty differential between crude oil and finished petroleum. In response private companies constructed three small cracking plants. The bulk of requirements of finished products, however, continued to be imported.

Alluding to the example of France, the Italian government in 1934 enacted the licensing system with 20-year and three-year licenses for crude-oil and finished-product imports, respectively, making refining quasi-mandatory for such marketing companies as wished to retain their established competitive position. An American company which over many years had built up a leading position as marketer of American high-grade lubricants and which until then had not refined locally saw itself confronted with the choice of either refining or exposing its import business to the uncertain issue of short-term licenses.

It chose to construct a complete and modern refinery with a catalytic cracking unit and a solvent lub-oil treating plant. Under the direction of American engineers, this plant began successful operations in 1937 although, with all fuel imported, certain operating costs were high.

It eventually became apparent, however, that the government, after encouraging private companies to set up refining, anticipated for its own company, the A.G.I.P., the major share in the expansion and future of the industry. The A.G.I.P. not only modernized its Fiume refinery but also by the outbreak of the Second World War had constructed another refinery exceeding the combined capacity of all other refineries in the country and in addition had constructed two hydrogenation plants at Bari and Leghorn.

Experience in Brazil.—During the period 1933–1936, the kerosene market in Brazil became very competitive as a result of the operation of a number of small refineries, most of which were located in São Paulo. With elementary equipment they produced an inferior kerosene from diesel oil that paid import duties of only 10 reis per kilo, as against 286 reis per kilo for regular kerosene.

To meet this competition, an American company purchased a site on the outskirts of the city of São Paulo at a cost of $266,800 and erected a refinery at a cost of $176,600—a total investment of $443,400. The refinery had a capacity of 2,160 bbl. daily of Cumarebo crude and would have supplied 65 to 70 per cent of the company's gasoline requirements in the state of São Paulo, 100 per cent of the refined-oil and diesel-oil requirements, and 15 per cent of the fuel-oil requirement.

The necessary licenses to build and operate this refinery had been secured from the competent government authorities prior to erection, and the Minister of Agriculture in particular had given every assurance of his support. Notwithstanding this, a Decree Law No. 395 was issued on Apr. 29, 1938, stipulating that the ownership and operation of petroleum refineries must be entirely national, and thereby the operation of the company's refinery became impossible and it was forced to suspend operations.

Not long after the issuance of the decree law that stopped the operation of the refinery, the Brazilian government placed a production tax upon products of local manufacture, which had the effect of making local refining considerably less profitable.

Examples Illustrate Postwar Problem.—These examples serve to illustrate (a) the measures used to induce or force American oil companies to build refineries abroad, and (b) the way in which government-sponsored or -owned companies tend ultimately toward a complete national monopoly at the expense of foreign oil interests. They are important today because they illustrate a postwar problem confronting American oil companies in many foreign countries, for the trend toward nationalization is as pronounced as, if not more pronounced than, it was before the Second World War.

Large Producing Countries Demand Local Refineries.—Furthermore, to contrast the situation in countries without adequate home crude-oil supplies, there is a growing tendency in certain foreign countries with large home production to be just as insistent that refining industries be built within their own borders.

Venezuela is probably the foremost example of this trend. For some time it has been the policy of the Venezuelan government not to grant any concessions in Venezuela without including a refinery obligation in the concession title. This obligation is that the concessionaire must refine within Venezuela an amount of crude equivalent to 10 per cent of the oil produced. Although the obligation is not imposed by law, it must be assumed before a petroleum concession can be secured under the Law of Hydrocarbons of 1943.

President Medina, in a statement to Congress in 1944, made the following statement relative to the refinery obligation: "The policy of the government is definitely to have refining within our own country; in all new concessions there will be an obligation to refine in Venezuela part of the petroleum exploited; . . . the petroleum of Venezuela should be refined in Venezuela or in those countries which will use it in the form of products or refined subproducts, but in no case should the petroleum of the new concessions be refined outside of Venezuela to supply other markets. . . ."

Several American companies have obligated themselves to construct refineries in Venezuela as a result of this policy.

The Creole Petroleum Corporation (American) will build a new 50-million-dollar refinery with a capacity to process at least 40,000 bbl. daily of Venezuelan crude oil. Also, the Royal Dutch–Shell in 1945 started work on a new refinery near Punta Cardon to be in excess of 40,000 bbl. daily capacity; this more than doubles its present refinery capacity in Venezuela. American-owned refineries in Venezuela at present total four, with 48,220 bbl. daily capacity.

Arthur T. Proudfit, Creole president, has explained that it is essential that the company's new refinery be placed where it can operate efficiently and can produce products from Venezuelan crude at a price that will make them strongly competitive in the world markets. This, he said, is vital, since the output of this and other new refineries to be built in the country will greatly exceed Venezuela's own needs, and the success of the refinery will depend, for the most part, on the demand for its products in foreign markets.

In other words, the position of American companies in foreign refining is complex to say the least—complex not only in nonproducing countries but also in large producing countries.

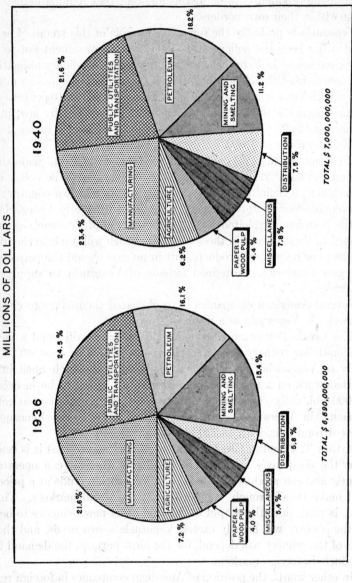

AMERICAN DIRECT INVESTMENTS ABROAD BY INDUSTRIAL GROUPS
MILLIONS OF DOLLARS

1936

TOTAL $ 6,690,000,000

- PETROLEUM — 16.1%
- MINING AND SMELTING — 15.4%
- DISTRIBUTION — 5.8%
- MISCELLANEOUS — 5.4%
- PAPER & WOOD PULP — 4.0%
- AGRICULTURE — 7.2%
- MANUFACTURING — 21.6%
- PUBLIC UTILITIES AND TRANSPORTATION — 24.5%

1940

TOTAL $ 7,000,000,000

- PETROLEUM — 18.2%
- MINING AND SMELTING — 11.2%
- DISTRIBUTION — 7.5%
- MISCELLANEOUS — 7.8%
- PAPER & WOOD PULP — 4.4%
- AGRICULTURE — 6.2%
- MANUFACTURING — 23.4%
- PUBLIC UTILITIES AND TRANSPORTATION — 21.6%

CHAPTER X

ADVANTAGES OF FOREIGN OIL OPERATIONS TO OUR ECONOMY

"The wise investment of United States capital abroad benefits the United States and the world at large," said Dean Acheson, then Assistant Secretary of State.[1] "It provides an important market for United States products and, by developing foreign countries, increases the purchasing power of the people of those countries for foreign products including those of the United States. It contributes directly to economic expansion, to full employment, and to high levels of national income, both here and abroad."

Oil Ranks Third in Our Foreign Investments.—American investments ("direct investment" or net worth) in foreign countries in all enterprises totaled 7 billion dollars in 1940, of which 1,277 million dollars or 18.2 per cent was in petroleum, according to the U. S. Department of Commerce.

Among the industrial groups into which the department divided American direct investments, "petroleum" ranked third. "Manufacturing" was given first place with 1.6 billion dollars and "public utilities and transportation" second place with 1.5 billion dollars. If "transportation" were listed separately, "petroleum" would easily have ranked second (Table 21).

More than one-third of the petroleum total was represented by investments in South America. In Venezuela alone the value was estimated at 250 million dollars, accounting for a major portion of the continent's total. Colombia, with 75 million dollars, held second position in American oil investment.

Investments in the petroleum industry in Europe were principally in the United Kingdom (71 million dollars), Germany (57 million dollars), France (43 million dollars), and Italy (38 million dollars). Investments in Asia (chiefly in the Middle East, Netherlands India, and China) and

[1] Before Subcommittee on Foreign Trade and Shipping of the House of Representatives Special Committee on Post-War Economic Policy and Planning, Nov. 30, 1944.

TABLE 21.—AMERICAN DIRECT INVESTMENTS ABROAD BY INDUSTRIAL GROUPS,
1940–1936

(In million dollars)

Industry	1940	1936
Manufacturing...................	1,618	1,442
Public utilities and transportation..	1,514	1,640
Petroleum......................	1,277	1,074
Mining and smelting.............	783	1,032
Distribution....................	522	391
Agriculture.....................	433	482
Paper and wood pulp.............	308	269
Miscellaneous...................	545	360
Total........................	7,000	6,690

TABLE 22.—SUMMARY OF RELATIVE OIL INVESTMENT ABROAD [1]

(Amounts in millions of dollars)

	1929					1940				
	Total all enterprises		Petroleum industry			Total all enterprises		Petroleum industry		
	Amount	% total foreign	Amount	% total foreign	% all enterprises	Amount	% total foreign	Amount	% total foreign	% all enterprises
Europe and Africa	1,447	19.2	262	23.4	18.0	1,551	22.2	356	27.9	23.0
Asia.............	403	5.4	114	10.2	28.9	422	6.0	177	13.9	41.9
Oceania.........	149	2.0	69	6.2	46.3	120	1.7	49	3.8	40.8
Western Hemisphere (excluding United States)........	5,529	73.4	672	60.2	12.3	4,874	69.6	691	54.1	14.2
International ..	.....	.....	.....	.....	....	33	0.5	4	0.3	12.1
Total foreign..	7,528	100.0	1,117	100.0	14.9	7,000	100.0	1,277	100.0	18.2

[1] Complete detailed figures are shown in Appendix Table 29. Source of data: U. S. Department of Commerce—*Trade Information Bulletin* 731, American Direct Investments in 1929; American Direct Investments in Foreign Countries, 1940.

"Petroleum operations abroad by American oil companies are integrated in the domestic oil industry to a remarkable degree. . . . Almost without exception the companies engage in foreign activity as part of their over-all operation." See page 125.

Part of a great Atlantic seaboard refinery at Baltimore which makes products for both domestic and foreign consumption.

Photograph at top by Vachon, at bottom by Parks, courtesy of Standard Oil Company (New Jersey).

eaboard refineries eceive foreign rude oil. A small anker delivers its argo to another eaboard refinery t Everett. The efinery receives s crude products om Texas, Baton Rouge, and Veneuela.

Thousands of Peruvian employees leaving Talara refinery at the end of day.

"In the foreign producing countries alone, American oil investment has created direc and indirect benefits to foreign economy over the 10-year period 1935–1944 to the exten of some $2,250,000,000."   See page 137.

Photographs by courtesy of Standard Oil Company (New Jersey); at bottom, by N. Morris.

The oil companies in Venezuela have built nearly 700 miles of roads. See page 144.

in Canada accounted for most of the remainder of American petroleum investments abroad [1] (Table 22).

Foreign Operations Integrated in Domestic Oil Industry.—Petroleum operations abroad by American oil companies are integrated in the domestic oil industry to a remarkable degree. Altogether, the total foreign investment of $2,499,257,000 (in 1939) reported by the 11 American

TABLE 23.—STOCKHOLDERS OF AMERICAN OIL COMPANIES WITH FOREIGN INVESTMENT *

(As of Dec. 31, 1944)

	Number of stockholders	Number of shares held
Individuals..................	816,361	59,466,337
Banks and/or trust companies.	42,139	30,104,842
Insurance companies..........	708	1,484,830
Charitable or educational foundations and/or institutions...	3,784	3,601,077
Others.....................	14,532	8,346,192
Total.....................	877,524	103,003,278

* Figures are combined stockholdings of the 11 companies reporting and include considerable duplication, the amount of which it is impossible to determine.

companies that answered the questionnaire of the Group on American Petroleum Interests in Foreign Countries represents actually 25 per cent of the combined gross assets shown on the annual reports by these same companies in the year of 1939.

Almost without exception the companies engage in foreign activity as part of their over-all domestic and foreign operation, either directly or through branches or subsidiaries and affiliates. Thus, generally speaking, there is no ready separation of foreign from domestic activities, although the foreign interest of a company may vary from a small percentage to a large proportion.

This being the case, the financial stability of these companies and the interest of their stockholders and employees are involved in their foreign as well as in their domestic operations. Similarly, the constant improvement in the quality of products marketed, the downward trend of prices

[1] See Appendix Table 29.

of petroleum products, the payment of high wages, and the ability of the industry to attract sufficient capital are proportionately made possible by the industry's participation in foreign oil operations.

Stockholdings in American Oil Companies Engaged in Foreign Operations.—Not only has the individual stockholder a stake in the foreign operations of these companies but also holders of insurance policies and investors in banks and other institutions inasmuch as such institutions have large investments in American oil companies with foreign interests.

TABLE 24.—DIVIDENDS RECEIVED AND BRANCH PROFITS REMITTED FROM FOREIGN OPERATIONS

Year	Amount
1935	$70,737,000
1936	64,549,000
1937	71,541,000
1938	81,007,000
1939	58,460,000
1940	86,668,000
1941	92,371,000
1942	63,618,000
1943	51,890,000
1944	82,605,000
	$723,446,000

Over 800,000 stockholders of record are reported by the 11 American oil companies engaged in foreign operations answering the group's questionnaire. These figures, of course, include duplications but are given as indicative of the wide public interest in oil investments (Table 23).

Dividends and Branch Profits from Foreign Operations.—Through foreign branch profits and dividends received from foreign subsidiaries and affiliates, foreign activities represent a flow of returns into this country that enters into American pay rolls, stockholders' dividends, and purchases in many fields.

Answers received from the same 11 American oil companies to another questionnaire sent out by this group show, for the 10-year period 1935–1944, dividends received and branch profits remitted from foreign operations totaling $723,446,000 (Table 24).

The amount of income taxes that the United States Treasury received from petroleum exports and also from foreign operations of American oil companies must be substantial. Such figures are not possible to determine inasmuch as companies engaging largely in domestic trade but with some export trade do not make separate returns for domestic and foreign income.

Employment of U. S. Nationals.—Petroleum export trade by the American oil industry has furnished employment for a great many American nationals not only abroad but in the United States.

Many in this country are engaged directly in foreign trade work in executive and clerical positions. Also, since a substantial part of the activities of many oil companies is in foreign countries, obviously the work of men and women employed by them here in producing, refining, transportation, and marketing and in technical divisions is proportionately dependent on these foreign activities. In view of the large quantity of petroleum exports and the large investments of American oil companies abroad, an estimate of salaries and wages paid by virtue of foreign business, if it were possible to make such apportionment, would run into a very substantial amount.

Oil-equipment Exports Stimulated.—The operations of American oil companies abroad directly contribute to the American oil-equipment supply business and to employment in those companies engaging in foreign trade.

The fact that American oil companies themselves are large purchasers for foreign account, coupled with American leadership in the manufacturing of oil-field, pipe-line, refinery, and distribution equipment, has directly meant large exports of petroleum equipment, contributing further to our favorable trade balance.

During the 12 years, 1930–1941, exports from the United States of crude-oil producing, pipe-line, and refinery equipment averaged $27,-500,000 annually and totaled $329,979,000 (Table 25).

American Oil Companies' Direct U. S. Purchase of All Supplies.—American oil companies operating in foreign countries buy in the United States for shipment abroad many materials other than and in addition to producing, pipe-line, and refinery equipment. These range from building and office supplies to hospital and personal articles.

Answers from the 11 American oil companies to a questionnaire requesting their total purchases of supplies and materials in the United States for foreign operations, excluding crude oil and petroleum products, indicated that these companies spent in the United States 330 million dollars, or an average of 33 million dollars a year, during the 10-year period 1935–1944.

Operations Abroad Create Buying of Other U. S. Commodities.—
Elsewhere it will be shown how the success of American oil companies in
building enterprises in foreign countries has aided in raising living standards in those countries (see Chap. XII). In this way increased purchasing power is created. In turn, larger purchases are made in the United

TABLE 25.—UNITED STATES EXPORTS OF CRUDE-OIL PRODUCING, PIPE-LINE, AND
REFINERY EQUIPMENT [1]

(In thousands of dollars)

Destination	Total 1930–1941	Average annual rate	Per cent of total
North America	32,415	2,701	9.82
South America	153,263	12,772	46.45
Western Hemisphere	185,678	15,473	56.27
Europe	27,854	2,321	8.44
Africa	6,019	502	1.83
Russia	26,673	2,223	8.08
Total for Europe, Africa, Russia	60,546	5,046	18.35
Near and Middle East	20,800	1,733	6.30
South and East Asia	33,527	2,794	10.16
Oceania	29,428	2,452	8.92
Eastern Hemisphere	144,301	12,025	43.73
Grand total	329,979	27,498	100.00

[1] See also Appendix Table 30. Authority: Bureau of Foreign and Domestic Commerce, U. S. Department of Commerce.

States flowing into many industries and businesses other than petroleum. The great extent to which the United States economy benefits
from this source is not generally appreciated.

How investments abroad in productive enterprises breed trade may
be illustrated by examples of investment not only in oil abroad but also
in other activities. For instance, investments by Americans in the sugar
and fruit businesses in the West Indies and Central America in the early
part of the century, like the development of petroleum and mining

properties in Mexico and South America, were based on the productive use of natural resources that before the advent of the foreigners remained mostly untouched. The combination of American ingenuity, engineering, and capital applied to the technique of producing, handling, and marketing sugar and fruit resulted in these industries' creating vast quantities of new wealth. By transforming natural resources into useful products and finding markets for them the foreign investors added materially to the income of the people in these countries.

Buying of Factory, Office, and Home Supplies.—That American consumers benefited from the supplies of sugar and fruit from these regions is obvious. Less understood is the fact that the development of these properties abroad created vast new markets for American products.

A large part of the increase was due to the general economic improvement in these countries resulting from productive activities of foreign capital. The building up of properties acquired by foreigners called for large quantities of capital goods manufactured in the United States. Plantations required extensive purchases of American agricultural machinery. When roads were built, the demand for American trucks and automobiles grew. The construction of sugar mills called for costly machinery for grinding the cane and extracting the sugar, and for all of the accessories of industrial plants such as boilers and lighting and power plants. As operations expanded, a steady demand for replacements was created.

Practically all these materials came from the United States and not only stimulated business at home but added to the profits of American shipping companies in the Latin-American trade. Furthermore, the American personnel sent down to handle technical problems and take part in the management had to be housed according to American or European standards. In a sense they took a piece of America with them. They naturally used American office equipment and furnishings and demanded American radios, passenger automobiles, foodstuffs, etc. Thus they helped to popularize many types of American goods in the countries to which they went. The people among whom they lived came to know and to want the goods the Americans brought with them, and, as their living standards improved, thanks largely to the activities of the foreign companies, they began to be able to afford to buy more American goods.

The latent wealth made productive through the use of foreign capital—wealth that otherwise would have stagnated in undeveloped resources—improved local living conditions, increased local buying power, stimulated local business activities, and, at the same time, expanded trade with the investing nation and the rest of the world.

Example of Oil in Mexico.—What happened in the case of the development of sugar and fruit plantations in Cuba and Central America by Americans also happened in the opening up of mines and the development of oil fields in Mexico. Large quantities of American machinery of all kinds were required in making the initial installations, and extensive replacements followed year by year. It has been estimated, for example, that the petroleum industry in its own development in Mexico was directly responsible for the shipment of nearly 750 million dollars, worth of American products to Mexico in the period 1916–1938. Thus, the sale of American capital goods was stimulated—to the profit of American industry and labor and to the benefit of Mexico.

The indirect contributions of the oil industry to the increase of exports from the United States to Mexico were also great. Although it is, of course, impossible to obtain official figures on the amount of exports of American consumers' goods to Mexico directly attributable to the increased activities in that country due to the oil business, it has been estimated that during this same 22-year period 340 million dollars' worth of additional purchases was made in the United States by Mexicans and Americans. In the same period the oil companies disbursed in Mexico in the form of wages, taxes of all kinds, freights, etc., four times this amount—$1,360,000,000.

It is obvious, of course, that the great increase in shipments of American goods to Mexico helped United States railroads and shipping companies, banks, cable companies, and all those interests that directly or indirectly contributed to the production or transportation of the goods that were shipped.

It is similarly true today as a reflection of American oil investment in Venezuela and other foreign countries. This is one of the great services of foreign trade—that it stimulates productivity in many lines at home, thus improving business conditions generally.

Oil Contributes to Favorable Trade Balance.—The American petroleum industry, both domestic and foreign, has been since its birth one of the most important factors in giving the United States a favorable trade balance.

Petroleum exports accounted for from 9 to 13 per cent of the total value of all merchandise exports by the United States from 1921 to the outbreak of the Second World War. During this period the value of petroleum exports varied from 200 million dollars in 1932 to over 550 million dollars in 1926. For a great many years petroleum and petro-leum-products exports were second only to cotton in the earlier period and to the export category "machinery of all classes" in recent years.

The favorable balance of merchandise trade that the United States has enjoyed during these two decades has varied widely, but in several years of this period—specifically, 1923, 1926, 1935, 1936, and 1937—the value of petroleum exports equaled or exceeded the net balance due this country from merchandise shipments.

In 1940–1941 there was a sharp decline in the ratio of petroleum ex-ports to total U. S. exports partly because of the Atlantic submarine blockade directed against tankers. However, indications point to a de-clining proportion as foreign oil sources are built up and as the United States market draws increasingly on these sources to meet domestic demands (Table 26).

Imports by American Oil Companies.—Practically all the oil imported into this country is produced in foreign countries by American oil com-panies and shipped here by them. The benefits to the American econ-omy from this fact are difficult to evaluate but may be broadly referred to.

It can be said generally that some of the money paid to foreign coun-tries covering oil imports returns to United States nationals in the form of dividends, branch profits, interest on bonds, and taxes paid to the United States government—returns that would not accrue were other than American companies importing the oil.

Inasmuch as this country may have to depend increasingly on im-ports of petroleum, it is fortunate for security, as well as economic, rea-sons that American oil companies are in a position in foreign fields to provide the bulk of such requirements.

National Defense and Economic Need for Foreign Operations.—Mr. Rayner, in his role as Petroleum Adviser of the Department of State, pointed out in his testimony before the Special Senate Committee In-vestigating Petroleum Resources on June 27, 1945, that in 1938, the last normal prewar year, our domestic requirements for petroleum amounted to 3,115,000 bbl. daily, an increase of 2 million since the First World War. In the last five years of this period the yearly increase amounted to 145,000 bbl. daily.

"This steady upward trend in domestic demand should be considered in the light of annual new discoveries of domestic reserves which have shown a definite tendency to approach if not to fall below annual do-mestic requirements," he said. "Extraordinary war needs have, of

TABLE 26.—TOTAL U. S. EXPORTS AND IMPORTS AND PERCENTAGE OF CRUDE
PETROLEUM AND PETROLEUM PRODUCTS [1]

(In thousands of dollars)

Year	Total U. S. exports	Petroleum exports	Per cent petroleum	Total U. S. imports	Petroleum imports	Per cent petroleum
1913	2,448,288	160,584	6.6	1,813,008	12,997	0.7
1914	2,071,056	149,040	7.2	1,893,926	11,501	0.6
1915	3,493,236	159,792	4.6	1,674,170	10,564	0.6
1916	5,422,644	221,136	4.1	2,197,884	13,887	0.6
1917	6,169,620	275,148	4.5	2,659,355	20,605	0.8
1918	6,047,880	371,184	6.1	2,945,655	25,670	0.9
1919	7,749,816	377,124	4.9	3,904,365	31,441	0.8
1920	8,080,476	592,872	7.3	5,278,481	65,903	1.3
1921	4,378,932	401,232	9.2	2,509,148	78,844	3.1
1922	3,765,096	345,504	9.2	3,112,747	88,485	2.8
1923	4,090,716	366,792	9.0	3,792,066	78,713	2.1
1924	4,497,648	443,784	9.9	3,609,963	101,357	2.8
1925	4,818,720	474,024	9.8	4,226,589	107,694	2.6
1926	4,711,716	555,432	11.8	4,430,888	124,556	2.8
1927	4,758,864	486,768	10.2	4,184,742	113,434	2.7
1928	5,030,100	526,740	10.5	4,091,444	132,842	3.3
1929	5,157,084	562,116	10.9	4,399,361	143,557	3.3
1930	3,781,176	495,264	13.1	3,060,908	145,116	4.7
1931	2,377,980	271,284	11.4	2,090,635	92,741	4.4
1932	1,576,152	208,992	13.3	1,325,093	60,630	4.6
1933	1,647,216	200,688	12.2	1,449,559	25,693	1.8
1934	2,100,132	228,312	10.9	1,636,003	36,521	2.2
1935	2,243,076	251,124	11.2	2,038,905	37,346	1.8
1936	2,418,972	264,540	10.9	2,423,977	40,570	1.7
1937	3,298,932	378,132	11.5	3,009,852	44,586	1.5
1938	3,057,170	390,216	12.8	1,949,624	39,461	2.0
1939	3,123,343	385,068	12.3	2,276,099	43,541	1.9
1940	3,934,182	310,140	7.9	2,540,656	70,110	2.8
1941	5,019,877	284,653	5.7	3,221,954	82,455	2.6

[1] Sources: *Survey of Current Business Foreign Commerce and Navigation, Statistical Abstract of United States.*

course, accentuated this trend, but, nevertheless, the fact remains that, failing a substantial increase in the discovery of new reserves, the United States, long an exporter on balance, is facing the definite probability of becoming a net importer of oil.

"It is therefore extremely important to examine the share that American nationals hold in the foreign oil resources of the world not only as a safeguard to our own national security and economic well-being but as a source from which to maintain and expand our international oil trade in the consuming markets of the world. . . .

"In a report of the Committee on Petroleum Economics to the Petroleum Industry War Council, dated Oct. 24, 1944, there was presented a résumé of the papers published up to that time by industry representatives dealing with the probable postwar demand for petroleum and its products. The five studies included in this review indicated that during the postwar years 1946–1950 the total United States demand for petroleum products might average 4.7 million bbl. daily. Two of the studies in the same report forecast a decline of 54 per cent in our exports to 129,000 bbl. daily from an estimated high of 282,000 bbl. daily. In 1938 our exports of petroleum products amounted to 517,000 bbl. daily.

"If we are to maintain domestic consumption levels at 4.7 million bbl. daily and at the same time to continue to produce about what we produced in 1943 (4.2 million bbl. daily) or in 1944 (4.6 million bbl. daily), the deficit of domestic supply would have to be met from average imports ranging between 100,000 to 500,000 bbl. daily. Such imports would be equivalent to from 2 to 12 per cent of our 1943 production. In 1939 (the peak prewar year for imports) our imports of petroleum amounted to 4.7 per cent of our 1939 domestic production of 3.5 million bbl. daily.

"During the five-year period 1935–1939 our average imports of petroleum and petroleum products were 159,000 bbl. daily and were obtained principally from Venezuela, Dutch West Indies, and Mexico; Colombia provided only about 1 per cent of our total imports and other countries less than 1 per cent. . . .

"Whether or not the quantities of petroleum to be obtained from new domestic sources will steadily decline or will increase is a question which no one can answer with certitude. Educated guesses indicate that our reserves are being depleted at a rate which warrants our undertakings in conservation and technical research in new fuels.

"It is not in the interest of the United States to run down its oil resources to a point where in times of emergency we would become importantly dependent on foreign sources even to a greater extent than other major consuming countries. But this is a danger to which we expose ourselves unless we are prepared to import petroleum in quantities commensurate with the postwar levels of domestic production and consumption.

"The commercial policy of this government, moreover, aiming as it does at an expanding trade, seeks to contribute by practicable measures to maintain those conditions of peaceful economic relations with other countries which serve to prevent threats to peace arising from economic isolationism and its consequent enmities and dangers to national defense."

CHAPTER XI

ECONOMIC ADVANTAGES TO FOREIGN NATIONALS

The history of American foreign investments including petroleum shows that they provide for the continuing creation of new wealth and purchasing power. Thus a steady expansion of trade opportunities results, profitable alike to the country in which the capital has been put to productive use and to the country furnishing the capital. When Americans build up enterprises in foreign lands such as mining, oil, public utilities, and the like, they increase the wealth of those countries and thereby raise standards of living.

History is also eloquent in showing that where productive foreign investments abroad after establishment have been discriminated against, crippled, or otherwise rendered sterile, the internal economy of the producing country suffers and trade with the investing country fall off. The purchasing power is lowered and standards of living decline. This in turn reacts adversely on industry and labor in the investing country because the demand for goods from it is slackened.

Only by the production and sale of more and more at constantly lessening costs both at home and abroad can the benefits of modern industrial civilization be most widely shared. In this process of production, American foreign investments play an important part. By raising the purchasing power of foreign nations they enable these nations to buy more from the United States (see Chap. X). At the same time they help to discover, make available, and introduce to the American people an increasing amount of foreign goods.

Benefit to the Country in Which Investments Are Made.—It is no exaggeration to say that the people in the countries in which American capital has been invested have profited even more from these investments than have those Americans who furnished the capital. The development of such necessary services as railroads, tramways, telephones, cables, and electric power, together with shipping and aviation, has done much to raise general economic levels wherever capital has been put to productive use.

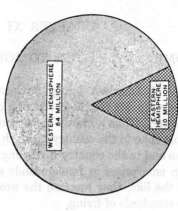

ANNUAL AVERAGE
ROYALTIES AND
TAXES PAID
(BY AMERICAN INTERESTS)

1935-1939

DOLLARS

WESTERN HEMISPHERE
64 MILLION

EASTERN HEMISPHERE
10 MILLION

TOTAL—74,000,000 DOLLARS

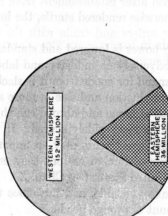

ANNUAL AVERAGE
CRUDE PRODUCTION
(BY AMERICAN INTERESTS)

1935-1939

BARRELS 42'S

WESTERN HEMISPHERE
152 MILLION

EASTERN HEMISPHERE
36 MILLION

TOTAL—188,000,000 BBLS. 42'S

In many parts of Latin America the creation of new wealth has speeded up the process of improving the standards of living. One of the most valuable functions of capital in the modernization of society is that it enables a country to increase production and so to add to the people's wealth and well-being.

The same thing happened when foreign capital was invested in the development of the United States. A large proportion of America's railroads were built, and mining and other productive enterprises were developed with the help of British and Dutch capital.

Most of the money invested in the United States by foreigners was used for productive purposes. It helped create new sources of wealth. The railroads opened up new farm areas. The mines produced new supplies of much-needed raw materials. As a result, the development of less settled regions of the United States was hastened, and the general standards of living and economic well-being of the American people were improved. The settlers who followed the line of advance and who took advantage of the economic benefits resulting from good transportation and from the development of natural resources profited more than did the Eastern or European capitalists who put up the original money with which the railroads were built.

How American oil investment along with national activities has aided living standards in foreign countries makes for fascinating study (see Chap. XII). Economically also, the gains are dramatic in their humanitarian implications, their influence on the habits and well-being of the nationals coming directly and indirectly within their orbit (see Chap. XI).

Ten-year Total of 2¼ Billion Paid.—For instance, in foreign producing countries alone, American oil investment has created direct and indirect benefits to foreign economy over the 10-year period 1935–1944 to the extent of some $2,250,000,000, as measured by pay rolls, purchases, royalties, and taxes paid by American oil companies (Table 27).

Employment for Nationals.—In foreign oil-producing countries, the function of exploration for, and production of, crude oil requires substantial numbers of skilled and unskilled personnel, an extensive employment of nationals within the operating areas. Out of a total of 67,000 employees in 1944 in all foreign producing countries (only a small proportion in other than the production of crude), American companies employed 63,000 foreign nationals. Of these, about 17 per cent were employed in supervisory and technical capacities—10,000 were supervisory and office personnel, and 1,000 were geologists, engineers, and doctors or were engaged in other technical work.

In the 10-year period 1935–1944 total wages paid by American oil companies in foreign producing countries exclusive of Europe (not reported owing to war conditions) amounted to some 625 million dollars, with 1944 the peak year at 90 million dollars. The high proportion of the 60-million-dollar pay roll in South America in 1944 reflects the large extent of the producing activity there, while wage payments and employment of personnel in Asia and Oceania have almost attained prewar proportions.

TABLE 27.—PAY ROLLS, PURCHASES, ROYALTIES, AND TAXES OF AMERICAN COMPANIES

(In thousands of dollars)

	1944	10-year total, 1935–1944
Total pay roll	89,993	624,632
All purchases	130,991	720,333
Royalties	37,996	194,059
Taxes	104,321	736,490
Total foreign [1] producing countries	363,301	2,275,514

[1] Figures for European countries are not available because of war conditions. See also Appendix Tables 31–37.

The Venezuelan Labor Law requires employment of stipulated percentages of nationals. Today Venezuelan drillers are found on practically every drilling well. Venezuelan drivers man the trucks and tractors, weld the pipe lines behind their weird masks, and operate the typewriters and comptometers and the most complicated electric bookkeeping and accounting machines in all the offices of the oil companies throughout Venezuela.

How Peruvians Have Benefited.—In the case of Peru, nationals working in the oil fields and refinery there today represent the third generation with this vocation.

The principal Peruvian oil fields lie along the northern coast of the country, which forms the most westerly extremity of the South American continent. A cold antarctic current flows past these shores—hence the sandy desert bounded on the west by the roaring surf of the Pacific and on the east by foothills that gradually rise to the snow-clad peaks of the Andes.

When Pizarro arrived at this desert point, he found the fishermen of that day defying the breakers on frail rafts of balsa wood. Three hundred years later, material for oil exploration was landed on the Peruvian shores with the help of similar rafts.

Today Peru has at Talara what is perhaps the best equipped harbor on the west coast of South America. In anchorage the mightiest tankers can lie in safety. The bare hogback that provided this shelter is now the site of a thriving town, grown up around a 16,000-barrel refinery, with great storage tanks.

Administrative offices, houses for national and foreign workers, schools, hospitals, clubs, cinema and stores, the bustling harbor with its huge concrete mole, visited by ocean liners, tramp steamers and tank ships, the puffing locomotives, the clang and clamor of machine shops and the derricks on the surrounding *tablazo* present a vivid picture of the beehive of industry oil brings in its wake.

When the International Petroleum Company started operations in Talara and Negritos, there was no wharf or dockage, not a foot of railroad or road of any kind, no drinking water, no vegetation except for a few trees. Everything had to be imported from North America. Landing supplies and heavy machinery was attended with much risk and occasional losses.

The pioneer operators obtained a supply of brackish water from the Parinas Valley and carried it on mule back to the scene of their operations. In 1905 a condensing plant was built at Negritos, followed by a similar installation at Talara, and these, at a cost of about a quarter of a million dollars annually, met the water needs of the field for some time.

In 1922 a filtration and pumping plant was constructed on the Chira River, some 25 miles south of Negritos and connection made with every part of the developed field. In 1927 the plant was enlarged and removed to higher ground at Portachuelo and is an inestimable boon to a territory that experiences a real, honest-to-goodness rain only once in every 30 years or thereabouts.

As Talara grew up and acquired the city complex, it looked with increasingly lifted eyebrows at "Fishtown," nestling on its doorstep. The houses in this village, built of the flotsam and jetsam of land and sea, defied every known law of gravity and sanitation. Gradually these eyesores were acquired, demolished, and replaced by structures that are standard for national workers throughout the estate.

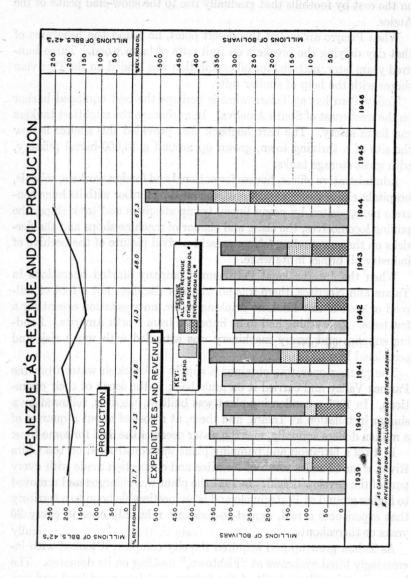

VENEZUELA'S REVENUE AND OIL PRODUCTION

While Talara is the site of the refinery and port, Negritos is the center of field activity and both are model towns. Schools are operated for the children of nationals and foreign children; the hospitals are equipped along up-to-date lines and staffed by fully qualified doctors and nurses. Sports grounds are provided for football, to which the Peruvian has taken kindly, for baseball, tennis, and golf. Cinema houses are found in both towns and the comfortable club rooms are the centers of social activity.

Each town has its police force and fire brigade; in fact the communities possess many of the advantages of town life as we know it and escape some of the disadvantages that tend to complicate our North American existence. Smaller camps, such as Lagunitos and La Brea, are dotted over the estate, connected with the central activity by road and railway and akin in their community life.

Indirectly, the whole country has benefited for petroleum and its products constituted about 30 per cent of the value of the country's total merchandise exports in the period from 1935 to 1941.

Foreign Investment in Venezuela 62 Per Cent American.—Venezuela furnishes an outstanding example of the favorable economic results to both a country and private business of an open-door oil policy backed up by equitable and stable laws.

Total foreign investments in the petroleum industry of Venezuela were estimated in 1940 to be about 400 million dollars, of which American capital accounted for 250 million dollars, or 62½ per cent. In that year Venezuela ranked third among the countries of the world in the production of petroleum, only slightly behind Russia, and was first in exports.

Between 1935 and 1941 petroleum and its products accounted for from 80 to 90 per cent of the value of total exports from Venezuela. Without these petroleum exports, it would have been impossible for Venezuela to finance the volume of imports she has received in recent years.

The sale of foreign exchange in Venezuela by the oil companies to cover wages, taxes, and other production costs in that country is generally sufficient to cover entirely the import balance in nonpetroleum trade plus the amounts owed abroad for freight, insurance, and other service items and to leave, in addition, a substantial net credit balance before gold and capital movements. Much of this stems from the intensive development enjoyed by the country rather than from exceptional resources, and in contrast other nations with far greater area for oil exploration have had but slight oil development because of less equitable policies and laws.

Direct and Indirect Revenue Payments by Oil Companies.—Approximately half the proceeds from the sale of drafts in Venezuela by the petroleum companies is applied to the payment of taxes levied upon the industry, including surface and royalty taxes on petroleum concessions and oil produced therefrom, duties on material imports by the oil companies, stamp taxes, and income taxes. It is estimated that between 1935 and 1942 about one-third of the government's total revenue was contributed by the petroleum industry, and for the fiscal year 1943–1944 the petroleum industry's share was 48 per cent.

In addition to these direct tax payments the petroleum companies have, of course, made many indirect contributions to the economy through accelerated industrialization, expanded employment, and construction of roads, schools, hospitals, port works, etc., all of which have aided materially the development and general welfare of the country and its people.

Oil 48 Per Cent of Venezuela's Total Revenue in 1943.—Of the total revenue of 340,226,000 bolivars of the Venezuelan government in 1943, actual oil-industry payments are estimated at 163,425,000 bolivars,[1] or 48 per cent.

Government profits on dollar sales by the oil industry amounted to 17,388,000 bolivars in 1943 compared to 14,911,000 bolivars in 1943 (Table 28).

Venezuela's Revenues Show Transformation since Oil Development Started.—"The figures of Venezuela's revenues show clearly the transformation that took place as the country's oil resources were developed," Nicholas Roosevelt writes.[2] "During the period 1900–1920—the last two decades before the intensive production of oil—the annual expenditures of the government averaged about 51 million bolivars. Revenues during this period were sufficient to cover expenses. By 1925 revenues had jumped to 120 million bolivars and expenses to 115,500,000 bolivars. By 1931 the figures were, respectively, 210,300,000 bolivars and 260,-900,000 bolivars. There was a sharp decline both in revenues and expenditures during the period 1931–1934, but by 1938 revenues had risen to 330 million bolivars and expenses to 313 million. The estimated revenues and expenditures for 1940 are 361 million bolivars each.

[1] 3.09 bolivars = $1 U. S. currency at present exchange rate.
[2] *Venezuela's Place in the Sun*, pp. 60–64.

"During the decade 1930–1940 petroleum royalties and import duties each furnished in the neighborhood of one-third of the government's revenues. Furthermore, the expenditure of millions of dollars in the form of wages, which in turn have gone to buy goods and services, together with the increase in expenditures accompanying the improved economic conditions of the country, directly stimulated Venezuela's

TABLE 28.—VENEZUELAN REVENUES [1]

(In thousands of bolivars)

	1939	1940	1941	1942	1943
Total revenue	350,855	330,072	359,263	291,819	340,226
Total disbursements	378,076	369,175	334,032	303,539	335,859
Revenue from oil (as carried by government)	91,832	83,502	131,887	83,306	99,269
Revenue from oil included under other headings	19,360	30,000	43,341	37,275	64,156
Grand total oil revenue	111,192	113,502	179,228	120,581	163,425
Per cent oil revenue of total revenue	31.7	34.3	49.8	41.3	48.0
Production (thousand barrels)	205,434	186,134	228,131	147,984	179,399
Production (barrels daily)	562,834	508,562	625,017	405,436	491,505
Bolivars per barrel of oil produced left in the country		1.25	1.19	1.45	1.59
Dollar equivalent (3.09)		0.40	0.38	0.47	0.51

[1] Compiled from *Memoria de Fomento* and private sources.

imports and thus contributed directly to the Venezuelan government's revenues. Although it would be difficult to specify the precise amount of Venezuela's revenues that may be attributed to the oil industry, it is apparent that it is considerably larger than the sums paid directly in royalties.

Expenditures for Modernization.—"As the revenues of the Venezuelan government began to rise sharply when the development of the oil industry assumed important proportions, the Venezuelan government was enabled to inaugurate its much-needed program of public works. In the decade prior to 1920, the average annual expenditure on roads, waterworks, sewers, and public buildings was about 7 million bolivars. During the period 1920–1937 these expenditures averaged about 26 million bolivars. The sum set aside for public works in the budget for 1940 amounts to a little under 74 million bolivars.

"This money has gone in the first place for the development of roads. President Gomez began the work of building suitable paved roads for automotive traffic. This work has been steadily pushed since 1920, but much still remains to be done. The Venezuelan government has made it a practice to keep its public-works expenditures as much as possible within revenues and has endeavored to work out a system of priority under which the most needed links in the country's road system are the first to be completed. As already explained, the government has entered into contracts with the oil companies through which the latter make part of the payments which they owe to the government in the form of construction of much-needed public works."

Roads and Harbors Built in Venezuela.—The oil companies in Venezuela have built nearly 700 miles of roads. While these have been laid out to meet their own needs, they have been opened to the general public. It is notable that, wherever such roads have been built, the general level of prosperity has risen and business activities of all kinds have increased. Some of these roads are already more used by the public than by the companies. In addition, the companies have entered into contracts with the Venezuelan government to build certain stretches of public roads not connected with the oil fields and to put in other public works.

In eastern Venezuela the task of building roads has been made particularly difficult because of the swampy nature of the jungle in the lowlands. Thus, in addition to the difficulty of laying out and clearing roads in dense tropical country, it has been necessary to deal with questions of drainage and filling, some of which have added considerably to the cost of construction. In the more open regions of the Orinoco Delta, road construction has been made difficult because of seasonal floods. Even in those regions where the actual road building has presented few complications, the extent of the country to be crossed has added materially to the problems.

This is notably true of the road recently opened between the harbor of Puerto la Cruz near Barcelona and the oil fields near Oficina, a hundred miles to the south. In this instance, it was necessary not only to import from the United States the road-building machinery but also to construct a port and harbor facilities in order to be able to handle the large volume of equipment that was necessary both in constructing the road and in building the camps, machine shops, storehouses, and power

Members of pipe-laying crew, Jusepin, Eastern Venezuela.

Venezuelan drilling crew, Jusepin.

"Out of a total of 67,000 employees in 1944 in all foreign producing countries . . . American companies employed 63,000 foreign nationals." **See page 137.**

Photographs by Vachon, courtesy of Standard Oil Company (New Jersey).

See page 138.

Jose A. Ramirez, running saponification test in the Tropical Oil Company's refinery laboratory, Barranca Bermeja, Colombia.

Photographs by Collier, courtesy of Standard Oil Company (New Jersey).

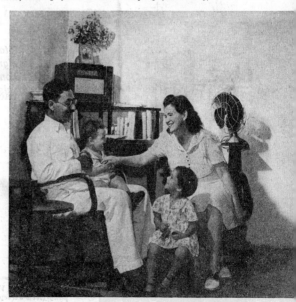

Sr. Alfonso Lopez, Tropical Oil Company's refinery foreman, at home with his family in Barranca Bermeja.

Roads and Harbors Built by American Oil Companies Abroad

While these (roads) have been laid out to meet their own (the companies') needs, they have been opened to the general public." See page 144.

Section of Puerto La Cruz-Oficina, Eastern Venezuela, all-weather road built by Meme Grande Oil Company and associated companies, 100 miles.

Oil-loading lines, bonded warehouse No. 1 in background. Puerto La Cruz Terminal, operated by American oil companies.

Oil-loading dock, Puerto La Cruz Terminal.

Cargo dock and warehouse, showing 25-ton crane, Puerto La Cruz Terminal.

Modern tractors and earth movers in Colombian jungles.

"It is notable that, wherever such roads have been built, the general level of property has risen and business activities of all kinds have increased. Some of these roads are already used more by the public than by the companies." See page **144.**

Combating the rapidly growing tropical vegetation is a year-round job in Colombia.

arranca Bermeja, Colombia. The Galan
umping station of the Andean National
ipeline which carries Tropical's crude to
he terminus on the Caribbean.

Tanker loading oil at Momenal, tidewater
terminus of the Andean National Pipeline,
15 miles from Cartagena.

Andean National Hospital at Momenal, Colombia.

New home of the Tropical Oil Company, Barranquilla.

Charter boat which is employed to carry case oil up and down the Magdalena River.

Tropical Oil bulk plant on the Magdalen River, Barranquilla.

*American oil interests abroad have inaugurated and advanced social
nd public improvements in cooperation with the governments of the
espective countries."* See page 153.

il worker's house at Caripito, Eastern Venezuela.

*"Modern housing for staff, oil field, and
refinery workers has been provided in all
cases."* See page 153.

Four-room bachelors' houses at Caripito.

*Photographs by courtesy of Standard Oil Company
(New Jersey).*

Workers' houses at Leona oil field camp.

Workers' camp at Lagunillas, Western Venezuela.

plant in the neighborhood of the oil fields. This road was pushed through a low mountain range and then straight down across plains that resemble Texas and New Mexico to the open country where the Oficina oil fields are located. The road is paralleled by a pipe line laid to carry the production of the field to the port.

It permits travel from Guanta on the Caribbean all the way to Ciudad Bolívar on the Orinoco, and it will be seen by a glance at a map how great a territory this road opens up. Today cars and trucks travel over this road at the usual speeds, and by this route the interior is now shipping cattle, hides, and agricultural products that are aiding the economic well-being of the nation.

Another important road in eastern Venezuela completed recently and one that is worthy of special mention is the Jusepin–Puerto la Cruz road, approximately 68 miles long. This road has opened up an area relatively unpopulated, and new villages are already commencing to spring up along the route.

Modern Community Comes to the Jungle of Colombia.—In the development of the De Mares concession in Colombia by the International Petroleum Company, a complete modern community has been built at El Centro, close by the Infantas oil fields. It has schools, hospitals, clubs, golf courses, a water system, a power plant, commissaries, comfortable homes, and all the other paraphernalia of healthful and secure urban existence. All these emerged from a steaming, tropical jungle.

Bogotá, because of slow river travel, was almost as remote as the secret city of Tibet. The Magdalena River was the only road to the coast. A more uncertain and hazardous route could scarcely be imagined. Snags and sand bars abounded in the shifting course and there were long periods when low water completely obstructed traffic. Specially designed towboats and barges were needed, and also a railway from the river terminal at Barranca Bermeja to the oil fields at Infantas and to El Centro.

The zone of oil operations was almost uninhabited and remote from any populous centers; therefore, the labor problem was a difficult one. Where Quesada and his few followers pitched their little camp, the engineers and other technicians of the Tropical Oil Company (first American company to open the territory) had to create a complete community; to house, feed, and provide otherwise for the staff of 5,500 workers assembled at the peak of constructive effort.

Building the first road from the river port on the east bank of the Magdalena to well No. 1 of the Infantas field was a herculean task. At first all the road clearing and grading were done by hand. The jungle swarmed with timbermen wielding axes and machetes and shook to the explosions of tons of dynamite. Earth-moving gangs followed, using picks, shovels, and wheelbarrows to grade the road. To speed up the work a narrow-gauge track was laid, along which dump cars moved the excavated earth. After months of work the narrow road was finished complete with wooden culverts and bridges.

But the engineers' troubles were not over. For the first 11 kilometers of the road, no grades exceeding 15 per cent were encountered, but then the road suddenly descended into the "Paso del Diablo" ("Devil's Pass") on a grade of 28 per cent, much too steep for anything but tractors to traverse. In the rainy seasons part of the road frequently was flooded. The engineers were called in again to take out the sharp curves and to raise the grades, and the tractor road was converted into an all-weather road over which automobiles and trucks could be driven with safety.

As the De Mares concession was developed further, the need for road-building equipment became apparent. In 1921 the Tropical Oil Company purchased a ½-cu.-yd. steam shovel. As time passed, more equipment was secured until today the latest and best of road-building equipment, such as bulldozers, graders, carryalls, power shovels, and oil-spraying machines, are pushing roads through the jungle in the quest for oil.

In all, over 330 miles of oil-field roads have been built by the International Petroleum Company in the past 20 years. Many bridges had to be built, of which 19 of steel construction span the rivers and larger streams, while scores of smaller wooden bridges carry the roads over the creeks that crisscross the concession.

The jungle isn't tamed easily. Gangs of men are constantly at work on the roads, swinging their machetes to fight back the fast-growing tropical vegetation. In the summer, or dry season, fires are a constant menace. In the rainy seasons rivers and creeks frequently rise over their banks, flooding the surrounding areas. But to the best of man's ability, the jungle of the De Mares concession has been tamed. In the space of 20 years' time, the tortuous mule trails have been converted to good serviceable roads over which cars and trucks pass with ease. While they cannot compare with our modern high-speed roads, these jungle highways serve well the purpose for which they were intended—providing efficient and economical oil-field transportation. Where in the old days it took a good rider an entire day to travel 50 kilometers of a trail by saddle mule, autos now can travel the same distance safely and comfortably in little more than an hour.

Economic Contribution to Colombia.—Although petroleum has provided a somewhat smaller percentage of the total merchandise exports of Colombia than of Venezuela or Peru, the narrow margin by which Colombia's total exports normally exceed her imports emphasizes the importance of the petroleum trade. Eliminating petroleum exports, Colombia would have found it necessary to curtail the volume of her imports in each year of the 1935–1941 period.

Active development of Colombia's oil was a stabilizing factor during the years of world-wide depression, as illustrated by the fact that in connection with the De Mares concession from 1926 to 1936 the Tropical Oil company and Andian National Corporation transferred $17,-501,000 in cash to Colombia and imported into the country $25,732,000 in machinery, materials, and supplies and a further 6 million dollars in foreign products for resale within the republic. In the same period these companies paid $40,960,000 in royalty and taxes to the Colombian government. Their income-tax payments approximated one-third of the republic's total income-tax collections. Expenditures of $36,654,-588 for Colombian goods and labor were a strong prop to local industry at a time when internal trade and employment were at low ebbs.

Oil Revenue 18 Per Cent of Total in Colombia.—The oil industry (largely American-controlled companies) of Colombia not only makes substantial investments in concessions, equipment, drilling machinery, and test wells as evidenced by the data on wildcats completed and sums invested, but it is likewise a substantial contributor to the fiscal revenues of the nation.

During 1939, of the total government income of 91,359,288 pesos or $52,200,000, the oil industry paid $9,275,900, or 18 per cent, of the fiscal revenues.[1] This was paid by 15 different oil enterprises, of which only four were operating commercially. The others were engaged solely in exploratory work (Table 29).

In 1926 when the oil industry started commercial exploitation, represented by the first pipe-line shipments and the sale of Colombian oil in the world market, the fiscal income from the oil industry did not amount to more than 1.5 per cent of total revenues of the government.

[1] E. Ospina-Racines, *World Petroleum*, September, 1941.

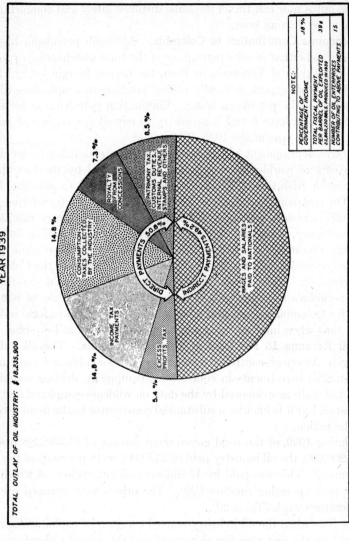

Oil Important Factor in Colombia's Favorable Trade Balance.—Formerly dependent on foreign oil, Colombia's commercial needs are now supplied by products manufactured within the republic from its own crude. The virtual elimination of oil imports was an important contribution to Colombia's favorable balance of trade over past years, and at a critical time it eased the country's foreign-exchange burden.

TABLE 29.—OIL INDUSTRY'S DIRECT PAYMENTS TO COLOMBIAN GOVERNMENT, 1939

(U. S. currency)

Surface rentals and storage depots.................... $	72,900
Royalties from concessions..........................	1,320,000
Income-tax payments...............................	2,710,000
Estimated income-tax yield accruing to government from total wages and salaries paid to oil-industry personnel, 1 per cent of 24,447,451 pesos—244,474 pesos........	140,000
Capital-assets levy (patrimony tax)..................	606,000
Excess-profits taxes................................	978,000
Customs duties.....................................	383,000
Rights on common carrier...........................	148,000
Internal-revenue stamps, official paper, etc............	208,000
Gasoline, greases, and lubricants consumption tax collected by the industry............................	2,710,000
Wages and salaries paid to nationals..................	8,960,000
Total outlay of the oil industry, 1939...............	$18,235,900
Total paid to the government.......................	9,275,900
Percentage of government income, 1939...............	18
Total fiscal payments per barrel of oil exploited: 23,860,230 barrels produced in 1939.................	0.39
Number of oil enterprises contributing to above payments	15

A dependable supply of petroleum products at prices radically lower than those that used to prevail has further stimulated the country's social and industrial progress.

Royalties and Taxes Paid in Foreign Producing Countries.—In foreign producing countries alone, American oil companies paid royalties and taxes amounting to 930 million dollars in the 10-year period 1935–1944 (Table 30).

Over 4 Billion Dollars in Royalties and Taxes in All Foreign Countries.—As a direct contribution to the revenue of foreign countries, American oil companies paid in the 10 years 1935–1944 the huge sum

TABLE 30.—TOTAL ROYALTIES AND TAXES PAID BY AMERICAN OIL COMPANIES IN
FOREIGN PRODUCING COUNTRIES ONLY, 1935–1944 *

(In millions of dollars)

	North America	South America	Western Hemisphere	Europe and Africa †	Asia and Oceania ‡	Eastern Hemisphere ‡	Total foreign ‡
1935	20	29	49	....	2	2	51
1936	23	30	53	....	9	9	62
1937	26	44	70	....	14	14	84
1938	30	48	78	....	10	10	88
1939	26	44	70	....	14	14	84
Total 1935–1939	125	195	320	....	49	49	369
Average per year	25	39	64	....	10	10	74
Per cent total foreign	33.8	52.7	86.5	....	13.5	13.5	100.0
1940	34	42	76	....	19	19	95
1941	47	61	108	....	16	16	124
1942	48	41	89	....	4	4	93
1943	47	57	104	....	2	2	106
1944	51	88	139	....	4	4	143
Total 1940–1944	227	289	516	....	45	45	561
Total 1935–1944	352	484	836	....	94	94	930

* See Appendix Table 36.   † Data are unobtainable because of war conditions.
‡ Incomplete for the 1940–1944 period because of war conditions.

TABLE 31.—TOTAL ROYALTIES AND TAXES PAID BY AMERICAN OIL COMPANIES IN ALL FOREIGN COUNTRIES, 1935–1944 [1]

(In millions of dollars)

	North America	South America	Western Hemisphere	Europe and Africa [2]	Asia and Oceania [2]	Eastern Hemisphere	Total foreign [2]
1935	24	38	62	258	260	518	580
1936	28	39	67	234	291	525	592
1937	33	52	85	266	336	602	687
1938	36	58	94	227	284	511	605
1939	34	53	87	219	285	504	591
Total 1935–1939	155	240	395	1,204	1,456	2,660	3,055
Average per year	31	48	79	241	291	532	611
Per cent total foreign	5.1	7.9	13.0	39.4	47.6	87.0	100.0
1940	41	53	94	55	126	181	275
1941	55	75	130	24	95	119	249
1942	56	48	104	23	66	89	194
1943	54	66	120	22	75	97	217
1944	57	98	155	8	90	98	252
Total 1940–1944	263	340	603	132	452	584	1,187
Total 1935–1944	418	580	998	1,336	1,908	3,244	4,242

[1] See Appendix Table 32.
[2] Incomplete for the 1940–1944 period because of war conditions.

of 4.2 billion dollars in royalties and taxes alone in *all* foreign countries. (Table 31).[1] The peak year was 1937 when the total was 687 million dollars. Higher payments may well have been reached during the 1940–1944 period had not war conditions rendered these reports incomplete. Complete world analysis can be made only for the 1935–1939 period during which five years average annual payments of 611 million dollars in royalties and taxes were made. The Eastern Hemisphere represents some 87 per cent of total foreign, reflecting the high duties on imports of products, and excise taxes and municipal taxes in the marketing of oil products, particularly in the European area. Income taxes, also included in these data, often are payable on fixed minimum bases irrespective of actual earnings.

Increasing Burden of Taxation.—Looked at from the side of government income, certainly these payments have been substantial. But the benefit to certain countries is questionable where taxation has grown to such proportions as to keep national consumption of petroleum products from a natural expansion and as to discourage foreign enterprise within such countries.

---

[1] Through answers to the questionnaire distributed by the Group on American Petroleum Interests in Foreign Countries to American oil companies with foreign investments and representing an estimated 93 per cent of all such investments, it is possible to give for the first time authentic figures on royalties and taxes paid and on purchases by these companies in all foreign countries. Also made available in addition to these figures are statistics showing total and native employment and wages paid in foreign oil-producing countries in which American companies have investments. The figures for producing countries are exclusive of European oil-producing countries' figures, which were not available because of war conditions.

CHAPTER XII

SOCIAL AND EDUCATIONAL ADVANTAGES TO FOREIGN NATIONALS

During the past 25 years American oil interests abroad have inaugurated and advanced social and public improvements in cooperation with the governments of the respective countries in which they are active. They may well be proud of the contribution they have made to the better living in sister republics of the Western Hemisphere, in countries of the Middle East, and in the islands of the Far East.

Modern housing for staff, oil-field, and refinery workers has been provided in all cases. In Venezuela and Colombia, for example, thousands of oil-company employees and their families live in company-built and -operated camps. Schools, churches, hospitals, model farms, irrigation and sanitation projects, and recreational facilities have been built. Health and sanitary standards of the nationals have been improved because of these facilities.

Vocational Training of Nationals.—In Latin America, in the Middle East, and in the Dutch East Indies, Americans have trained nationals to take skilled positions in the shops, fields, and offices. Today in Peru, Colombia, and Venezuela, virtually all such workers as well drillers, shopmen, and pump-station operators are citizens of those countries who have been educated and trained by the American oil companies.

True, in Venezuela and Colombia labor laws require that a stipulated percentage of employment be of nationals, and that specialized and general educational and medical facilities in certain instances be provided. But in large degree American companies anticipated these requirements. They provide them as a matter of good business reasoning based upon having a labor supply physically fit, interested, and of constantly improved skills. The necessity of this is apparent when it is considered that, except for certain areas in Europe, most of the great foreign oil fields have been found in remote and sparsely populated areas. Often they are located in swamp and jungle or in poorly grassed plateaus or in deserts where it has been necessary to bring in workers and to make operations almost entirely self-sufficient.

The oil companies recognized that the advent of petroleum development in such areas, creating as it does unfamiliar activity and a necessary concentration of population, raises problems of housing and education that did not exist before. The facilities provided by the oil companies to meet them were, at least in part, a voluntary contribution to assist in solving the problems that they themselves had created.

They also recognized that the introduction of a new industry such as petroleum requires workmen of many skills and that the training for such employment contributes not only to the welfare of the individuals but also to the profitable operation of the companies themselves. The benefits of higher wages paid their own workers extended to the businessman, tradesman, and farmer by raising living standards and purchasing power.

Participation in Public Works.—The oil companies have participated in public-works projects such as road building in these countries. Many service utilities directly or indirectly benefiting the public, such as modern wharves where large seagoing vessels receive and discharge cargo and passengers, customs warehouses, power and light plants, fresh-water and sanitary systems, have been promoted or aided by them. They have dredged and maintained channels for seagoing vessels into some of the principal ports.

In fact, one of the outstanding general benefits from the work of oil companies in developing their concessions has been the opening up of new areas by roads or new ports and the stimulation of economic development as a result. In the South American countries this is favorably spoken of by many government officials. It is no less true in the Middle East. Bringing new areas into touch with the rest of the world is important both socially and economically.

Improved Transportation Facilities.—Directly, the advent of an oil industry makes available to the people of these countries petroleum products at a much lower cost than the imported product.

Most of these countries have extremely poor transportation facilities. It is good business, therefore, for the companies to encourage the construction of new highways not only on their own initiative but in participation with the government. These new highways require asphalt and eventually will be used by all types of automotive equipment consuming gasoline made by the local refining industry.

In numerous instances new highways have been constructed through outlying agricultural regions and undeveloped fertile valleys that stimulated new agricultural endeavors. Agricultural products, therefore, were made available to the consuming urban population and oil-company camps alike at a much lower cost than the produce formerly imported or available.

In many countries oil companies today operate social-security plans supplementary to those required by law. The industry has cooperated very extensively and generously in Latin American countries with local governmental charity and social organizations in the raising of funds to build small hospitals and clinics in areas outside the oil fields, the maintenance of lunchrooms for school children, the building of roads and bridges in rural areas, the establishment and maintenance of churches, the carrying on of health and sanitary surveys, the aiding of national schools for the training of geologists and engineers and schools for adult illiterates, as well as centers for manual and domestic-science training. The industry has likewise furnished scholarships to many nationals in engineering, medicine, agriculture, accounting, finance, and other courses in United States schools and colleges.

Basis of Sound Business.—"The inauguration of a new industry in any country is of benefit not only to the nationals of the country but to the government through increased revenue and to the foreign concern which is able to make a return on its capital investment which creates dividends for the shareholder," an American oil company executive with Venezuelan interests said at a recent stockholders' meeting, "and it is sound business to aid in improving the health of the nationals of the country. It also seems to be good business to train them for the many highly specialized jobs required by the petroleum industry.

"I personally feel that industry has certain obligations in the promoting of economic, social, and cultural welfare of various countries," this executive said.

"Public works that we have financed have been largely roads and hospitals. . . . We are required by law, of course, to build a certain number of hospitals. Even if we weren't, we would proceed with the program which we are following.

"I think that the various people who have been in Venezuela can show you the advantage from a purely dollars-and-cents standpoint of developing your workmen. . . . We know from the statistics we have compiled that a man today can do considerably more work than he could formerly, and we think that is largely due to the fact that we have helped take care of him physically.

"So we think our statistics prove pretty conclusively that hospitals are a good investment, even though we spend a substantial amount of money in hospitals."

Stability of Industry Essential Factor.—As a matter of fact, the oil companies operating in Venezuela in collaboration with the government authorities have done more to better the condition of the worker in health, housing, medical attention, educational facilities, and the encouragement of sport and thrift than has been done, perhaps, anywhere else in the world by a government or by government and industry in cooperation. No one, least of all the oil-company officials in charge of this work, assumes that it springs from a purely philanthropic motive.

It was realized from the beginning that, for genuine stability of the industry over the long-term development that was contemplated, the industry must be manned by Venezuelan workers. The companies assumed the obligation not only to return to the government a fair share of the value of oil produced in taxes and royalties but also to furnish employment opportunities to the Venezuelan worker. For an adequate domestic supply of contented and efficient labor in a country as little developed as Venezuela was 20 or 25 years ago, pleasant and healthy living conditions were essential. At all times the attitude of the government has been entirely cooperative and the work of the companies has borne fruit in a greatly increased standard of living and standard of health. And as the health and contentment of the workers improved, they have proved themselves adept at even the more complicated tasks of oil-field development.

Already many of the higher positions are occupied by Venezuelans. In the field they have learned to be oilmen. In the machine shops they have become welders, electricians, mechanics. On the roads they are truck drivers and chauffeurs. At the ports they attend to the loading and unloading. In the offices they work as stenographers, file clerks, draftsmen, and accountants. They serve on the staffs of the companies as lawyers, engineers, geologists, and doctors.

Latin Americans Trained in United States.—As a result of an agreement between the Ministry of Education and some of the oil companies, scholarships have been awarded to geological students attending the Geological Institute in Caracas. Today there are many South Americans (not all of them university students) receiving scientific or trade education in the United States financed wholly or in part by practically all American oil companies operating in Latin America under the Inter-American Commission Plan.

For example, the Creole Petroleum Corporation's Latin-American educational program began as a matter of business expediency to develop a supply of competent personnel. It was given impetus by the

"Americans Have Trained Nationals to Take Skilled Positions in the Shop, Fields, and in the Offices."   See Page 153.

Concordia school for workers and wives.

Daily classes in instrument department at Aruba refinery.

Photographs at upper left and bottom by Vachon, at upper right by N. Morris, courtesy of Standard Oil Company (New Jersey).

Venezuelan workers on pile driver on Lake Maracaibo.

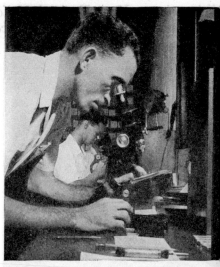

Venezuelan oil worker at lunch hour, La Salina.

Venezuelan technicians examining core samples, Caripito.

Photographs by Vachon, courtesy of Standard Oil Company (New Jersey).

". . . they have proved themselves adept at even the more complicated tasks of oil field development. . . . They serve on the staffs of the companies as lawyers, engineers, geologists, and doctors." See page 156.

Photograph by Collier, courtesy of Standard Oil Company (New Jersey).

Alfonso Lopez, Tropical Oil Company's refinery foreman leaving for work, Barranca Bermeja, Colombia.

Venezuelan geologist examining core samples, La Salina.

E. F. Blakesley of Tropical Oil refinery staff dictating to his secretary, Miss Maria Ferreira, Barranca Bermeja, Colombia.

Photographs at top and bottom, left, by Vachon, right by Collier, courtesy of Standard Oil Company (New Jersey).

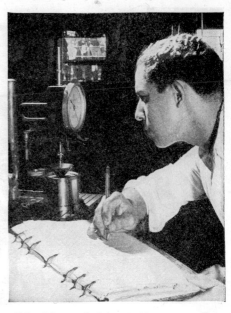

Venezuelan laboratory technicians, La Salina.

Colombian technician testing grease, Barranca Bermeja.

Schools Provided by American Oil Companies

Going to school at Caripito.　　　National science class at Concordia.

Photographs by courtesy of Standard Oil Company (New Jersey).

"Many of the oil fields are located in isolated areas that had no schools. Six years before the passage of the 1936 (Venezuelan) Labor Law obliging companies to maintain schools, they had already begun their educational program." See page 157.

Photograph by courtesy of Mene Grande Oil Company.

Venezuelan teachers and pupils of the second and third grades of San Tome school.

Physical exercises at Concordia school.

Recess time at Punta Gorda school.   Playtime at Tia Juana school.

Care Given Workers' Families

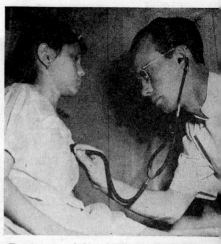

Doctor examining child at La Salina clinic

Maternity hospital, Caripito, built by
Creole Petroleum Corp.

*Photographs by courtesy of Standard Oil Company (New
Jersey).*

". . . [companies] *found it necessary from the beginning to take every possible step
not only to prevent the spread of illnesses of all kinds, but also to improve the physical
condition and health of their employees. . . . Hospitals are caring for employees and
their families."* See page 159.

Photograph by courtesy of Mene Grande Oil Company.

Mene Grande Oil Company hospital at San Tome.

This commissary at San Tome is run by the Mene Grande Oil Company on a nonprofit basis and is stocked with a wide variety of both Venezuelan and American edibles and household articles.

"It is sound business to aid in improving the health of the nationals of the country who because of undernourishment and tropical disease are often found incapable of doing more than the equivalent of a half-day's work." See page 155.

Photographs by courtesy of Mene Grande Oil Company.

Sons and daughters of workers having lunch at San Tome school.

Antimalarial drainage ditches constructed by N.K.P.M. in Dutch East Indies.

Drainage system for tidewater, Tandjong Oeban, D.E.I.

Photographs by courtesy of Standard-Vacuum Oil Company.

Bedding being aired outside bachelor quarters, Soengei Gerong.

The team and the rooters. Mene Grande Oil Company Venezuelan workmen baseball team.

Mene Grande Oil Company employees ready for game.

Photographs by courtesy of Mene Grande Oil Company.

Venezuelan and American children, sons and daughters of Mene Grande Oil Company employees engage in competitive sports.

"Sports, Recreation, and Social Facilities Are Provided for Employees." See Page 159.

Baseball is popular in Venezuela. Mene Grande Oil Company employees in midst of an exciting game with usual interested spectators.

Club house for American and technical Venezuelan employees at San Tome. The club house was erected by the Mene Grande Oil Company, but its operation is in the hands of the employees. Moving picture shows are furnished free by company.

Swimming pool at Caripito. A delightful and popular place.

Photograph at bottom by courtesy of Standard Oil Company (New Jersey); others by courtesy of Mene Grande Oil Company.

Football game at refinery field, Palembang South Sumatra, Dutch East Indies.

Refinery football field and grandstand, Palembang.

Refinery workers watching football game, Sumatra.

Hospitals Provided by American Oil Companies

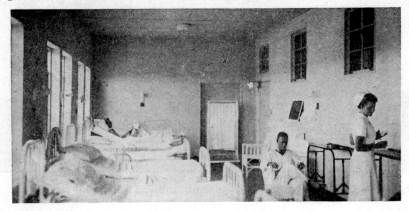

Ward in Mene Grande Oil Company's San Tome Hospital.

Staff of San Tome Hospital. All doctors and nurses are Venezuelans except three foreign registered nurses.

Photographs by courtesy of Mene Grande Oil Company.

Ambulance maintained and operated by company without cost to employees.

Creole Petroleum Corporation's hospital at Caripito would do credit to a city of 50,000 people in the United States.

"During 1944, Creole Petroleum Corporation's clinics gave 122,693 treatments to employees, 116,839 to members of their families, and 25,931 to others in near-by communities." See page 160.

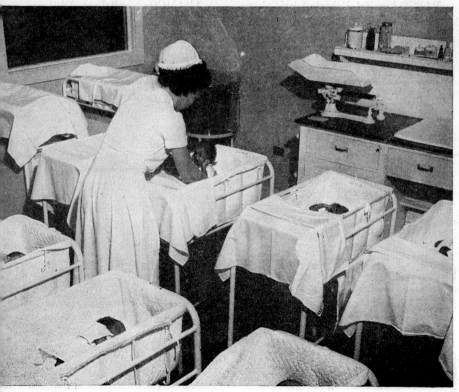

Nursery section of Aruba refinery hospital.

Facilities Provided by American Oil Companies in Middle East

BAPCO hospital, Bahrein Island.

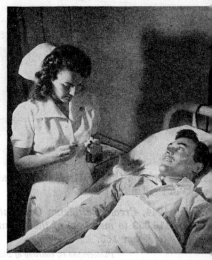

ARAMCO hospital at Dhahran, Sau
Arabia.

*"In Saudi Arabia, Bahrein Island, and
Kuwait . . . American oil companies already have spent considerable sums for
social and educational purposes."* See
page 162.

*Photographs by courtesy of The Bahrein Petroleum Company, Limited; upper right by Robert Yarnall Richie, courtesy
of Arabian American Oil Company.*

BAPCO school playground.

BAPCO auditorium, destroyed by fire.

adoption in several southern nations of legislati
lan statute providing that all companies empl
should provide three scholarships to Venezuelan
far beyond statute requirements as a policy of
ment.

School Facilities Provided.—Many of the oil
isolated areas that had no schools. Six years befo
1936 Labor Law obliging the companies to mainta
already begun their educational program. The teacl ⁓ venezuelans
and are carefully selected. Their salaries, as well as the cost of building
and maintaining the schools, are paid by the companies. Vocational
schools to teach manual training, agriculture, and animal husbandry to
boys have been established.

Creole Petroleum Corporation has built 16 schools and has spent over
$550,000 on them. Several thousand children have received instruction
in these schools. Opportunities are furnished for mechanical and clerical
instruction at company expense, and English classes are conducted.
All drillers in settled fields are Venezuelans, and only wildcat drilling is
confined to foreign experts. Scholarships for the Geological College and
for the Trade School in Caracas are set up by the company.

Mene Grande Oil Company has established a school in Cabimas and
another in Lagunillas with a capacity for 200 pupils in each. The buildings are modern construction, equipped with furniture imported from
the United States, and each school is staffed by a principal and five
teachers. These schools are under the direct supervision of the governmental education authorities, but all operating expenses are borne by
the Mene Grande Oil Company.

At Taparito an ultramodern school has been erected and is operated
jointly by Mene Grande, Creole, and Venezuelan Oil Concessions
(British-Dutch).

In eastern Venezuela the Mene Grande Oil Company operates schools
for the children of Venezuelan workmen at Oficina, Santa Ana, and the
San Tome camp.

Creole's Educational Report.—"Boys and girls attending our schools
in 1944 numbered 2,654," the Creole Petroleum Company's 1944 report
states. "We continued to offer courses to adult workers to prepare them
for advancement in the company, and some 968 adults took advantage
of the opportunity. By way of illustration it is interesting to note that
in one area of our operations the number of employees who could read
and write increased from 12 out of 100 to 88 out of 100 in about 10 years;

ped that by the application of the Laubach method of adult initiated in Venezuela by the government, and in which Creole operating through the training of two of its teachers, further great rides will be made toward teaching every adult in our fields of operation to read and write.

"The company provides scholarships for numerous employees and sons and daughters of employees aspiring to the higher technical positions. During 1944 we had 50 scholarship students in such courses as petroleum engineering, geology, nursing, medicine, and navigation. Seventeen of these scholars were studying in United States universities and colleges.

"To cooperate in the preparation of well-trained teachers, the company provides normal-school training on scholarships, and there were five young women and one man studying on these scholarships in Venezuela in 1944.

"As a result of the continuing job-training program, our supervisory and foreman force is now comprised almost entirely of Venezuelans. One interesting result of this program is that all of our drilling foremen now are well-qualified Venezuelans who readily acquired specialized knowledge for this job."

Mene Grande's Educational Report.—The Mene Grande Oil Company's 1944 report to the Minister of Fomento says: "The elementary schools maintained by the company in San Tome and El Tigre continued to function efficiently during the year. . . . These schools have the following personnel: five normal-school graduate teachers; one teacher with a Degree of Bachelor of Philosophy; two teachers with Certificates of Primary Instruction presently pursuing correspondence studies with the Extension Center of the Minister of National Education; and one graduate of the Superior School of Arts for Women in Caracas; also, a professor of physical education who gives instruction in sports, calisthenics, etc. The El Tigre school has been limited to the teaching of the first grade. The children in the other grades are all enrolled in the San Tome school. This practice was adopted this year because of the better teaching organization, special course in domestic science, collation, physical education, library, practical agriculture, etc., which are not feasible in a school with a small number of pupils.

"For the transportation of the children we have put in service a modern bus with all necessary safeguards. These children bring their lunches, and at school they are served a supplementary lunch consisting of a soup and a glass of milk.

"The company furnishes everything necessary to give a collation daily to all students consisting of chocolate beverage or milk, fruits, and cookies prepared in the department of domestic science by the children themselves."

Sports and Recreation.—Sports, recreation, and social facilities are provided for employees. Various baseball tournaments are carried out between teams of neighboring communities and other petroleum camps. In general, effort has been made to stimulate sports activities and physical education among the workmen organized under company auspices.

Special premises for centers of social life, playing fields, and swimming pools have been provided. Football and baseball fields of regulation size and athletic tracks are a familiar sight.

Needless to say, there are comfortable cinemas where the best films and latest newsreels to come into the country are exhibited at a nominal price.

Sanitary and Medical Work by Oil Companies.—American and British-Dutch companies prospecting for oil in Venezuela found it necessary from the beginning to take every possible step not only to prevent the spread of illnesses of all kinds but also to improve the physical condition and health of those of their employees who had long been debilitated by tropical diseases. This meant not only the establishment of hospitals and medical services but also the providing of safe water supplies and the installation of proper drainage and sewage facilities.

It meant also constant and close inspection of all supplies of fresh foods and, in those regions where malaria was most prevalent, the carrying on of systematic campaigns to cover all standing water with oil so as to discourage the breeding of malarial mosquitoes, and to screen all houses or to furnish all employees with mosquito nets.

From the original limited beginnings the health and sanitary services of the oil companies have grown into facilities of the first importance.

Hospital Facilities Provided.—Hospitals, some individually and one jointly built and operated by American and British-Dutch oil companies, are caring for employees and their families. There is a jointly owned and operated hospital at Lagunillas. The Lagunillas hospital has accommodations for 15 inpatients, 4 doctors, 22 nurses, 2 pharmacists, and a laboratory technician.

At the Mene Grande field, Shell has built a 90,000-dollar hospital with 40 beds and a staff of 2 doctors, 1 pharmacist, a laboratory technician, and 11 nurses.

Creole Petroleum Corporation also has spent hundreds of thousands of dollars to build dispensaries at La Salina and Cumarebo in western Venezuela and at Caripito and Quiriguire in eastern Venezuela. In Maracaibo it uses the facilities of the Shell hospital through a special administrative agreement.

During 1944 the Creole Petroleum Corporation's clinics gave 122,693 treatments to employees, 116,839 to members of their families, and 25,931 to others in near-by communities. The hospitals cared for 5,714 inpatients, and 491 children were born in company hospitals.

Sinclair Oil Corporation's subsidiary has constructed a large modern hospital at Santa Barbara.

The Mene Grande Oil Company has a large, modern hospital at Maracaibo. As the company carried on important operations in eastern Venezuela, where their Oficina field was being rapidly developed, they operated medical facilities there, too, and constructed two more hospitals. Clinics have been maintained by Mene Grande at Barcelona, San Tome, Oficina, and Ciudad Bolívar. Limited hospitalization was available at Barcelona, Oficina, and Ciudad Bolívar. Serious cases were transported by air to the Creole company's Caripito hospital or to the company's own hospital at Maracaibo.

"Our workmen and members of their immediate families sought the professional service of our doctors in 13,732 cases of nonprofessional sickness during the year," says the company's 1944 report. "During the previous year there were 9,915 similar treatments."

Physicians Also Given Training.—Besides the engineering students, physicians are given opportunity for United States study. These are usually young men who have received their medical degrees from South American institutions and who have served the equivalent of an internship in one of the company's medical centers, of which 10 are maintained in Venezuela alone, ranging from a 94-bed unit at Caripito to single-bed dispensary units at field camps.

The chiefs of the hospitals select the South American nationals for study in the United States in some specialty such as tropical diseases and public health.

Examples of Expenditures for Social and Educational Purposes. Two American-owned oil companies in Venezuela alone have made capital expenditures for social and educational purposes totaling $36,599,000, and their annual operating expense for such activities amounts to $10,-404,000.

The Creole Petroleum Corporation, subsidiary of the Standard Oil Company (New Jersey), has made capital expenditures totaling $23,-

108,608, and in 1944 its operating expense for these purposes was $7,413,-
000, representing 29.27 per cent of its total annual operating expenses
in Venezuela.[1]

The Mene Grande Oil Company, a subsidiary of Gulf Oil Corporation,
has made capital expenditures totaling $13,491,496, and in 1944 its
operating expense for these purposes was $2,991,186, representing 22.2
per cent of its total annual operating expenses in Venezuela.[2]

An Investment in National Welfare in Colombia and Peru.—To relate
what the petroleum companies have done in Colombia and Peru would
be somewhat repetitive of the social and educational contributions
made by the oil industry in Venezuela. Of course, it also should be
borne in mind that oil development in these two countries in no way
compares with Venezuela in magnitude.

Colombia's advanced social legislation has had the wholehearted support of the International Petroleum Company (American-controlled),
principal operator in that country and in Peru.

Separately the affiliated Tropical Oil Company and the Andian National Corporation operate two hospitals, among the finest in Colombia,
and there is a thoroughly efficient sanitary organization.

Expenditures for social and educational purposes by the Tropical Oil
Company and the Andian National Corporation, Limited, operating the
De Mares concession in Colombia, have totaled since and including 1922
$18,300,000 and amount to $1,100,000 annually.[3]

In Peru, the International Petroleum Company put up hospitals in
Talara and Negritos and subsequently established six medical dispensaries in the less populous districts. In these hospitals and dispensaries
from 600 to 800 patients are treated daily. Each of the hospitals is
equipped with the most modern installations, including a complete
range of surgical instruments, an X-ray set, pharmacies, and a total of
190 beds. Eight doctors and a diplomaed laboratory and X-ray technician are in attendance, assisted by 84 nurses who give all possible care
to their patients. Workmen receive free medical attention at their
homes or in the hospitals, are operated on free of charge, and pay nothing for medicine. This service and the upkeep of hospitals and dispensaries involve a yearly expenditure of $275,000.

The upkeep of schools in Talara and Negritos—11 in all with 125
teachers—amounts to approximately $75,000 yearly.

[1] See Appendix Table 38.
[2] See Appendix Table 39.
[3] See Appendix Table 40.

As part of its educational service and with a view to fitting Peruvian employees to become skilled technicians the company grants scholarships to promising pupils leaving its schools so that they can go to Lima to finish their studies. Scholarships also are awarded to graduates of the Lima School of Engineering, enabling them to acquire advanced technical training in Canada or the United States.

Social and Educational Facilities in Middle East.—In Saudi Arabia, Bahrein Island, and Kuwait and participating in the oil development in Iraq, American oil companies already have spent considerable sums for social and educational purposes although their operations, still on a comparatively small basis, were affected by the Second World War.

Good Progress in Saudi Arabia.—For example, projects were sponsored by the Arabian American Oil Company and The Bahrein Petroleum Company, Limited, both jointly owned by the Standard Oil Company of California and The Texas Company, in the interest of advancement of the social and educational welfare of the native population in Saudi Arabia and in Bahrein Island.

Training and Education in Saudi Arabia and on Bahrein Island.—In Saudi Arabia the Arabian American's efforts during the first few years were devoted almost entirely to the training of the local Arabs in mechanical crafts. Thousands of Arabs hitherto totally unskilled now do semiskilled and skilled mechanical work, some with remarkable proficiency. As rapidly as the Arab workers have developed their skills, the company has increased their wages accordingly.

Schools for education other than craft training have been introduced in Al Khobar and at Dhahran camp. In view of the general illiteracy of the population, the only subjects so far offered have been English, written and oral, Arabic writing and grammar, and arithmetic. The company schools have been open to the public, to employees and nonemployees, of all ages.

The schools were started with local Arab teachers under the supervision of the company personnel department. In 1943 the company engaged an American educator to act as superintendent of schools and to take charge of the company's educational program. Additional schools were opened in Ras Tanura in the area of the new refinery during 1944.

Encouraged by the successful results to date and realizing the importance of this work in the future, the company in its future program envisages a great improvement and enlargement of the present school system as rapidly as the demand develops.

On Bahrein Island, The Bahrein Petroleum Company, Limited, similarly from the very beginning of its operations has sponsored social and educational projects, working in conjunction with local governmental agencies and members of the ruling family of this independent sheikdom.

For the past several years it has sponsored the government's Technical School for Arab boys interested in various mechanical vocations. Upon completion of training the students are employed by the company, and their training along mechanical lines is continued. In addition, the company selects from its employees those demonstrating aptitude for various types of work involved in its operations and develops them as qualified craftsmen and operators; as they progress, their rates of pay are increased correspondingly.

Housing and Hospitals.—Both in Saudi Arabia and on Bahrein Island the companies have provided housing for employees in the vicinity of operations. The type varies from the native *Barasti* variety of palm-leaf and reed construction to more permanent stone or cement structures that provide central cooking facilities, electric lighting, water supply, and sanitary facilities.

For several years the Arabian American has maintained a hospital for Arab employees in the company's camp at Dhahran. Medical attention is provided for all employees free of charge. A gradually increasing number of nonemployees have also been availing themselves of the company's medical facilities. A nominal charge for medical care is made to nonemployees although the charge is waived in the case of individuals whom the government certifies as indigent.

The company doctors have been making constant efforts to reduce disease through the education of employees and for the past several years have been carrying on a campaign to eliminate malaria in Dammam and El Hobar, the two towns nearest the Dhahran camp. The campaign has been largely successful but not entirely so owing to the lack of full cooperation on the part of the Arab residents.

In all their Middle East operations the companies have successfully trained their employees in safe practices. A large part of the education campaign has been carried out through the use of illustrative posters.

The Bahrein Petroleum Company, Limited, at the start of operations subsidized the American Mission Hospital at considerable expense to enable it to take care of the medical needs of Arabian employees and their families. This subsidy has been continued.

The company now plans to convert one of the present buildings into a modern, well-equipped, adequately staffed hospital for natives, under the general direction and supervision of the company's medical officers.

Public Projects.—The Arabian American Oil Company has given assistance to the Saudi Arab government from time to time in the development of water and of agriculture. The most notable project in which the company has participated has been the Al Kharj project, about 50 miles southeast of Riyadh. This project was started by the government itself and carried forward by them until 1941, at which time they appealed to the company for technical advice in the enlargement of the project. In the spring of 1941 company engineers made a complete survey and made recommendations to the government as to steps that should be taken to increase the water supply and place additional land under cultivation. The recommendations were followed and the company placed orders in the United States for additional pumping equipment recommended.

Work on the project was carried on under the advice of company engineers during 1942, and in 1943 company engineers and construction men took over complete supervision of the project with the government supplying the labor. For this purpose the company engaged an American irrigation engineer previously with the United States government Indian Service.

The project was completed at the end of 1944. The work consisted of the installation of modern centrifugal pumps at the edge of a large limestone pit that is fed by a source of water some 600 ft. below the surface, the pumps being installed in 36-in. wells drilled into an overhanging wall of the pit. It also involved the construction of an 11-mile canal and the leveling and grading of some 2,000 acres of land as an initial unit of the new area to be placed under cultivation.

The company has drilled test wells for water in various parts of the country, some of which were successful and some unsuccessful. Successful water wells have been completed and are being maintained by the company at Maagala, Rhauda al Hani, Khobar, Dammam, Qatif, and Jubail. At many other points good water wells that the company discovered in its structure drilling and seismograph work have been completed and are maintained for the benefit of the local Bedouin. A number of wells have been drilled by the company at Riyadh to be used for irrigation purposes.

As a further assistance in the advancement of agriculture in Saudi Arabia, the company now has a project under way for the development of a farm of its own in the area of its operations. A qualified agricul-

Arab employees' recreation, Dhahran.

Employee swimming pool, Dhahran.

"The company schools have been open to the public, to employees and nonemployees of all ages." See page 162.

BAPCO club.

Arab school boys.

Projects and Living Quarters Provided

Old Donkey well, Riyadh.

Camels watering at Hofuf.

*"The Arabian American Oil Company h
given assistance to the Saudi Arab gover
ment from time to time in the developme
of water and of agriculture."* See page 16

Photographs by Robert Yarnall Richie, courtesy of Arabian American Oil Company.

Al Hani water well; truck service station.

Irrigation project, Al Kharj.

Vorkers' quarters, Kuwait.

Starting work on "married quarters."

Photographs by courtesy of Kuwait Oil Company, Limited.

Temporary housing for Arab employees.

American housing at Ras Tanura.

Photographs by Robert Yarnall Richie, courtesy of Arabian American Oil Company.

Old-type Arab quarters.

Barasti house and Arab caretaker.

"The companies have provided houses for employees in the vicinity of operations. The type varies from the native Barasti variety of palm leaf and reed construction to more permanent stone or cement structures that provide central cooking facilities, electric lighting, water supply, and sanitary facilities." See page 163.

See page 163.

Photographs by courtesy of The Bahrein Petroleum Company, Limited.

Concrete tile for Arab quarters.

Tile houses for Arab workers.

Arab drillers, Bahrein Island.

Arab "roughnecks," Damman field.

"Thousands of Arabs hitherto totally unskilled now do semiskilled and skilled mechanical work, some with remarkable proficiency. As rapidly as the Arab workers have developed their skills, the company has increased their wages accordingly." See page 162.

Photograph at upper right by Robert Yarnall Richie, courtesy of Arabian American Oil Company; others by courtesy of The Bahrein Petroleum Company, Limited.

Arab working in drum plant, Bahrein Island.

Arabs working in aviation acid-testing pump house, Bahrein Island.

Service Awards for Arabian Employees

Ten-year service awards to ARAMCO employees.

Ten-year service awards to BAPCO employees.

Photograph at upper left by Robert Yarnall Richie, courtesy of Arabian American Oil Company; others by courtesy of The Bahrein Petroleum Company, Limited.

BAPCO refinery employees checking out at gate.

Employees at BAPCO cracking plant.

turist has been engaged for this purpose, and for the past year or so he has been making studies of agriculture, soil, water sources, etc., of the area. The company's hope is that by conducting a farm of this kind under its own control, experiments of various kinds can be carried out and that any of these which may be successful can be passed on to the local people in the form of a demonstration and example that they can easily follow.

For several years the company has maintained a small stock farm, used primarily for the fattening of locally purchased cattle and sheep. Some experiments have been conducted there in the raising of crops. These experiments will be greatly enlarged upon in the new farm that is under contemplation.

The company has also been of considerable assistance to the Saudi Arab government in providing technical services and petroleum supplies. Wireless facilities have been installed for the government, and the company has contributed substantially to the maintenance of government automotive equipment. It also built facilities at Jidda to handle cargoes of gasoline and supervised the construction of service stations between the port of Jidda and Riyadh, the capital of Saudi Arabia.

The Bahrein Petroleum Company, Limited, has sponsored agricultural developments and has imported at various times selective seeds from the United States and has distributed these to the more interested local farmers and gardeners in the interest of improving their produce. Similarly, the company has sponsored irrigation projects through freshwater conservation measures and by the provision of artesian wells.

Vacations and Benefits.—Recognizing the value of vacations in the interest of health, the Arabian American and Bahrein companies have established the policy of an annual paid vacation for Arabian employees corresponding to American domestic vacations normally granted employees of industry.

The companies also have adopted a sickness and injury disability and retirement and death benefit plans. In fact, the various projects in which the companies have engaged mean that the standard of living, health, and hygienic conditions are undergoing a constant change of rapid improvement.

Social and Educational Work in Dutch East Indies.—Before the Japanese occupation in February, 1942, the N. V. Nederlandsche Koloniale Petroleum Maatschappij, subsidiary of the Standard-Vacuum Oil Company, had spent $3,198,000 for social and educational purposes in the Dutch East Indies, and its average yearly expense for these purposes during the last years previous to the Japanese invasion was approximately $319,000.[1]

The social and educational facilities provided by the N.K.P.M. in the Dutch East Indies for its employees prior to the Japanese invasion were well established and extensive.

The company built for the Indonesians in all its producing camps and refineries substantial multiple dwellings either of dressed lumber in the temporary camps or of plastered brick with concrete floors in the permanent establishments. Both types of dwelling were covered with corrugated iron or asbestos roof, thus avoiding any danger of fire. These dwellings were provided with electric light, separate kitchens, bathing and toilet facilities with running water, and separate laundry facilities. The native foremen and clerks were often provided with quarters in duplex houses with all modern conveniences.

The houses for Europeans, which include both Eurasians and Hollanders, were provided with all modern conveniences such as electric lights, baths, and toilets with running water, as well as comfortable servants' quarters. All of these houses were furnished with screens in the windows and doors. In recent years air-conditioning units were provided by the N.K.P.M. in some of the offices and in several of the rooms in the hospital.

One of the most beneficial steps toward improved living conditions was the construction by the company of large, airy, clean markets where the local merchants could display their wares for the benefit of Indonesian employees. These markets were built at the refinery near Palembang in the native quarters and also centrally located in the producing fields in south Sumatra.

General stores also were provided by the N.K.P.M. for the convenience of the Indonesian and Holland personnel. A forward step was the construction of cold-storage facilities at the refinery and at the main producing field so that meat and vegetables could be properly kept in storage. Despite the necessity for ice and refrigeration facilities in this tropical land, they were not very common in the Dutch East Indies, and the Americans have done a great deal to bring these modern advantages to the population.

Hospitals and Medical Care.—The task of bringing medical care and hospital facilities to employees was a difficult one because of the extensive territory involved and the isolated situation of many of the producing fields. This, coupled with the tropical climate and native

[1] See Appendix Table 41.

habitat, demonstrates some of the unfavorable circumstances under which industrial medicine must be practiced in this far-off territory.

An example of the increase in use of company medical service rendered to employees and their families is the fact that clinical visits during 1939 at the refinery totaled 102,742 as compared with 52,161 during 1938. Graduate first-aid men were sent out with many of the geological exploration parties and to the wildcat wells, and during 1939 they handled 8,900 cases with 41,477 visits.

The N.K.P.M.'s medical services were spread over an extensive area and into many isolated localities. The number of persons from employees and their families served by the N.K.P.M. medical staff during 1939 amounted to 15,793. These people were taken care of by a staff of 4 doctors, 15 nurses, and 35 other assistants and laboratory technicians.

There was a total of 229 hospital beds scattered from Borneo to north Sumatra, including those in the base hospitals at the refinery at Soengei Gerong, near Palembang and the main producing field in south Sumatra.

Besides the visits to clinics and hospital admissions, the N.K.P.M. furnished its employees and their families with the required drugs and medicines.

The company also maintained and operated medical laboratories in connection with its hospitals at the refinery and at the main producing field. Much of the laboratory work is carried out in the control of malaria and dysentery, two diseases very prevalent in this tropical climate.

Primary and Industrial Education.—Primary schooling for the children of Indonesian and Holland employees was provided by the N.K.P.M. at the refinery and main producing field. Buildings and equipment as well as a capable teaching staff were furnished by the company. The Indonesian schools were conducted in Malay in accordance with the practice of the country, and the schools for European employees, including Eurasians, were conducted in the Holland language.

The industrial education of natives was particularly noticeable during the company's operations in the Dutch East Indies. They were trained so that they became skilled in many mechanical trades, such as boiler making, pipe fitting, and machine-tool operation. Several hundred Hollanders have been sent to the United States for training in the drilling, production, and refining of oil.

For the operation of the refinery it was necessary to train completely unskilled Indonesians to assist in many of the complicated technical processes, so that they were used to a large extent in the routine refinery operations as gaugers and pumpmen.

The company furnished correspondence courses to the Hollanders, Eurasians, and Indonesians to help them improve their knowledge of modern operating techniques.   Indonesian drillers and machinists are now very proud of their increased knowledge and ability.

Recreational and Social Facilities.—The Hollanders introduced association football (soccer) to Netherlands India, and the natives are all very fond of this game.   Consequently, the company built football fields at all its permanent installations. Large crowds of Indonesians and Europeans witness the games.   The company has built and maintains many tennis courts for the use of the employees.

Clubhouses were built by the N.K.P.M. at the refinery and the main producing fields for both the Indonesian and European personnel. These are equipped with ping-pong tables, billiard tables, dance floors, bar and refreshment facilities, and complete moving-picture outfits with sound equipment.   At least twice a week movies are shown.   Several times a month special additional features are arranged for the Indonesians, who are fond of the Tarzan pictures as well as American westerns.

Modern Services.—Although in the larger cities in the Dutch East Indies modern services have been available for many years, the company's operations in outlying districts brought to the Indonesian and Holland population the advantages of electric lights, ice, and refrigeration, as well as pure running water that had been settled and chlorinated in modern waterworks.   Besides this, modern sewage disposal and properly drained camps improved the health of the population.

Improved housing, particularly for the Indonesians, as well as adequate bathing and laundry facilities has raised the standard of living. Improved roads and bridges, as well as company-operated trucks and busses, helped solve the problem of transportation.   A company-operated radio communications and telephone services in the principal camps increased the ease of communication, much to the advantage of the local population as well as to the efficient operation of the company's business.

CHAPTER XIII

OUR FUTURE FOREIGN OIL PARTICIPATION

The increasing demand for petroleum products and the rather disappointing rate at which new reserves have been discovered in the United States during the past few years point to the necessity and importance of American participation in foreign oil production on an ever-increasing scale.

When American oil companies first began to go abroad for oil production, there was no thought that petroleum in this country might in time be exhausted or become inadequate to meet domestic needs. Rather, their interest stemmed from their world-wide activities in marketing. It has been pointed out that

1. Prior to 1914, Americans were represented in the oil-production columns of only two countries—Rumania and Mexico.

2. Predictions after the First World War of an oil famine and of foreign oil domination caused our government strongly to urge that American oil interests go abroad.

3. In fulfilling this mandate, American operators, with the strong diplomatic support of their government, embarked on exploratory and development activities in all parts of the world with the result that today much of the available knowledge of oil prospects in many inaccessible and undeveloped regions of the earth stems back to these far-flung American ventures of the early twenties.

4. Even in the face of an oversupply at home right up to the outbreak of the Second World War, American oil companies have continued and expanded their foreign activities. In fact, the only major producing countries in which American companies have not been represented to at least some degree are Russia, Burma, Japan, Iran, and British Borneo. Absence from these is due to restrictions by national governments.

5. Nevertheless, despite these continuing and expanding activities the percentage of foreign production outside Russia controlled by American companies has declined since the twenties from 57 per cent in 1922 to 39 per cent in 1941.

6. American oil companies that continued foreign operations and attempted to protect investments through the years were faced, particularly during the last decade, with lack of strong, effective support from the government.

7. There were expropriation in Mexico, seizure in Bolivia, and the trend toward increasing taxation in other countries to the extent of making producing operations uneconomical.

8. Examples illustrate the trend toward complete national monopolies at the expense of foreign oil interests in many European and Latin-American countries.

9. These also illustrate a postwar problem confronting American oil companies in many foreign countries, for the trend toward nationalization is as pronounced if not more pronounced than it was before the Second World War.

10. Just as the First World War left many nations that had no important indigenous oil resources supersensitive of their dependence on imports, so it is after the Second World War.

11. The "sterling area" is a potential source of serious problems, encompassing as it does a large volume of trade and the production and consumption of a great quantity of oil.

12. Again the vital role of oil in the scheme of war, national defense, and national economies is in the forefront of international considerations.

Uncertainties Following the Second World War.—It should be added that large investment in foreign countries by American oil companies has been jeopardized by the fact that substantial foreign interests of the American petroleum industry were located in the European and Far Eastern theaters of war. Some of these properties have been damaged or destroyed; others are located in territories that either have experienced or might experience a change of sovereignty. American corporations, directly or through subsidiaries, own property located in parts of the war-torn areas of Finland, Germany, Rumania, Austria, Hungary, and Poland, and also in the Dutch East Indies, to mention only a few countries visited by the ravages of war where Americans have interests.

Presumably, war risks to foreign investors are offset by principles of international law regarding removal of private property from the category of legitimate war booty, and by provisions for payment of requisitioned goods and restoration of damaged or seized properties. Such provisions usually are incorporated in armistices or peace treaties. Yet the fact remains that full compensation for war losses thus incurred is highly improbable.

Prospects for restitution of losses in the Second World War are further clouded by the political complexion of successor governments in both victor and vanquished countries, many of whom incline toward nationalized economies. A further complication is the quasi-separate armistices concluded, terms of which, involving war-loss settlements, are being fulfilled in advance of a general peace treaty.

American-controlled Foreign Oil Aided Victory.—For national-security reasons it is important that we continue our foreign oil participation. When victory came to the United Nations in 1945, Brigadier General Howard L. Peckham, then director of the Fuels and Lubricants Division of the Offices of the Quartermaster General, said: "The Army is happy to pay tribute to all who have contributed to the continuous flow of motor fuel to the front. . . . This has been a joint undertaking of America's great petroleum industry and various governmental agencies including the Quartermaster's Corps of the Army."

The important contribution of American petroleum industry both in domestic and foreign operations was made possible through the organization and coordination and planning of wartime petroleum supply abroad under the Petroleum Administration for War and the large number of industry committees, headed by the Petroleum Industry War Council. PAW and industry committees were staffed largely by men whose services were contributed by the industry. The coordination of tanker operations with available petroleum supplies was helped by the Tanker Division of the War Shipping Administration and staffed by industry men who worked in close cooperation with the United States Navy. The Army-Navy Petroleum Board was also to a large extent staffed by the American oil industry.

Oil produced by American companies in foreign countries during the Second World War played its direct part in victory, for the United Nations were dependent upon these as well as United States sources to fill the tremendous needs of the armed services. Without the oil produced abroad by American interests, serious shortages that would have adversely affected the aggressive prosecution of the war and the economy of the United States would have been inevitable.

The recent world conflict called for technical skills not only behind the lines but also in the operation of war implements and the transport and use of war material. It was proved in all war theaters that technical oil know-how was one of America's formidable weapons in battle. By the same token, the existence, continuance, and further development of such knowledge are national-defense insurance.

Our government had at its fingertips the personnel and facilities of American oil companies abroad and the knowledge and skill of its nationals in petroleum to draw upon when the emergency—the Second World War—came. Products made at American-owned refineries in the Caribbean and the Persian Gulf areas were available to ourselves and our Allies. Oil companies operating abroad furnished our armed forces with maps, geographic data, photographs, and other information of foreign areas that were of vital concern to them.

Knowledge of Foreign Areas Proved Valuable.—The Air Transport Command selected American oilmen because of their foreign knowledge for the important task of laying down supplies on the now famous air route across North Africa to its eastern terminus near the Red Sea and also on airfield routes in India, South Africa, Australia, and the Far East.

When American and British troops invaded Africa in 1942, two submarine pipe lines, important as means of supplying gasoline to the armed forces of the United Nations, were quickly completed on the west coast of Africa with the help of American oilmen's knowledge of local conditions. With the completion of the sea pipe lines, the tankers discharged to shore tankage through a long submerged pipe line. Similarly, seasoned oil pipe lines laid military lines across France after the Normandy invasion and in the Philippines and other campaigns against the Japanese.

American Aid in War Projects Abroad.—Among the many military pipe lines, the world's longest—from Calcutta, India, to American airfields in Yunnan, China, covering a distance of over 2,000 miles—was engineered by men from America's petroleum companies who prior to the actual work took a course in laying pipe lines under simulated battle conditions. This India-Burma-China pipe line was the same type of line first found so effective militarily in North Africa and France to which American pipe-line know-how contributed.

Americans Aid in War Gasoline Expansion Abroad.—American refinery experts aided in an overseas 100-octane gasoline-plant expansion to meet the needs of the Second World War. Early in the war, when it became evident that the demand for 100-octane gasoline would increase tremendously, plans were made for the major construction of new facilities both in British refineries and in overseas refineries of American ownership.

In addition to the contribution of American technical know-how, a large part of the equipment for these plants was obtained in the United States.

Steaua Romana refinery bombed, Rumania.

"Large investment in foreign countries by American oil companies has been jeopardized . . . full compensation for war losses thus incurred is highly improbable. . . . restitution of losses is further complicated by the political complection of successor governments in both victor and vanquished countries, many of whom incline toward nationalized economies." See *page* 170.

Photographs by courtesy of U. S. Army Air Forces.

Damages to acid towers, Teleajen refinery, Rumania.

Fueling a fighter plane.

Landing oil drums at beachhead.

"Our government had at its fingertips the personnel and facilities of American oil companies abroad and the knowledge and skill of its nationals in petroleum to draw upon when the emergency—the Second World War—came." See page 172.

Photographs by courtesy of Signal Corps, U. S. Army.

Fueling U. S. Army trucks on their way to the front.

Pipe flown over "hump" for Burma-China line.

Testing unit for aviation gasoline,
Elizabeth, N. J.

Toluene plant, Baytown, Tex.

Photographs by courtesy of Standard Oil Company (New Jersey).

Famous "Big Inch" war pipe line, Texas to New York.

Photograph by courtesy of World Petroleum.

Assurance of Adequate Oil Supplies

Pipe-line transportation in the making.   Tanker loading.

"The American oil industry recognizes that again a mandate has been given it to make secure an adequate share in world oil development for American needs and, with this [government] support, it will succeed to this end."   See page 179.

Naphtha-fractionating unit and spheroid tanks, Baytown, Tex., refinery.

Tankers on the Supply Lines.—One of the most notable achievements was the industry's assistance in the design and construction of the high-speed national-defense type of tanker, many of which were in operation before Dec. 7, 1941. Also before our entry into the war, the industry established a shuttle service between Gulf and north-of-Hatteras ports in which many American tankers gave much help during England's darkest hour.

Again in the prewar days the industry diverted from customary trade routes and made available all its foreign-flag tanker tonnage. This marked the beginning of civilian oil rationing in the United States, which actually was the direct result of the transportation shortage caused by this country's desire to aid Britain.

With the entrance of the United States into the Second World War and the general requisition of all tankers over 3,000 tons dead weight, the tanker industry evidenced what an official statement said was "a spirit of wholehearted devotion to the aims of this Administration for which this Administration is profoundly grateful."

Tankers were the target of submarine warfare, and acts of heroism by crews have been numerous. A big job was done in the management of tankers. New and important records on "turn-around" have been made, and loading and unloading time has been cut to new lows. This greater efficiency in management of tankers did the work that several hundred more tankers would have had to do, or, to state it another way, this efficiency accounted for the transportation of many hundreds of millions of additional gallons that sent tens of thousands more men and trucks and armor against the enemy.

American petroleum know-how is one of the best assurances that there will be enough oil to go around in an oil-thirsty world.

Revival of Oil-shortage Scare in 1943–1944.—American oil participation in foreign countries received attention in 1943–1944 when there was a revival of the oil-shortage scare reminiscent of that immediately following the First World War. It centered, as did the earlier one, on the heavy drain being placed on United States oil to meet military requirements and fear for our national security.

Petroleum Administrator for War Harold L. Ickes announced the formation of the Petroleum Reserves Corporation, government-sponsored, at the annual meeting of the American Petroleum Institute in November, 1943, saying that in the past American oil companies "have established themselves in the foreign oil business, obtained rights to oil reserves, constructed refining and pipe-line facilities, and engaged in world-wide distribution of oil and its products—all entirely as a result of proved initiative, with the government simply extending its good offices." On the other hand, he said, "The other principal nations, or most of them, have conducted their foreign oil business through corporations or agencies entirely or partly owned or in effect controlled by the government itself."

He said that, since government assistance and participation may be necessary for American companies from now on, "the Petroleum Reserves Corporation is available for this purpose." Directors named were the Secretaries of State, War, Navy, and Interior and the Administrator of the Foreign Economic Administration.

Later announcement was made of a projected Arabian pipe line sponsored by the Petroleum Reserves Corporation under a proposed agreement between it and the Arabian American Oil Company and the Gulf Exploration Company.[1] Under this agreement, the government upon "recommendation of the War Department, Navy Department, Joint Chiefs of Staff, and the Army and Navy Petroleum Board and with the approval of the Department of State" agreed "to construct and to own and maintain a main trunk pipe-line system, including requisite facilities, for the transportation of crude petroleum from a point near the presently discovered oil fields of Saudi Arabia and Kuwait to a port at the eastern end of the Mediterranean Sea," the companies maintaining and operating the line.

After wide public discussion of the proposed project, it was reported dropped in the middle of 1944. The project as proposed did not materialize.

Anglo-American Oil Agreement.—Further attention was given to American oil participation abroad during the proposals for an Anglo-American Oil Agreement. In July, 1944, representatives of the British government met with those of the United States government in Washington in a series of oil conferences that resulted in the promulgation of an Anglo-American Oil Agreement dated Aug. 8, 1944 (see Appendix, page 186). The agreement was "to assure the orderly development of petroleum resources for international trade and to provide the basis for a multilateral world-wide oil accord in the postwar era." It was signed by the State Department, Edward R. Stettinius, Jr., Acting Secretary, and Lord Beaverbrook, Lord Privy Seal.

---

[1] Text of proposed agreement, Report 10, Part 15, of Special Senate Committee (Truman Committee) Investigating the National Defense Program, 78th Cong., 2nd Sess., Government Printing Office, 1944, pp. 77–79.

President Roosevelt submitted the agreement to the Senate in the form of a treaty for ratification on Aug. 24, 1944. After wide discussion the agreement was withdrawn by the President from the Senate for further study. Revisions were made and a new Anglo-American oil agreement,[1] also designed to form the basis of a multilateral agreement to which other countries would affix their signatures, was signed Sept. 24, 1945, in London by United States Petroleum Administrator Ickes and Great Britain's Fuel Minister, Emanuel Shinwell. Late in 1945 President Truman submitted this agreement to the Senate for approval as a treaty. No action has been taken at this writing.

CONCLUSIONS

Conclusions relative to our future foreign oil participation reached by the Group on Petroleum Interests in Foreign Countries in its report to the Senate Committee Investigating Petroleum Resources follow in full:

"Participation in the development of oil production and reserves and in petroleum refining, transportation, and marketing in foreign countries by American oil companies has had a sixfold importance.

"First, it has enabled us to maintain abroad an American business of large proportions with resulting benefits to our nation.

"Second, it has made it possible for this country to supplement United States reserves in carrying on a world petroleum trade in which American capital pioneered and still has a tremendous investment.

"Third, only by such activities could American interests meet foreign competition that derives oil supplies from both foreign and United States sources.

"Fourth, with respect to Western Hemisphere development, it is insurance of contiguous, readily marketable supplies against the day when to fill the United States' needs will require greater supplement from abroad.

"Fifth, participation in foreign oil development is a means toward world peace in guaranteeing American-controlled supplies for national defense in strategically located parts of the globe and is so recognized by our State, War, and Navy Departments.

"Sixth, the United States, accounting for about two-thirds of the entire world's petroleum consumption, is compelled to control an ade-

[1] For text of new Anglo-American Oil Agreement, see Appendix, p. 186.

quate share of foreign oil production and reserves to ensure high living standards in its domestic economy.

"At the same time participation by American oil companies in foreign business has also afforded broad social and economic benefits to the foreign countries themselves. Among such results are the following:

"1. That the development of natural resources with the aid of foreign capital greatly benefits the people of the country in which the investments are made.

"2. That these activities create new productive wealth.

"3. That this, in turn, stimulates trade not only with the investing nation but also with the rest of the world.

American Position Not Unfavorable.—"The American oil industry has had the foresight, the enterprise, and the courage to go into foreign oil development and markets. Its foreign position is not unfavorable, but if new domestic oil discoveries do not keep pace relatively with increasing United States demand (as has been the tendency in recent years), foreign reserves under American control must be expanded in order to maintain reserves in safe balance with our requirements.

"There are four great oil-producing regions in the world in addition to the United States, namely, the Caribbean region, the Caspian basin region of southern Russia, the Persian Gulf region of the Middle East, and the Dutch East Indies.

"American companies lead in the first with British-Netherlands interests in second place. In the second, Russia has exclusive state control. In the third, British interests dominate although American companies hold extensive properties with large proved reserves. In the fourth, British-Netherlands interests lead with American companies becoming increasingly important.

"All these areas are expected to be actively and increasingly exploited as, with the war's close, producing fields long occupied by the enemy or destroyed are reoccupied and rehabilitated and as foreign civilian markets for petroleum products return. In this revived activity there will be the keenest international competition.

Obstacles in Meeting Severe Competition.—"The future of foreign investments by American oil companies depends to a large degree on their ability to compete freely in the sale of crude oil and products in the markets of the world, as well as in their obtaining a share in foreign oil production and reserves.

"The principal obstacles to this free competition are financial and political in character. Exchange restrictions are of so great concern that the petroleum industry asks that the fundamental conditions which have given rise to exchange control be corrected.

"It has been shown that political risks are even more onerous than economic and physical risks in foreign activities. A national oil policy encouraging to American enterprise abroad would aid materially in decreasing political risks.

Same Freedom of Action as Competitors Asked.—"It is recognized that nationalization or the threat thereof, the throwing up of trade barriers, governmental cartels, and the like—expected to be carried over into the postwar era in even more pronounced form—do not lend themselves to easy diplomatic solution. Nevertheless, if American companies are not allowed the same freedom of action as their foreign competitors to operate in accordance with the laws and customs of foreign countries, regardless of their merits, loss of our foreign oil development and markets cannot but result. It is essential, therefore, that the industry be freed insofar as it is possible from the uncertainty as to the conflict between American laws and the laws and customs of foreign countries.

"Moreover, if it is true that the American oil industry is expected to participate in foreign oil development as a measure of national security, the problem ceases to be one solely involving the industry but in addition becomes one vital to our government and to the American people.

Foreign Activities National-defense Insurance.—"The war has brought home to us the importance of having far-flung bases of supply abroad. To ensure that these facilities are available to our military forces in time of emergency we must have peacetime markets. The contribution of American development of oil reserves accessible to the United States to the insurance of United States peacetime consumption demands has been noted, and its bearing on added national-defense insurance also should be stressed.

"It would seem advisable that our government be especially vigilant in encouraging and assisting American interests in the principal regions referred to. The Caribbean area oil proved valuable in the winning of the war. Oil in the Middle East aided victory and won that area recognition by our government for its strategic importance.

"As a result of the firm attitude taken by the United States government in the early 1920's for the right of its nationals to participate in the petroleum resources of the Dutch East Indies, the Netherlands accorded to American interests available producing rights which they otherwise undoubtedly would not have obtained, and just prior to the Japanese invasion of the Dutch East Indies, American interests were producing at the rate of about 41,000 bbl. daily. Had it been possible to prevent the occupation of the Japanese, that source of oil, which included aviation gasoline and other military and navy fuels, would have been strategically placed for use by the United States military forces in the war against Japan.

"With our victory over Japan and in consideration of our future bases in the Pacific, our participation in oil development in the Persian Gulf, Dutch East Indies, and all other present and potential oil regions of Asia and Oceania becomes increasingly a matter of national concern.

Diplomatic Action Asked against Exclusion except on Minority Basis. "As it now stands, American interests are excluded, except on a minority basis, in such countries as British India, Baluchistan, Burma, China, the Philippines, Brazil, Chile, Trinidad, Mexico, Bolivia, and Uruguay. It is submitted that the precedent set in the Dutch East Indies, where a firm American attitude against discrimination toward American oil interests was successful in obtaining the elimination of such discrimination, establishes the fact that such might be obtained by a similar attitude toward other discriminatory measures in other countries.

"Particularly would this positive position seem tenable inasmuch as the United States does not discriminate against foreign interests in the development of its own resources.

"Furthermore, it is believed that, without the diplomatic assistance of the United States government, American interests will continue to be prevented from participation in petroleum exploration and development in various countries except on a minority basis.

Severe Setbacks in Recent Years.—"After the First World War the government gave the American petroleum industry a mandate to find and develop oil abroad. How well this mandate was carried out is amply demonstrated, as shown in this report, by the record of discovery and development by American companies during the years 1919–1925, to which activity today we owe much of our present favorable position in foreign oil.

"But there have been severe setbacks in the last 10 years. American as well as other foreign capital has been the victim of discriminatory laws and of arbitrary and unjust treatment in many countries. It has been deprived by expropriation or confiscation of title to property legally acquired.

"Failure on the part of the diplomatic agents of the countries making foreign investments to bring about justice and ensure respect for lawfully acquired rights of their nationals exposes capital to injurious treatment by political groups wherever there is desire to undermine foreign investment.

"American oil companies with investment abroad find themselves today in the position of fighting for their legal and economic existence in many countries and, as has been stated, the experiences they have had, in which extensive and legitimate rights have been eliminated or seriously reduced by the action of foreign governments, make it evident that the problem now is not only how to acquire initial rights abroad but also how to keep secure those which we now hold or which we may subsequently acquire in foreign production, reserves, transportation, refining, and marketing.

"This situation is further complicated in the postwar period because of the large American oil investments in countries located in the European and Far Eastern theaters of war. Some of these properties were damaged or destroyed; some located in territories which either have experienced or might experience a change of sovereignty or which are in the hands of certain of the United Nations and which therefore present special problems for our State Department. The difficulties in working out a solution in such cases are recognized by the oil industry, which, however, feels that a solution must be found that will be in keeping with international law and justice.

Strong Backing Should Be Proclaimed.—"The traditional policy of the United States government has been to recognize the value of foreign investments and foreign trade in the development of American economic life. This is the policy existing today, but it needs reiteration. The government of the United States should proclaim to the world its backing of its nationals in their search for and development of foreign oil resources and make clear that it will expect its nationals to receive treatment not less favorable than that accorded to nationals of foreign countries and to competing government-controlled companies.

"The American oil industry recognizes that again a mandate has been given it to make secure an adequate share in world oil development for American needs, and, with this support, it will succeed to this end.

"Given the same freedom of action as their foreign competitors to operate in accordance with the laws and customs of foreign countries, the American oil industry has no fear of fulfilling the mandate. The presence in the world picture of a number of aggressive companies representing commerce-minded nations provides assurance in itself not only that adequate supplies will be available to all nations but that those supplies will be provided at reasonable prices established on the basis of competition. The very independence of these companies, competing as they are for both supplies and markets, gives the best possible assurance that the world will continue to receive all it requires of the 'essential fuel of peacetime' at economical prices."

APPENDIX

APPENDIX

GROUP ON AMERICAN PETROLEUM INTERESTS IN FOREIGN COUNTRIES

B. Brewster Jennings, president, Socony-Vacuum Oil Co., *Chairman*
R. H. Colley, president, The Atlantic Refining Co.
H. D. Collier, president, Standard Oil Co. of California
J. Frank Drake, president, Gulf Oil Corp.
George A. Hill, Jr., president, Houston Oil Co. of Texas
Eugene Holman, president, Standard Oil Co. (New Jersey)
W. Alton Jones, president, Cities Service Co.
Don R. Knowlton, manager of the Foreign Department, Phillips Petroleum Co.
W. S. S. Rodgers, chairman of the board, The Texas Co.
Reese H. Taylor, president, Union Oil Co. of California
A. E. Watts, executive vice-president, Sinclair Oil Corp.

Statistical Subcommittee

A. D. Stewart, Socony-Vacuum Oil Co., *Chairman*
W. C. Allen, The Texas Co.
C. J. Bauer, Standard Oil Co. (New Jersey)
V. L. Elliott, The Atlantic Refining Co.
H. A. Hassan, Sinclair Oil Corp.
E. P. Hinds, Cities Service Co.
W. G. Moore, Gulf Oil Corp.
B. Saurino, Sun Oil Co.

PROVED U. S. CRUDE-OIL RESERVES

(REPORT OF THE AMERICAN PETROLEUM INSTITUTE'S COMMITTEE ON PETROLEUM RESERVES)

The American Petroleum Institute's Committee on Petroleum Reserves herewith submits its report as of Dec. 31, 1945.

The committee estimates that the proved reserves of crude oil in the United States, as of Dec. 31, 1945, amounted to 20,826,813,000 bbl. This is derived as follows (Table *A*):

TABLE *A*.—TOTAL PROVED RESERVES, 1945

(In thousands of barrels)

			Barrels
Total proved reserves as of Dec. 31, 1944			20,453,231
Revisions of previous estimates..	+248,891		
Extensions of old pools	1,441,424	1,690,315	
New reserves (new pools) discovered in 1945		419,984	2,110,299
Total proved reserves as of Dec. 31, 1944 and new proved reserves added in 1945			22,563,530
Subtract production during 1945			1,736,717
Total proved reserves as of Dec. 31, 1945			20,826,813
Increase in reserves since Dec. 31, 1944			373,582

183

The estimates in this report, as in all previous annual reports of this committee, refer solely to proved or blocked-out reserves of crude oil, including condensate [1] produced as oil on the lease or through cycling plants. They include only oil recoverable under existing economic and operating conditions. In previous years this condensate has been included in the committee's total estimate of reserves. Thus, in the 20,453,231,000 bbl. as of Dec. 31, 1944, 668,701,000 bbl. were condensate. The 20,826,813,000 bbl. as of Dec. 31, 1945, include 884,967,000 bbl. of condensate.

The estimates in this report do *not* include:

1. Casinghead gasoline extracted at natural-gasoline plants.[2]
2. Oil under the unproved portions of partly developed fields.
3. Oil in untested prospects.
4. Oil that may be present in unknown prospects in regions believed to be generally favorable.
5. Oil that may become available by secondary-recovery methods from fields where such methods have not yet been applied.
6. Oil that may become available through chemical processing of natural gas.
7. Oil that can be made from oil shale, coal, or other substitutes.

Proved reserves are both drilled and undrilled. The *proved drilled reserves* in any pool include the oil estimated to be recoverable by the production systems now in operation, whether primary or secondary, and from the area actually drilled up on the spacing pattern in vogue in that pool. The *proved undrilled reserves* in any pool include reserves under undrilled spacing units, which are so close and so related to the drilled units that there is every reasonable probability that they will produce when drilled.

In the case of new discoveries, which are seldom fully developed in the first year and in fact for several years thereafter, the estimates of proved reserves necessarily represent but a part of the reserves that may ultimately be assigned to the new reservoirs discovered each year. For a one-well field, where development has not yet gone beyond the discovery well, the area assigned as proved is usually small in regions of complex geological conditions but may be larger where the geology is relatively simple. In a sparsely drilled field, the area between wells is only considered to be proved if the information regarding the geology of the field and the productive horizon is adequate to assure that such area will produce when drilled. The total of *new oil* through discoveries estimated as proved in any given year is comparatively small, and the total of *new oil* through extensions is comparatively large. As knowledge of the factors affecting production and well performance become available and as these factors are studied, reserves in older fields can be estimated with greater precision and revised accordingly. Therefore, the oil assigned to new discoveries plus the oil proved through extensions comprise the total quantity of the new proved reserves for the year.

The committee again wishes especially to stress the fact that its estimates of proved reserves cannot be used as a measure of the rate at which these reserves can be produced with or without physical waste. Oil cannot be produced from the permeable rocks in which it occurs at any desired rate, because the flow of oil through the pores of the oil-bearing rocks is definitely controlled by the physical factors of the reservoir. As a matter of fact, today's *known oil* can be recovered only over a period of many

---

[1] Produced as a result of condensation of reservoir gases.

[2] Estimates of casinghead-gasoline reserves will probably be available next year.

years and at gradually declining annual rates. This has been widely demonstrated by past performance under all kinds of operating conditions. Therefore, only incorrect conclusions as to the life of these estimated reserves can be obtained by dividing these reserves by the current rate of production.

For comparative purposes we append a summary tabulation (Table *B*) of the overall figures contained in the committee's annual reports covering the period from 1937 to 1945, inclusive. Figures for 1935 and 1936, which were the first developed by the committee, are not available separately.

TABLE *B*.—SUMMARY OF COMMITTEE'S ANNUAL REPORTS COVERING THE PERIOD 1937 TO 1945

(In thousands of barrels)

Year	New oil blocked out during year			Production during year	Estimated proved reserves as of end of year	Increase over previous year
	Through revisions of previous estimates and extensions to known fields	Through new pools discovered during year	Total through new discoveries, extensions, and revisions			
1936	....	....	....	....	13,063,400	
1937	2,792,790	928,742	3,721,532	1,277,664	15,507,268	2,443,868
1938	2,243,571	810,493	3,054,064	1,213,186	17,348,146	1,840,878
1939	2,058,455	340,667	2,399,122	1,264,256	18,483,012	1,134,866
1940	1,607,012	286,338	1,893,350	1,351,847	19,024,515	541,503
1941	1,538,989	429,974	1,968,963	1,404,182	19,589,296	564,781
1942	1,618,925	260,051	1,878,976	1,385,479	20,082,793	493,497
1943	1,202,368	282,418	1,484,786	1,503,427	20,064,152	−18,641
1944	1,556,192	511,308	2,067,500	1,678,421	20,453,231	389,079
1945	1,690,315	419,984	2,110,299	1,736,717	20,826,813	373,582

As in the past, this committee wishes to emphasize the fact that every effort has again been made to secure a fair, unprejudiced, and representative opinion. Each member in his district appointed a number of subcommittees to gather and study the necessary data. All previously determined factors pertaining to the various pools were examined and adjusted in the light of new information. The subcommittees, which were largely responsible for the data, were comprised of especially trained geologists and petroleum engineers with long experience in this class of work. We wish to acknowledge the valuable assistance and information received from these men and others, and to thank all for their cooperation.

THE ANGLO-AMERICAN OIL AGREEMENT

A revised agreement on petroleum between the government of the United Kingdom of Great Britain and Northern Ireland and the government of the United States of America was announced Sept. 24, 1945. It superseded the Anglo-American agreement on petroleum which was signed in Washington on Aug. 8, 1944, but which was not brought into force. The agreement follows in full:

Preamble: The Government of the United States of America and the Government of the United Kingdom of Great Britain and Northern Ireland, whose Nationals hold, to a substantial extent jointly, rights to explore and develop petroleum resources in other countries, recognize—

1. That ample supplies of petroleum, available in international trade to meet increasing market demands, are essential for both the security and economic well-being of nations.

2. That for the foreseeable future the petroleum resources of the world are adequate to assure the availability of such supplies.

3. That the prosperity and security of all nations require the efficient and orderly development of the international petroleum trade.

4. That the orderly development of the international petroleum trade can best be promoted by international agreement among all countries interested in the petroleum trade, whether as producers or consumers.

The two Governments have therefore decided, as a preliminary measure to the calling of an international conference to consider the negotiation of a multilateral petroleum agreement, to conclude the following agreement.

Article I: The signatory Governments agree that the international petroleum trade in all its aspects should be conducted in an orderly manner on a worldwide basis with due regard to the considerations set forth in the preamble, and within the framework of applicable laws and concession contracts, to this end and subject always to considerations of military security and to the provisions of such arrangements for the preservation of peace and prevention of agression as may be in force, the signatory Governments affirm the following general principles with respect to the international petroleum trade:

a. That adequate supplies of petroleum, which shall in this agreement mean crude petroleum and its derivatives, should be accessible in international trade to the Nationals of all countries on a competitive and nondiscriminatory basis;

b. That, in making supplies of petroleum thus accessible in international trade, the interests of producing countries should be safeguarded with a view to their economic advancement.

Article II: In furtherance of the purposes of this agreement, the signatory Governments will so direct their efforts:

a. That all valid concession contracts and lawfully acquired rights shall be respected and that there shall be no interference directly or indirectly with such contracts or rights;

b. That with regard to the acquisition of exploration and development rights the principle of equal opportunity shall be respected;

c. That the exploration for and development of petroleum resources, the construction and operation of refineries and other facilities, and the distribution of petroleum shall not be hampered by restrictions inconsistent with the purposes of this agreement.

Article III: 1. With a view to the wider adoption of the principles embodied in this agreement, the signatory governments agree that as soon as practicable they will propose to the governments of all interested producing and consuming countries the negotiation of an international petroleum agreement which *inter alia* would establish a permanent international petroleum council.

2. To this end the signatory governments agree to formulate at an early date plans for an international conference to negotiate such a multilateral petroleum agreement. They will consult together and with other interested governments with a view to taking whatever action is necessary to prepare for the proposed conference.

Article IV: 1. Numerous problems of joint, immediate interest to the signatory governments with respect to the international petroleum trade should be discussed and resolved on a co-operative interim basis if the general petroleum supply situation is not to deteriorate.

2. With this end in view, the signatory governments agree to establish an international petroleum commission to be composed of six members, three members to be appointed immediately by each government. To enable the commission to maintain close contact with the operations of the petroleum industry, the signatory governments will facilitate full and adequate consultation with their nationals engaged in the petroleum industry.

3. In furtherance of and in accordance with the purposes of this agreement, the commission shall consider problems of mutual interest to the signatory governments and their nationals, and with a view to the equitable disposition of such problems it shall be charged with the following duties and responsibilities:

a. To study the problems of the international petroleum trade caused by dislocations resulting from war;

b. To study past and current trends in the international petroleum trade;

c. To study the effects of changing technology upon the industrial petroleum trade;

d. To prepare periodic estimates of world demands for petroleum and of the supplies available for meeting the demands, and to report as to means by which such demands and supplies may be correlated so as to further the efficient and orderly conduct of the international petroleum trade;

e. To make such additional reports as may be appropriate for achieving the purposes of this agreement and for the broader general understanding of the problems of the international petroleum trade.

4. The Commission shall have power to regulate its procedure and shall establish such organization as may be necessary to carry out its functions under the agreement. The expenses of the Commission shall be shared equally by the signatory governments.

Article V: The signatory governments agree:

a. That they will seek to obtain the collaboration of the governments of other producing and consuming countries for the realization of the purposes of this agreement, and to consult with such governments in connection with activities of the Commission;

b. That they will assist in making available to the Commission such information as may be required for the discharge of its functions.

Article VI: The signatory governments agree:

a. That the reports of the Commission shall be published unless in any particular case either government decides otherwise;

b. That no provision in this agreement shall be construed to require either government to act upon any report or proposal made by the Commission, or to require the nationals of either government to comply with any report or proposal made by the Commission, whether or not the report or proposal is approved by that government.

Article VII: The signatory governments agree:

a. That the general purpose of this agreement is to facilitate the orderly development of the international petroleum trade, and that no provision in this agreement, with the exception of Article II, is to be construed as applying to the operation of the domestic petroleum industry within the country of either government;

b. That nothing in this agreement shall be construed as impairing or modifying any law or regulation, or the right to enact any law or regulation, relating to the importation of petroleum into the country of either government;

c. That, for the purposes of this article, the word "country" shall mean

1. In relation to the Government of the United Kingdom of Great Britain and Northern Ireland, the United Kingdom, all British colonies, overseas territories, protectorates, protected states, and all mandated territories administered by that government and

2. In relation to the Government of the United States of America, the continental United States and all territory under the jurisdiction of the United States, lists of which, as of the date of this agreement, have been exchanged.

Article VIII: This agreement shall enter into force upon a date to be agreed upon after each government shall have notified the other of its readiness to bring the agreement into force and shall continue in force until three months after notice of termination has been given by either government or until it is superseded by the international petroleum agreement contemplated in Article III.

FOREIGN OIL STATISTICS

Source of the following tables is the Report of the Group on Petroleum Interests in Foreign Countries to the Special Senate Committee Investigating Petroleum Resources, previously cited.

TABLE 1.—INVESTMENT BY AMERICAN OIL COMPANIES IN FOREIGN COUNTRIES, 1918-1944 [1]

(In thousands of dollars)

Part I—Total Assets Employed [2]

End of year	Western Hemisphere			Eastern Hemisphere								Total foreign
	North America	South America	Total	Europe	Africa	Europe and Africa	Near and Middle East	South and East Asia	Oceania	Total Near, Middle, and Far East	Total	
1918	85,391	56,904	142,295	107,032	8,772	115,804	277	60,211	20,013	80,501	196,305	338,600
1919	112,997	66,692	179,689	91,369	10,871	102,240	6,585	91,276	19,641	117,502	219,742	399,431
1920	122,789	137,611	260,400	119,019	10,733	129,752	3,164	110,646	22,670	136,480	266,232	526,632
1921	188,774	136,044	324,818	127,663	12,394	140,057	4,670	104,590	38,683	147,943	288,000	612,818
1922	209,274	151,113	360,387	127,711	11,308	139,019	5,826	95,956	39,962	141,744	280,763	641,150
1923	219,249	166,437	385,686	126,796	11,102	137,898	6,110	96,821	40,899	143,830	281,728	667,414
1924	246,927	188,094	435,021	165,571	12,928	178,499	5,429	110,402	44,603	160,434	338,933	773,954
1925	247,541	233,979	481,520	184,406	16,336	200,742	6,306	110,973	51,120	168,399	369,141	850,661
1926	265,784	291,435	557,219	224,343	21,901	246,244	5,681	111,225	62,831	179,737	425,981	983,200
1927	260,275	335,372	595,647	252,883	23,267	276,150	6,071	91,851	75,656	173,578	449,728	1,045,375
1928	277,868	430,988	708,856	290,402	29,177	319,579	8,880	102,040	96,785	207,705	527,284	1,236,140
1929	302,407	476,208	778,615	337,764	39,164	376,928	10,341	115,512	124,618	250,471	627,399	1,406,014
1930	315,522	515,439	830,961	480,574	48,337	528,911	10,468	110,602	142,638	263,708	792,619	1,623,580
1931	290,522	541,333	831,855	419,003	48,345	467,348	10,636	99,121	129,783	239,540	706,888	1,538,743
1932	310,435	711,265	1,021,700	457,295	47,138	504,433	12,377	79,729	131,608	223,714	728,147	1,749,847
1933	316,163	745,223	1,061,386	650,303	50,873	701,176	29,792	75,112	139,239	244,143	945,319	2,006,705
1934	333,262	716,211	1,049,473	649,179	50,109	699,288	39,921	85,132	140,592	265,645	964,933	2,014,406
1935	325,034	728,251	1,053,285	678,366	54,105	732,471	46,973	81,927	147,357	276,257	1,008,728	2,062,013
1936	321,721	763,432	1,085,176	635,611	58,685	694,296	54,302	84,372	148,568	287,242	981,538	2,066,714
1937	321,855	987,959	1,309,814	704,608	64,861	769,469	60,434	91,753	166,947	319,134	1,088,603	2,398,417
1938	303,060	984,413	1,287,473	679,091	67,070	746,161	73,558	77,377	168,268	319,203	1,065,364	2,352,837
1939	297,096	1,058,280	1,355,376	714,911	72,465	787,376	93,100	83,361	180,044	356,505	1,143,881	2,499,257
1940	310,071	1,099,433	1,409,504	497,087	78,575	575,662	103,897	92,090	190,056	386,043	961,705	2,371,209
1941	351,397	1,167,289	1,518,686	331,382	85,674	417,056	117,748	78,347	197,465	393,560	810,616	2,329,302
1942	363,459	1,147,106	1,510,565	335,764	91,262	427,026	126,443	49,630	108,775	284,848	711,874	2,222,439
1943	362,590	1,206,765	1,569,355	353,691	98,988	452,679	147,507	56,669	115,977	320,153	772,832	2,342,187
1944	373,714	1,312,180	1,685,894	200,682	90,760	291,442	202,918	74,205	115,531	392,654	684,096	2,369,990

[1] For breakdown by major activities, 1935-1944, see Appendix, Table 2. Breakdown was not available prior to 1935. Source of data: Tabulation of data from 11 American oil companies and their subsidiaries and affiliates. It is not complete for Europe, Africa, South and East Asia, and Oceania in 1940-1944 (incl.) since information submitted was incomplete because of war conditions.

[2] Covers all assets and investments, including current assets and gross fixed capital assets.

TABLE 1.—INVESTMENT BY AMERICAN OIL COMPANIES IN FOREIGN COUNTRIES, 1918-1944 [1]—Continued

(In thousands of dollars)

Part II—Net Assets Employed [2]

End of year	Western Hemisphere			Eastern Hemisphere								Total foreign
	North America	South America	Total	Europe	Africa	Europe and Africa	Near and Middle East	South and East Asia	Oceania	Total Near, Middle, and Far East	Total	
1918	81,431	53,727	135,158	98,822	8,286	107,108	277	60,088	19,625	79,990	187,098	322,256
1919	104,426	62,834	167,260	86,581	10,416	97,297	6,585	91,193	19,143	116,921	214,218	381,478
1920	108,713	133,565	242,278	111,872	10,125	121,997	3,160	110,642	22,167	135,969	257,966	500,244
1921	165,578	131,278	296,856	116,240	11,648	127,888	4,529	98,847	37,984	141,360	269,248	566,104
1922	176,252	144,875	321,127	114,460	10,439	124,899	5,603	89,967	39,079	134,649	259,548	580,675
1923	182,146	158,116	340,262	114,284	10,171	124,455	5,753	90,319	39,353	135,425	259,880	600,142
1924	202,950	176,686	379,636	149,205	11,841	161,046	4,987	103,088	42,478	150,553	311,599	691,235
1925	195,489	215,777	411,266	164,419	15,148	179,567	5,781	103,085	48,544	157,410	336,977	748,243
1926	211,570	267,659	479,229	195,793	20,475	216,268	4,886	102,558	59,409	166,853	383,121	862,350
1927	205,757	301,470	507,227	216,339	21,336	237,675	5,250	83,033	69,722	158,005	395,680	902,907
1928	217,872	383,002	600,874	243,790	26,754	270,544	7,962	92,587	89,083	189,632	460,176	1,061,050
1929	236,625	410,018	646,643	276,060	35,761	311,821	9,325	104,119	114,192	227,636	539,457	1,186,100
1930	242,554	434,427	676,981	309,562	43,770	413,332	9,591	99,227	128,025	236,843	650,175	1,327,156
1931	217,022	448,419	665,441	309,741	43,498	352,239	9,658	86,582	107,128	203,368	555,607	1,221,048
1932	222,625	538,763	761,388	335,471	39,737	375,208	11,418	66,364	102,506	180,288	555,496	1,316,884
1933	221,840	534,984	756,824	470,264	41,711	511,975	28,546	60,821	101,303	190,670	702,645	1,459,469
1934	236,616	491,630	728,246	467,067	40,823	507,890	38,153	69,998	96,369	204,520	712,410	1,440,656
1935	228,249	481,652	709,901	484,776	43,102	527,878	43,910	65,914	97,529	207,353	735,231	1,445,132
1936	221,746	494,729	716,475	430,566	46,798	477,364	50,313	67,438	93,676	211,427	688,791	1,405,266
1937	222,023	686,864	908,887	498,705	52,053	550,758	54,317	74,290	107,116	235,723	786,481	1,695,368
1938	206,037	662,548	868,585	461,124	53,195	514,319	64,981	59,450	103,152	227,583	741,902	1,610,487
1939	195,144	708,698	903,842	484,952	57,293	542,245	79,867	64,035	109,003	252,905	795,150	1,698,992
1940	205,018	716,767	921,785	346,528	62,137	408,665	88,070	71,624	113,623	273,317	681,982	1,603,767
1941	232,889	751,637	984,526	241,056	67,889	308,945	98,542	58,975	118,293	275,810	584,755	1,569,281
1942	245,000	708,868	953,868	241,654	72,467	314,121	103,369	43,472	80,281	227,122	541,243	1,495,111
1943	236,018	742,690	978,708	256,728	79,432	336,160	121,230	50,094	86,580	257,904	594,064	1,572,772
1944	240,146	813,651	1,053,797	147,907	73,770	221,677	173,658	67,218	85,098	325,974	547,651	1,601,448

[1] For breakdown by major activities, 1935-1944, see Appendix, Table 2. Breakdown was not available prior to 1935. Source of Data: Tabulation of data from 11 American oil companies and their subsidiaries and affiliates. It is not complete for Europe, Africa South and East Asia, and Oceania in 1940-1944 (incl.), since information submitted was incomplete because of war conditions.

[2] Covers all assets and investments, including current assets and fixed capital assets at depreciated values.

Table 2.—Investments by American Oil Companies in Foreign Countries by Major Activities, 1935–1944 [1]

(In thousands of dollars)

Part I—Total Assets Employed [2]

	1935	1936	1937	1938	1939	1940	1941	1942	1943	1944
North America										
Exploration and production	33,558	29,803	31,931	23,143	23,638	25,279	26,921	34,112	38,363	40,821
Refining	72,644	75,974	73,986	72,579	74,014	80,861	88,244	85,624	85,429	90,253
Transportation	41,568	47,320	37,979	43,620	48,229	52,324	67,149	73,475	66,295	66,321
Marketing	101,711	102,844	102,884	98,453	103,185	104,703	112,087	114,727	112,085	111,697
All others [3]	75,553	65,803	75,075	65,265	48,030	46,904	56,996	55,521	60,418	64,622
Total gross assets [1]	325,034	321,744	321,855	303,060	297,096	310,071	351,397	363,459	362,590	373,714
South America										
Exploration and production	411,588	444,082	585,927	663,036	732,133	764,157	801,388	800,651	816,644	913,352
Refining	85,260	86,824	96,110	113,620	133,330	139,490	149,248	145,789	158,426	159,293
Transportation	30,773	31,006	30,627	40,601	51,069	51,110	50,422	50,361	65,989	65,354
Marketing	76,193	87,462	78,673	88,340	83,811	86,753	95,656	81,583	89,275	90,122
All others [3]	124,437	114,058	196,622	78,816	57,937	57,923	70,575	68,722	76,431	84,059
Total gross assets [1]	728,251	763,432	987,959	984,413	1,058,280	1,099,433	1,167,289	1,147,106	1,206,765	1,312,180
Western Hemisphere										
Exploration and production	445,146	473,885	617,858	686,179	755,771	789,436	828,309	834,763	855,007	954,173
Refining	157,904	162,798	170,096	186,199	207,344	220,351	237,492	231,413	243,855	249,546
Transportation	72,341	78,326	68,606	84,221	99,298	103,434	117,571	123,836	132,284	131,675
Marketing	177,904	190,306	181,557	186,793	186,996	191,456	207,743	196,310	201,360	201,819
All others [3]	199,990	179,861	271,697	144,081	105,967	104,827	127,571	124,243	136,849	148,681
Total gross assets [1]	1,053,285	1,085,176	1,309,814	1,287,473	1,355,376	1,409,504	1,518,686	1,510,565	1,569,355	1,685,894

Europe and Africa										
Exploration and production	9,163	7,394	7,085	7,501	33,530	35,601	31,913	28,126	28,300	27,972
Refining	57,494	58,953	58,013	57,200	69,668	100,853	94,708	94,221	87,631	106,766
Transportation	11,690	11,667	11,555	11,551	16,916	31,229	27,744	22,215	18,222	18,726
Marketing	200,016	209,725	194,560	194,244	271,606	420,057	387,925	392,978	362,690	391,601
All others[3]	13,079	164,940	153,256	146,244	183,942	199,636	203,871	231,929	197,453	187,406
Total gross assets[1]	291,442	452,679	427,026	417,056	575,662	787,376	746,161	769,469	694,296	732,471
Total Near and Middle East, South and East Asia, and Oceania										
Exploration and production	76,834	73,928	68,041	103,770	94,075	85,029	67,798	57,148	56,021	43,358
Refining	79,250	31,408	21,537	61,054	59,931	57,244	52,364	47,236	39,918	35,856
Transportation	13,181	12,664	12,738	15,546	14,253	14,152	12,793	11,637	11,355	20,805
Marketing	179,391	165,745	150,859	186,020	196,356	183,754	176,339	196,536	175,226	173,812
All others[3]	43,998	36,408	31,673	27,170	21,428	16,326	9,909	6,577	4,722	2,426
Total gross assets[1]	392,654	320,153	284,848	393,560	386,043	356,505	319,203	319,134	287,242	276,257
Eastern Hemisphere										
Exploration and production	85,997	81,322	75,126	111,271	127,605	120,630	99,711	85,274	84,321	71,330
Refining	136,744	90,361	79,550	118,254	129,599	158,097	147,072	141,457	127,549	142,622
Transportation	24,871	24,331	24,293	27,097	31,169	45,381	40,537	33,852	29,577	39,531
Marketing	379,407	375,470	347,976	380,580	467,962	603,811	564,264	589,514	537,916	565,413
All others[3]	57,077	201,348	184,929	173,414	205,370	215,962	213,780	238,506	202,175	189,832
Total gross assets[1]	684,096	772,832	711,874	810,616	961,705	1,143,881	1,065,364	1,088,603	981,538	1,008,728
Total foreign										
Exploration and production	1,040,170	936,329	909,889	939,580	917,041	876,401	785,890	703,132	558,206	516,476
Refining	386,290	334,216	310,963	355,746	349,950	365,441	333,271	311,553	290,347	300,526
Transportation	156,546	156,615	148,129	144,668	134,603	144,679	124,758	102,458	107,903	111,872
Marketing	581,226	576,830	544,286	588,323	659,418	790,807	751,057	771,071	728,222	743,317
All others[3]	205,758	338,197	309,172	300,985	310,197	321,929	357,861	510,203	382,036	389,822
Total gross assets[1]	2,369,990	2,342,187	2,222,439	2,329,302	2,371,209	2,499,257	2,352,887	2,398,417	2,066,714	2,062,013

[1] For total assets for period 1918–1944 see Appendix, Table 1. It is not complete for Europe, Africa, South and East Asia, and Oceania in 1940–1944 (incl.) because of war conditions.

[2] Covers all assets and investments, including current assets and gross fixed capital assets.

[3] Includes investments in foreign subsidiary and affiliated companies of which breakdown by functional activities is not available.

Source of data: Tabulation of data from 11 American oil companies and their subsidiaries and affiliates. since information submitted was incomplete

TABLE 2.—INVESTMENTS BY AMERICAN OIL COMPANIES IN FOREIGN COUNTRIES BY MAJOR ACTIVITIES, 1935–1944 [1]—Continued

(In thousands of dollars)

Part II—Net Assets Employed [2]

	1935	1936	1937	1938	1939	1940	1941	1942	1943	1944
North America										
Exploration and production	24,092	20,638	21,314	15,842	15,383	16,189	17,076	22,097	23,534	23,188
Refining	38,906	40,276	34,709	31,602	31,281	36,313	39,804	40,227	38,558	42,031
Transportation	21,033	26,306	22,661	27,436	30,662	35,151	43,103	48,888	40,175	38,658
Marketing	74,459	74,184	73,384	69,179	73,164	74,091	79,726	82,326	77,456	75,829
All others [3]	69,759	60,342	69,955	61,978	44,654	43,274	53,180	51,462	56,295	60,440
Total net assets [1]	228,249	221,746	222,023	206,037	195,144	205,018	232,889	245,000	236,018	240,146
South America										
Exploration and production	240,083	255,859	380,065	433,441	479,346	483,864	493,546	475,124	474,536	545,466
Refining	54,087	51,742	56,542	69,238	86,451	89,068	95,516	87,990	96,153	90,788
Transportation	9,293	9,166	8,522	17,826	27,365	26,212	25,659	25,359	37,884	34,253
Marketing	54,074	64,196	58,480	63,619	58,299	60,738	68,073	53,362	59,678	61,374
All others [3]	124,115	113,766	183,255	78,424	57,237	56,885	68,843	67,033	74,439	81,770
Total net assets [1]	481,652	494,729	686,864	662,548	708,698	716,767	751,637	708,868	742,690	813,651
Western Hemisphere										
Exploration and production	264,175	276,497	401,379	449,283	494,729	500,053	510,622	497,221	498,070	568,654
Refining	92,993	92,018	91,251	100,840	117,732	125,381	135,320	128,217	134,711	132,819
Transportation	30,326	35,472	31,183	45,262	58,027	61,363	68,762	74,247	78,059	72,911
Marketing	128,533	138,380	131,864	132,798	131,463	134,829	147,799	135,688	137,134	137,203
All others [3]	193,874	174,108	253,210	140,402	101,891	100,159	122,023	118,495	130,734	142,210
Total net assets [1]	709,901	716,475	908,887	868,585	903,842	921,785	984,526	953,868	978,708	1,053,797

Europe and Africa

Exploration and production	18,382	18,141	16,927	19,502	21,575	19,852	6,849	6,621	6,925	8,588
Refining	89,847	67,283	68,427	65,419	66,760	45,258	38,293	38,623	39,185	38,897
Transportation	10,739	9,485	12,514	16,746	19,592	10,803	9,342	9,300	9,360	7,894
Marketing	275,217	238,506	266,236	257,926	283,671	199,569	150,457	151,496	162,843	154,406
All others³	133,693	143,949	186,654	154,726	150,647	133,183	104,004	108,081	117,847	11,892
Total net assets¹	527,878	477,364	550,758	514,319	542,245	408,665	308,945	314,121	336,160	221,677

Total Near and Middle East, South and East Asia, and Oceania

Exploration and production	30,451	41,667	40,579	49,095	63,463	70,037	77,028	58,644	63,165	64,503
Refining	18,366	19,877	24,715	26,770	27,934	27,347	26,661	14,854	23,520	70,172
Transportation	19,482	9,417	8,928	9,387	8,793	8,873	9,266	6,784	6,149	6,537
Marketing	136,652	135,761	154,967	132,508	136,508	145,793	135,888	115,411	128,944	141,087
All others³	2,402	4,705	6,534	9,823	16,207	21,267	26,967	31,429	36,126	43,675
Total net assets¹	207,353	211,427	235,723	227,583	252,905	273,317	275,810	227,122	257,904	325,974

Eastern Hemisphere

Exploration and production	48,833	59,808	57,506	68,597	85,038	89,889	83,877	65,265	70,090	73,091
Refining	108,213	87,160	93,142	92,189	94,694	72,605	64,954	53,477	62,705	109,069
Transportation	30,221	18,902	21,442	26,133	28,385	19,676	18,608	16,084	15,509	14,431
Marketing	411,869	374,267	421,203	390,434	420,179	345,362	286,345	266,907	291,787	295,493
All others³	136,095	148,654	193,188	164,549	166,854	154,450	130,971	139,510	153,973	55,567
Total net assets¹	735,231	688,791	786,481	741,902	795,150	681,982	584,755	541,243	594,064	547,651

Total Foreign

Exploration and production	313,008	336,305	458,885	517,880	579,767	589,942	594,499	562,486	568,160	641,745
Refining	201,206	179,178	184,393	193,029	212,426	197,986	200,274	181,694	197,416	241,888
Transportation	60,547	54,374	52,625	71,395	86,412	81,039	87,370	90,331	93,568	87,342
Marketing	540,402	512,647	553,067	523,232	551,642	480,191	434,144	402,595	428,921	432,696
All others³	329,969	322,762	446,398	304,951	268,745	254,609	252,994	258,005	284,707	197,777
Total net assets¹	1,445,13●	1,405,266	1,695,368	1,610,487	1,698,992	1,603,767	1,569,281	1,495,111	1,572,772	1,601,448

[1] For total assets for period 1918–1944 see Appendix, Table 1. Source of data: tabulation of data from 11 American oil companies and their subsidiaries and affiliates. It is not complete for Europe, Africa, South and East Asia, and Oceania in 1940–1944 (incl.) since information submitted was incomplete because of war conditions.
[2] Covers all assets and investments, including current assets and fixed capital assets at depreciated values.
[3] Includes investments in foreign subsidiary and affiliated companies of which breakdown by functional activities is not available.

TABLE 3.—NET WORTH [1] OF AMERICAN OIL COMPANIES' INVESTMENT IN FOREIGN COUNTRIES, 1918-1944 [2]

(In thousands of dollars)

| End of year | Western Hemisphere | | | Eastern Hemisphere | | | | | | | | Total foreign |
	North America	South America	Total Western Hemisphere	Europe	Africa	Europe and Africa	Near and Middle East	South and East Asia	Oceania	Total Near, Middle, and Far East	Total Eastern Hemisphere	
1918	74,051	35,976	110,027	61,865	7,261	69,126	210	49,361	10,746	60,317	129,443	239,470
1919	79,432	48,259	127,691	58,353	8,794	67,147	5,949	73,759	15,693	95,401	162,548	290,239
1920	85,848	108,709	194,557	88,809	8,821	97,630	2,545	90,017	18,480	111,042	208,672	403,229
1921	113,249	103,608	216,857	95,418	10,587	106,005	4,058	80,810	34,640	119,508	225,513	442,370
1922	122,753	110,619	233,372	92,843	8,169	101,012	5,338	72,741	32,028	110,107	211,119	444,491
1923	124,646	119,612	244,258	96,921	8,258	105,179	5,213	73,821	32,320	111,354	216,533	460,791
1924	143,088	133,613	276,701	128,324	10,817	139,141	4,458	84,916	38,327	127,701	266,842	543,543
1925	154,490	158,137	312,627	144,100	13,564	157,664	4,845	81,529	46,045	132,419	290,083	602,710
1926	162,420	188,202	350,622	171,212	18,492	189,704	4,411	82,887	58,370	145,668	335,372	685,994
1927	172,588	222,416	395,004	184,003	19,050	203,053	4,525	62,996	63,855	131,376	334,429	729,433
1928	186,720	287,665	474,385	204,160	23,352	227,512	6,962	71,183	71,011	149,156	376,668	851,053
1929	205,489	329,161	534,650	230,339	32,018	262,357	8,213	83,021	94,165	185,399	447,756	982,406
1930	208,684	330,351	539,035	281,309	38,388	319,697	8,473	80,911	109,697	199,081	518,778	1,057,813
1931	183,806	332,814	516,620	252,253	37,070	289,323	8,643	71,920	91,897	172,460	461,783	978,403
1932	183,066	378,630	561,696	256,056	32,282	288,338	10,619	55,439	81,206	147,264	435,602	997,298
1933	180,340	432,642	612,982	353,399	34,530	387,929	26,281	48,129	81,877	156,287	544,216	1,157,198
1934	217,311	409,215	626,526	313,914	33,779	347,693	34,796	55,246	78,134	168,176	515,869	1,142,395
1935	213,303	398,180	611,483	323,794	33,437	357,231	40,213	52,132	74,265	166,610	523,841	1,135,324
1936	198,901	405,638	604,539	323,165	38,855	361,620	36,447	51,362	72,890	160,699	521,719	1,126,258
1937	201,997	408,865	610,862	369,860	47,739	417,599	47,690	56,121	83,431	187,242	604,841	1,215,703
1938	188,705	431,959	620,664	366,879	47,191	414,070	56,914	43,682	88,607	189,203	603,273	1,223,937
1939	177,358	476,398	653,756	376,132	50,292	426,424	73,653	42,735	95,401	211,789	638,213	1,291,969
1940	179,489	490,542	670,031	235,734	53,152	288,886	79,854	49,156	93,187	222,197	511,083	1,181,114
1941	190,798	508,387	699,185	155,301	53,064	208,365	85,006	39,939	92,823	217,768	426,133	1,125,318
1942	201,957	499,563	701,520	153,615	49,371	202,986	93,948	21,948	65,498	181,394	384,380	1,085,900
1943	205,037	531,389	736,426	157,591	55,916	213,507	100,842	16,272	61,875	178,989	392,496	1,128,922
1944	188,668	541,503	730,171	101,052	48,232	149,284	139,268	17,214	65,482	221,964	371,248	1,101,419

[1] Includes capital stock, surplus, reserves other than evaluating reserves (appropriated surplus), net of accounts receivable and payable with parent company.

[2] Source of data: Tabulation of data from 11 American oil companies and their subsidiaries and affiliates. It is not complete for Europe, Africa, South and East Asia, and Oceania in 1940-1944 (incl.) since information submitted was incomplete because of war conditions.

TABLE 4.—ACCUMULATIVE TOTAL ASSETS AND NET ASSETS EMPLOYED BY MAJOR ACTIVITIES [1]

(In thousands of dollars)

	Exploration and production		Refining		Transportation		Marketing		All others [2]		Grand total	
	Total assets amount	Net assets amount	Total assets amount	Net assets amount	Total assets amount	Net assets amount	Total assets amount	Net assets amount	Total assets amount	Net assets amount	Total assets amount	Net assets amount
North America	82,338	49,723	90,253	42,031	59,913	31,972	110,060	74,258	86,949	76,955	429,513	274,939
South America	1,073,170	711,362	153,276	88,503	77,496	49,758	74,135	48,898	84,059	81,770	1,462,136	980,291
Western Hemisphere	1,155,508	761,085	243,529	130,534	137,409	81,730	184,195	123,156	171,008	158,725	1,891,649	1,255,230
Per cent total foreign	89.6	89.4	56.4	51.1	85.0	87.7	22.5	21.7	37.2	40.6	59.8	58.1
Europe-Africa	39,516	24,633	69,345	44,298	18,309	8,440	385,937	253,807	247,438	191,214	760,545	522,392
Per cent total foreign	3.1	2.9	16.1	17.3	11.3	9.1	47.1	44.6	53.8	48.9	24.1	24.2
Near and Middle East, South and East Asia, and Oceania	94,526	66,035	118,652	80,716	5,935	2,972	249,160	191,926	41,260	40,938	509,533	382,587
Per cent total foreign	7.3	7.7	27.5	31.6	3.7	3.2	30.4	33.7	9.0	10.5	16.1	17.7
Eastern Hemisphere	134,042	90,668	187,997	125,014	24,244	11,412	635,097	445,733	288,698	232,152	1,270,078	904,979
Per cent total foreign	10.4	10.6	43.6	48.9	15.0	12.3	77.5	78.3	62.8	59.4	40.2	41.9
Total foreign	1,289,550	851,753	431,526	255,548	161,653	93,142	819,292	568,889	459,706	390,877	3,161,727	2,160,209

[1] Total and net assets at end of 1944 before all amounts that may have been written off or revalued for various reasons since end of 1918. Source of data: Tabulation of data from 11 American oil companies and their subsidiaries and affiliates.

[2] Includes investments in foreign subsidiary and affiliated companies of which breakdown by functional activities is not available.

TABLE 5.—ACCUMULATIVE INVESTMENT [1] BY AMERICAN OIL COMPANIES IN FOREIGN
COUNTRIES [2]

(In thousands of dollars)

World area	Amount
North America....................	269,178
South America....................	711,683
Western Hemisphere.............,......	980,861
Per cent total foreign...........	58.9
Europe-Africa....................	369,253
Per cent total foreign...........	22.2
Near and Middle East, South and East Asia, and Oceania.......	314,765
Per cent total foreign...........	18.9
Eastern Hemisphere..............	684,018
Per cent total foreign...........	41.1
Total foreign.................1,664,879	

[1] Net worth of investment at end of 1944 before all amounts that may have been written off or revalued for various reasons since end of 1918.
[2] Source of data: Tabulation of data from 11 American oil companies and their subsidiaries and affiliates.

Table 6.—Total Assets Employed by Function in Each Area

(In thousands of dollars)

	1935		1939	
	Amount	% of grand total in each category	Amount	% of grand total in each category
Exploration and production				
North America.........	33,558	1	23,638	1
South America.........	411,588	20	732,133	29
Western Hemisphere..	445,146	21	755,771	30
Europe and Africa......	27,972	2	35,601	2
Asia and Oceania.......	43,358	2	85,029	3
Eastern Hemisphere..	71,330	4	120,630	5
Total foreign.......	516,476	25	876,401	35
Refining				
North America.........	72,644	4	74,014	3
South America.........	85,260	4	133,330	6
Western Hemisphere..	157,904	8	207,344	9
Europe and Africa......	106,766	5	100,853	4
Asia and Oceania.......	35,856	2	57,244	2
Eastern Hemisphere..	142,622	7	158,097	6
Total foreign......	300,526	15	365,441	15
Transportation				
North America.........	41,568	2	48,229	2
South America.......	30,773	1	51,069	2
Western Hemisphere..	72,341	3	99,298	4
Europe and Africa......	18,726	1	31,229	1
Asia and Oceania.......	20,805	1	14,152	1
Eastern Hemisphere..	39,531	2	45,381	2
Total foreign.......	111,872	5	144,679	6

TABLE 6.—TOTAL ASSETS EMPLOYED BY FUNCTION IN EACH AREA—*Continued*

(In thousands of dollars)

	1935		1939	
	Amount	% of grand total in each category	Amount	% of grand total in each category
Marketing				
North America	101,711	5	103,185	4
South America	76,193	4	83,811	3
Western Hemisphere	177,904	9	186,996	7
Europe and Africa	391,601	19	420,057	17
Asia and Oceania	173,812	8	183,754	7
Eastern Hemisphere	565,413	27	603,811	24
Total foreign	743,317	36	790,807	31
All others [1]				
North America	75,553	4	48,030	2
South America	124,437	6	57,937	2
Western Hemisphere	199,990	10	105,967	4
Europe and Africa	187,406	9	199,636	8
Asia and Oceania	2,426	...	16,326	1
Eastern Hemisphere	189,832	9	215,962	9
Total foreign	389,822	19	321,929	13
Total				
North America	325,034	16	297,096	12
South America	728,251	35	1,058,280	42
Western Hemisphere	1,053,285	51	1,355,376	54
Europe and Africa	732,471	36	787,376	32
Asia and Oceania	276,257	13	356,505	14
Eastern Hemisphere	1,008,728	49	1,143,881	46
Total foreign	2,062,013	100	2,499,257	100

[1] Includes investments in foreign subsidiary and affiliated companies of which breakdown by functional activities is not available.

TABLE 7.—TOTAL ASSETS EMPLOYED, VARIATION WITHIN AREAS

(In thousands of dollars)

	1935	%	1939	%	1944	%
North America						
Exploration and production......	33,558	10	23,638	8	40,821	11
Refining.....................	72,644	23	74,014	25	90,253	24
Transportation...............	41,568	13	48,229	16	66,321	18
Marketing....................	101,711	31	103,185	35	111,697	30
All others [1].................	75,553	23	48,030	16	64,622	17
Total.....................	325,034	100	297,096	100	373,714	100
South America						
Exploration and production......	411,588	57	732,133	69	913,352	70
Refining.....................	85,260	12	133,330	13	159,293	12
Transportation...............	30,773	4	51,069	5	65,354	5
Marketing....................	76,193	10	83,811	8	90,122	7
All others...................	124,437	17	57,937	5	84,059	6
Total.....................	728,251	100	1,058,280	100	1,312,180	100
Western Hemisphere						
Exploration and production......	445,146	42	755,771	56	954,173	56
Refining.....................	157,904	15	207,344	15	249,546	15
Transportation...............	72,341	7	99,298	7	131,675	8
Marketing....................	177,904	17	186,996	14	201,819	12
All others...................	199,990	19	105,967	8	148,681	9
Total.....................	1,053,285	100	1,355,376	100	1,685,894	100
Europe and Africa						
Exploration and production......	27,972	4	35,601	5		
Refining.....................	106,766	15	100,853	13		
Transportation...............	18,726	3	31,229	4	Data incomplete [2]	
Marketing....................	391,601	53	420,057	53		
All others...................	187,406	25	199,636	25		
Total.....................	732,471	100	787,376	100		
Asia and Oceania						
Exploration and production......	43,358	16	85,029	24		
Refining.....................	35,856	13	57,244	16		
Transportation...............	20,805	7	14,152	4	Data incomplete [2]	
Marketing....................	173,812	63	183,754	52		
All others...................	2,426	1	16,326	4		
Total.....................	276,257	100	356,505	100		
Eastern Hemisphere						
Exploration and production......	71,330	7	120,630	10		
Refining.....................	142,622	14	158,097	14		
Transportation...............	39,531	4	45,381	4	Data incomplete [2]	
Marketing....................	565,413	56	603,811	53		
All others...................	189,832	19	215,962	19		
Total.....................	1,008,728	100	1,143,881	100		
Total foreign						
Exploration and production......	516,476	25	876,401	35		
Refining.....................	300,526	15	365,441	15		
Transportation...............	111,872	5	144,679	6	Data incomplete [2]	
Marketing....................	743,317	36	790,807	31		
All others...................	389,822	19	321,929	13		
Total.....................	2,062,013	100	2,499,257	100		

[1] Includes investments in foreign subsidiary and affiliated companies of which functional activities is not available.

[2] Information submitted was incomplete because of war conditions.

EXAMPLES OF LARGE INITIAL INVESTMENT AND TIME LAG

TABLE 8

Colombia

Barco concession areas

    A. Date of first investment...................... October, 1916
    B. Date of first discovery........................ Mar. 5, 1933
        Total investment between (A) and (B) periods. $21,387,000
    C. Date of first oil commercially marketed......... Nov. 1, 1939
        Total investment between (A) and (C) periods.. $60,310,000

TABLE 9

Venezuela

Western and eastern Venezuela concessions

    A. Date of first investment...................... 1925
    B. Date of first discovery........................ May 30, 1937
        Total investment between (A) and (B) periods.. $17,227,000
    Date of first oil commercially marketed......... Dec. 5, 1939
        Total investment between (A) and (C) periods.. $44,015,000

TABLE 10

Venezuela

Venezuelan concession

    A. Date of first investment...................... 1934
    B. Date of first discovery........................ 1940
        Total investment between (A) and (B) periods.. $13,920,000
    C. Date of first oil commercially marketed......... May, 1944
        Total investment between (A) and (C) periods.. $26,900,000

TABLE 11

Venezuela

Field in state of Anzoátegui

    Cost of acreage or concession(s)................... $ 7,013,000
    Development-program commitment(s)............. 39,938,000
    Number of years involved....................... 15

TABLE 12

Venezuela

Creole Petroleum Company
Eastern portion of Venezuela

    Cost of acreage or concession(s).................. $3,508,000
    Development-program commitment(s)............... $7,600,000 [1]
    Number of years involved........................ 9

[1] Represents the initial investment cost in the Caripito refinery.

TABLE 13

Venezuela

Beacon Sun Company and subsidiaries
Venezuelan fields

Cost of acreage or concession(s).................... $ 886,342
Development-program commitment(s)............. $2,626,139
Number of years involved........................ 14 [1]

[1] No production. Most of concessions were surrendered, the concession retained being explored by another company. Beacon Sun Company and subsidiaries were liquidated.

TABLE 14

Iraq

Iraq Petroleum Company [1]
Kirkuk, Iraq

A. Date of first investment....................... 1925
B. Date of first discovery........................ 1927
C. Date of first oil commercially marketed........ 1934
    Total investment between (A) and (C) periods. $62,000,000 [2]

[1] American companies hold a 23¾ per cent interest.
[2] American share of expenditure, approximately $14,720,000.

TABLE 15

Dutch East Indies

A. Date of first investment........................ Apr. 24, 1912
B. Date of first discovery......................... July 24, 1922
    Total investment between (A) and (B) periods... $12,584,000
C. Date of first oil commercially marketed........... Oct. 12, 1926
    Total investment between (A) and (C) periods... $21,422,000

TABLE 16.—CRUDE-OIL PRODUCTION IN FOREIGN COUNTRIES, BY MAJOR NATIONALITIES

(In barrels daily)

	Western Hemisphere	% of area	Europe and Africa	% of area	Near and Middle East	% of area	Far East	% of area	Total foreign	% of area
1912										
American companies	25,905	49.8	4,003	1.6	.....	.....	.....	.....	29,908	8.4
British-Dutch companies	25,274	48.5	27,318	11.0	.....	.....	51,233	91.9	103,825	29.2
Other companies	868	1.7	47,784	19.3	.....	.....	4,533	8.1	53,185	14.9
Subtotal	52,047	100.0	79,105	31.9	.....	.....	55,766	100.0	186,918	52.5
Russian companies[1]	.....	.....	169,083	68.1	.....	.....	.....	.....	169,083	47.5
Total foreign	52,047	100.0	248,188	100.0	.....	.....	55,766	100.0	356,001	100.0
% of total foreign	14.6		69.7		.....		15.7		100.0	
1913										
American companies	40,313	51.4	6,459	2.6	.....	.....	.....	.....	46,772	12.1
British-Dutch companies	36,840	46.9	30,798	12.6	5,088	100.0	53,909	91.0	126,635	32.7
Other companies	1,320	1.7	44,810	18.4	.....	.....	5,315	9.0	51,445	13.3
Subtotal	78,473	100.0	82,067	33.6	5,088	100.0	59,224	100.0	224,852	58.1
Russian companies[1]	.....	.....	162,414	66.4	.....	.....	.....	.....	162,414	41.9
Total foreign	78,473	100.0	244,481	100.0	5,088	100.0	59,224	100.0	387,266	100.0
% of total foreign	20.3		63.1		1.3		15.3		100.0	
1914										
American companies	41,158	51.4	8,322	3.5	.....	.....	.....	.....	49,480	12.8
British-Dutch companies	38,107	47.7	48,309	20.5	7,973	100.0	53,631	88.1	148,020	38.5
Other companies	789	0.9	31,156	13.2	.....	.....	7,222	11.9	39,167	10.2
Subtotal	80,054	100.0	87,787	37.2	7,973	100.0	60,853	100.0	236,667	61.5
Russian companies[1]	.....	.....	148,148	62.8	.....	.....	.....	.....	148,148	38.5
Total foreign	80,054	100.0	235,935	100.0	7,973	100.0	60,853	100.0	384,815	100.0
% of total foreign	20.8		61.3		2.1		15.8		100.0	

	Value	%	Value	%	Value	%	Value	%	Value	%
1915										
American companies	55,506	54.8	7,562	3.1			57,549	87.8	63,068	15.1
British-Dutch companies	44,370	43.8	40,003	16.7			8,022	12.2	151,829	36.5
Other companies	1,439	1.4	32,799	13.7					42,260	10.1
Subtotal	101,315	100.0	80,364	33.5	9,907	100.0	65,571	100.0	257,157	61.7
Russian companies [1]			159,372	66.5					159,372	38.3
Total foreign	101,315		239,736		9,907		65,571		416,529	
% of total foreign	24.3		57.6		2.4		15.7		100.0	
1916										
American companies	63,344	55.2	6,207	2.6			60,659	88.2	69,551	16.0
British-Dutch companies	49,168	42.8	40,907	17.0			8,096	11.8	162,966	37.3
Other companies	2,266	2.0	28,818	11.9					39,180	8.9
Subtotal	114,778	100.0	75,932	31.5	12,232	100.0	68,755	100.0	271,697	62.2
Russian companies [1]			165,027	68.5					165,027	37.8
Total foreign	114,778		240,959		12,232		68,755		436,724	
% of total foreign	26.3		55.2		2.8		15.7		100.0	
1917										
American companies	104,464	62.2					60,962	88.6	104,464	22.7
British-Dutch companies	59,393	35.4	33,586	16.4			7,838	11.4	173,522	37.6
Other companies	3,994	2.4	29,122	14.3					40,954	8.9
Subtotal	167,851	100.0	62,708	30.7	19,581	100.0	68,800	100.0	318,940	69.2
Russian companies [1]			141,826	69.3					141,826	30.8
Total foreign	167,851		204,534		19,581		68,800		460,766	
% of total foreign	36.4		44.4		4.3		14.9		100.0	

[1] For years 1912–1918 inclusive, Russian companies' production includes an undeterminable quantity of British-Dutch production.

TABLE 16.—Crude-oil Production in Foreign Countries, by Major Nationalities—Continued

(In barrels daily)

	Western Hemisphere	% of area	Europe and Africa	% of area	Near and Middle East	% of area	Far East	% of area	Total foreign	% of area
1918										
American companies	129,714	66.8	230	0.2	....	....	....	....	129,944	32.1
British-Dutch companies	59,173	30.5	20,207	16.9	23,624	100.0	60,174	90.0	163,178	40.4
Other companies	5,384	2.7	35,344	29.5	....	....	6,688	10.0	47,416	11.7
Subtotal	194,271	100.0	55,781	46.6	23,624	100.0	66,862	100.0	340,538	84.2
Russian companies [1]	....	....	63,861	53.4	....	....	....	....	63,861	15.8
Total foreign	194,271	100.0	119,642	100.0	23,624	100.0	66,862	100.0	404,399	100.0
% of total foreign	48.1		29.6		5.8		16.5		100.0	
1919										
American companies	193,004	71.3	2,592	2.1	....	....	....	....	195,596	38.8
British-Dutch companies	73,046	27.0	9,619	7.4	27,778	100.0	69,551	91.9	179,994	35.7
Other companies	4,693	1.7	29,064	22.4	....	....	6,132	8.1	39,889	8.0
Subtotal	270,743	100.0	41,275	31.9	27,778	100.0	75,683	100.0	415,479	82.5
Russian government	....	....	88,233	68.1	....	....	....	....	88,233	17.5
Total foreign	270,743	100.0	129,508	100.0	27,778	100.0	75,683	100.0	503,712	100.0
% of total foreign	53.8		25.7		5.5		15.0		100.0	
1920										
American companies	326,277	70.1	4,070	3.5	....	....	....	....	330,347	47.5
British-Dutch companies	129,258	27.8	10,277	8.8	33,415	100.0	73,547	92.4	246,497	35.5
Other companies	9,996	2.1	26,525	22.7	....	....	6,041	7.6	42,562	6.1
Subtotal	465,531	100.0	40,872	35.0	33,415	100.0	79,588	100.0	619,406	89.1
Russian government	....	....	75,842	65.0	....	....	....	....	75,842	10.9
Total foreign	465,531	100.0	116,714	100.0	33,415	100.0	79,588	100.0	695,248	100.0
% of total foreign	67.0		16.8		4.8		11.4		100.0	

	Amount	%	Amount	%	Amount	%	Amount	%	Amount	%
1921										
American companies.....	409,842	71.1	5,274	4.3	.....	.....	98	0.1	415,214	50.2
British-Dutch companies.	145,690	25.2	11,123	9.1	45,679	100.0	75,689	92.6	278,181	33.7
Other companies......	21,228	3.7	26,788	21.8	.....	.....	5,956	7.3	53,972	6.5
Subtotal........	576,760	100.0	43,185	35.2	45,679	100.0	81,743	100.0	747,367	90.4
Russian government.....	.....	.....	79,364	64.8	.....	.....	.....	.....	79,364	9.6
Total foreign.......	576,760		122,549		45,679		81,743		826,731	
% of total foreign......	69.8		14.8		5.5		9.9		100.0	
1922										
American companies.....	417,130	76.4	4,583	3.1	.....	.....	145	0.2	421,858	50.4
British-Dutch companies.	109,214	20.0	13,651	9.4	60,951	100.0	79,469	93.3	263,285	31.4
Other companies......	19,363	3.6	29,508	20.3	.....	.....	5,538	6.5	54,409	6.5
Subtotal........	545,707	100.0	47,742	32.8	60,951	100.0	85,152	100.0	739,552	88.3
Russian government.....	.....	.....	97,786	67.2	.....	.....	.....	.....	97,786	11.7
Total foreign.......	545,707		145,528		60,951		85,152		837,338	
% of total foreign......	65.2		17.4		7.3		10.0		100.0	
1923										
American companies.....	307,711	66.4	3,430	2.2	.....	.....	274	0.3	311,415	39.6
British-Dutch companies.	139,307	30.1	13,534	8.6	69,123	100.0	90,938	94.7	312,902	39.8
Other companies......	16,267	3.5	33,868	21.4	.....	.....	4,821	5.0	54,956	7.0
Subtotal........	463,285	100.0	50,832	32.2	69,123	100.0	96,033	100.0	679,273	86.4
Russian government.....	.....	.....	107,252	67.8	.....	.....	.....	.....	107,252	13.6
Total foreign.......	463,285		158,084		69,123		96,033		786,525	
% of total foreign......	58.9		20.1		8.8		12.2		100.0	

[1] For years 1912–1918 inclusive, Russian companies' production includes an undeterminable quantity of British-Dutch production.

TABLE 16.—Crude-oil Production in Foreign Countries, by Major Nationalities—*Continued*

(In barrels daily)

	Western Hemisphere	% of area	Europe and Africa	% of area	Near and Middle East	% of area	Far East	% of area	Total foreign	% of area
1924										
American companies...	324,522	71.1	3,666	2.0	.....	.....	469	0.5	328,657	39.8
British-Dutch companies.	110,113	24.1	15,281	8.4	88,451	100.0	92,804	94.4	306,649	37.1
Other companies...	21,798	4.8	39,551	21.7	.....	.....	5,003	5.1	66,352	8.1
Subtotal...	456,433	100.0	58,498	32.1	88,451	100.0	98,276	100.0	701,658	85.0
Russian government...	.....	.....	123,921	67.9	.....	.....	.....	.....	123,921	15.0
Total foreign...	456,433	100.0	182,419	100.0	88,451	100.0	98,276	100.0	825,579	100.0
% of total foreign...	55.3		22.1		10.7		11.9		100.0	
1925										
American companies...	299,694	69.6	5,020	2.4	.....	.....	222	0.2	304,936	36.2
British-Dutch companies.	107,702	25.0	16,845	7.9	95,994	100.0	96,121	94.5	316,662	37.6
Other companies...	23,239	5.4	47,819	22.4	.....	.....	5,410	5.3	76,468	9.1
Subtotal...	430,635	100.0	69,684	32.7	95,994	100.0	101,753	100.0	698,066	82.9
Russian government...	.....	.....	143,359	67.3	.....	.....	.....	.....	143,359	17.1
Total foreign...	430,635	100.0	213,043	100.0	95,994	100.0	101,753	100.0	841,425	100.0
% of total foreign...	51.2		25.3		11.4		12.1		100.0	
1926										
American companies...	270,116	62.5	5,369	2.0	.....	.....	961	1.0	276,446	30.9
British-Dutch companies.	132,625	30.7	26,158	10.0	98,197	100.0	95,959	93.8	352,939	39.4
Other companies...	29,601	6.8	56,585	21.5	.....	.....	5,359	5.2	91,545	10.2
Subtotal...	432,342	100.0	88,112	33.5	98,197	100.0	102,279	100.0	720,930	80.5
Russian government...	.....	.....	174,958	66.5	.....	.....	.....	.....	174,958	19.5
Total foreign...	432,342	100.0	263,070	100.0	98,197	100.0	102,279	100.0	895,888	100.0
% of total foreign...	48.2		29.4		11.0		11.4		100.0	

1927

American companies	283,833	61.9	5,695	1.9			3,505	3.1	293,033	29.7
British-Dutch companies	151,163	33.0	26,062	8.6	109,660	100.0	104,760	91.9	391,645	39.7
Other companies	23,161	5.1	63,308	20.8			5,671	5.0	92,140	9.4
Subtotal	458,157	100.0	95,065	31.3	109,660	100.0	113,936	100.0	776,818	78.8
Russian government			208,943	68.7					208,943	21.2
Total foreign	458,157	100.0	304,008	100.0	109,660	100.0	113,936	100.0	985,761	100.0
% of total foreign	46.5		30.8		11.1		11.6		100.0	

1928

American companies	340,172	60.5	9,338	2.7			4,609	3.5	354,119	30.5
British-Dutch companies	201,679	35.8	30,215	8.7	120,694	100.0	117,994	91.0	470,582	40.5
Other companies	20,716	3.7	69,825	20.0			7,120	5.5	97,661	8.4
Subtotal	562,567	100.0	109,378	31.4	120,694	100.0	129,723	100.0	922,362	79.4
Russian government			239,571	68.6					239,571	20.6
Total foreign	562,567	100.0	348,949	100.0	120,694	100.0	129,723	100.0	1,161,933	100.0
% of total foreign	48.4		30.0		10.4		11.2		100.0	

1929

American companies	375,010	57.9	9,903	2.5			7,190	4.7	392,103	29.7
British-Dutch companies	251,915	38.9	35,724	8.7	117,652	100.0	135,920	89.6	541,211	41.0
Other companies	20,389	3.2	75,098	18.7			8,645	5.7	104,132	7.9
Subtotal	647,314	100.0	120,725	29.9	117,652	100.0	151,755	100.0	1,037,446	78.6
Russian government			282,194	70.1					282,194	21.4
Total foreign	647,314	100.0	402,919	100.0	117,652	100.0	151,755	100.0	1,319,640	100.0
% of total foreign	49.1		30.5		8.9		11.5		100.0	

TABLE 16.—Crude-oil Production in Foreign Countries, by Major Nationalities—*Continued*

(In barrels daily)

	Western Hemisphere	% of area	Europe and Africa	% of area	Near and Middle East	% of area	Far East	% of area	Total foreign	% of area
1930										
American companies...	345,754	54.8	10,485	2.0	......	......	11,946	7.5	368,185	25.7
British-Dutch companies.	266,586	42.3	43,141	8.4	127,572	100.0	136,326	85.4	573,625	40.1
Other companies...	18,368	2.9	89,550	17.4	......	......	9,501	6.0	117,419	8.2
Subtotal...	630,708	100.0	143,176	27.8	127,572	100.0	157,773	98.9	1,059,229	74.0
Russian government...	......	......	370,782	72.2	......	......	1,805	1.1	372,587	26.0
Total foreign...	630,708	100.0	513,958	100.0	127,572	100.0	159,578	100.0	1,431,816	100.0
% of total foreign...	44.1		35.9		8.9		11.1		100.0	
1931										
American companies...	302,518	54.0	14,732	2.4	......	......	15,300	11.0	332,550	23.2
British-Dutch companies.	238,701	42.6	47,262	7.8	123,578	100.0	113,001	80.4	522,542	36.5
Other companies...	19,254	3.4	100,136	16.4	......	......	9,640	6.9	129,030	9.0
Subtotal...	560,473	100.0	162,130	26.6	123,578	100.0	137,941	98.3	984,122	68.7
Russian government...	......	......	446,685	73.4	......	......	2,462	1.7	449,147	31.3
Total foreign...	560,473	100.0	608,815	100.0	123,578	100.0	140,403	100.0	1,433,269	100.0
% of total foreign...	39.1		42.5		8.6		9.8		100.0	
1932										
American companies...	293,671	53.0	16,703	2.8	......	......	17,952	12.2	328,326	23.0
British-Dutch companies.	241,278	43.6	54,528	9.2	137,164	100.0	117,207	79.3	550,177	38.4
Other companies...	19,048	3.4	101,709	17.1	......	......	8,853	6.0	129,610	9.0
Subtotal...	553,997	100.0	172,940	29.1	137,164	100.0	144,012	97.5	1,008,113	70.4
Russian government...	......	......	421,544	70.9	......	......	3,746	2.5	425,290	29.6
Total foreign...	553,997	100.0	594,484	100.0	137,164	100.0	147,758	100.0	1,433,403	100.0
% of total foreign...	38.6		41.5		9.6		10.3		100.0	

1933										
American companies....	299,360	52.9	16,410	2.8	86	0.1	24,271	15.2	340,127	23.2
British-Dutch companies.	243,235	43.0	51,486	8.7	150,565	99.9	122,162	76.5	567,448	38.6
Other companies........	23,035	4.1	105,752	17.8	......	......	8,412	5.3	137,199	9.3
Subtotal...............	565,630	100.0	173,648	29.3	150,651	100.0	154,845	97.0	1,044,774	71.1
Russian government.....	......	......	419,408	70.7	......	......	4,808	3.0	424,216	28.9
Total foreign..........	565,630	100.0	593,056	100.0	150,651	100.0	159,653	100.0	1,468,990	100.0
% of total foreign.....	38.5		40.4		10.2		10.9		-100.0	
1934										
American companies....	360,444	56.0	22,106	3.3	5,422	3.0	29,107	16.9	417,079	25.1
British-Dutch companies.	267,688	41.5	65,189	9.8	169,892	94.4	130,145	75.5	632,914	38.0
Other companies........	16,628	2.5	108,351	16.3	4,636	2.6	8,079	4.7	137,694	8.3
Subtotal...............	644,760	100.0	195,646	29.4	179,950	100.0	167,331	97.1	1,187,687	71.4
Russian government.....	......	......	470,425	70.6	......	......	5,069	2.9	475,494	28.6
Total foreign..........	644,760	100.0	666,071	100.0	179,950	100.0	172,400	100.0	1,663,181	100.0
% of total foreign.....	38.8		40.0		10.8		10.4		100.0	
1935										
American companies....	384,227	55.6	19,792	2.9	20,695	8.8	37,263	21.4	461,977	25.8
British-Dutch companies.	284,564	41.2	59,349	8.6	198,421	83.9	123,178	70.6	665,512	37.1
Other companies........	21,824	3.2	116,062	16.7	17,231	7.3	8,670	5.0	163,787	9.1
Subtotal...............	690,615	100.0	195,203	28.2	236,347	100.0	169,111	97.0	1,291,276	72.0
Russian government.....	......	......	497,554	71.8	......	......	5,178	3.0	502,732	28.0
Total foreign..........	690,615	100.0	692,757	100.0	236,347	100.0	174,289	100.0	1,794,008	100.0
% of total foreign.....	38.5		38.6		13.2		9.7		100.0	

TABLE 16.—CRUDE-OIL PRODUCTION IN FOREIGN COUNTRIES, BY MAJOR NATIONALITIES—*Continued*

(In barrels daily)

	Western Hemisphere	% of area	Europe and Africa	% of area	Near and Middle East	% of area	Far East	% of area	Total foreign	% of area
1936										
American companies.......	391,492	54.2	19,240	2.6	31,461	11.8	42,080	23.0	484,273	25.4
British-Dutch companies..	304,832	42.2	60,577	8.2	216,395	81.1	125,749	68.6	707,553	37.1
Other companies..........	26,270	3.6	123,411	16.8	18,828	7.1	9,929	5.4	178,438	9.3
Subtotal..............	722,594	100.0	203,228	27.6	266,684	100.0	177,758	97.0	1,370,264	71.8
Russian government.......	.....	.....	532,607	72.4	.....	.....	5,582	3.0	538,189	28.2
Total foreign........	722,594	100.0	735,835	100.0	266,684	100.0	183,340	100.0	1,908,453	100.0
% of total foreign......	37.9		38.5		14.0		9.6		100.0	
1937										
American companies.......	458,620	54.4	18,938	2.6	41,163	12.8	44,148	21.5	562,869	26.8
British-Dutch companies..	353,477	42.0	52,119	7.2	260,688	81.0	144,523	70.6	810,807	38.7
Other companies	30,422	3.6	100,685	13.8	19,964	6.2	10,063	4.9	161,134	7.7
Subtotal..............	842,519	100.0	171,742	23.6	321,815	100.0	198,734	97.0	1,534,810	73.2
Russian government.......	.....	.....	555,951	76.4	.....	.....	6,071	3.0	562,022	26.8
Total foreign........	842,519	100.0	727,693	100.0	321,815	100.0	204,805	100.0	2,096,832	100.0
% of total foreign......	40.2		34.7		15.3		9.8		100.0	
1938										
American companies.......	402,520	47.5	20,142	2.7	43,800	13.4	40,516	19.4	506,978	23.8
British-Dutch companies..	343,912	40.6	51,203	6.9	262,329	80.3	152,607	72.9	810,051	38.1
Other companies..........	100,881	11.9	94,437	12.7	20,588	6.3	9,750	4.7	225,656	10.6
Subtotal..............	847,313	100.0	165,782	22.3	326,717	100.0	202,873	97.0	1,542,685	72.5
Russian government.......	.....	.....	579,597	77.7	.....	.....	6,372	3.0	585,969	27.5
Total foreign........	847,313	100.0	745,379	100.0	326,717	100.0	209,245	100.0	2,128,654	100.0
% of total foreign......	39.8		35.0		15.4		9.8		100.0	

1939

American companies	441,616	48.3	20,272	2.6	49,813	15.7	43,198	19.2	554,899	24.9
British-Dutch companies	328,781	36.0	54,447	7.1	247,480	78.3	164,685	73.2	795,393	35.7
Other companies	143,731	15.7	96,784	12.5	18,966	6.0	9,149	4.1	268,630	12.0
Subtotal	914,128	100.0	171,503	22.2	316,259	100.0	217,032	96.5	1,618,922	72.6
Russian government	.....	.....	601,734	77.8	.....	.....	7,922	3.5	609,656	27.4
Total foreign	914,128	100.0	773,237	100.0	316,259	100.0	224,954	100.0	2,228,578	100.0
% of total foreign	41.0		34.7		14.2		10.1		100.0	

1940

American companies	421,557	48.2	21,121	2.6	43,353	16.4	41,848	18.5	527,879	24.3
British-Dutch companies	301,642	34.4	30,199	3.8	211,840	80.4	166,874	73.7	710,555	32.7
Other companies	152,189	17.4	124,256	15.4	8,331	3.2	8,926	4.0	293,702	13.6
Subtotal	875,388	100.0	175,576	21.8	263,514	100.0	217,658	96.2	1,532,136	70.6
Russian government	.....	.....	630,000	78.2	.....	.....	8,675	3.8	638,675	29.4
Total foreign	875,388	100.0	805,576	100.0	263,514	100.0	226,333	100.0	2,170,811	100.0
% of total foreign	40.3		37.1		12.2		10.4		100.0	

1941

American companies	512,553	51.5	23,319	2.8	33,722	16.8	40,724	20.1	610,298	27.3
British-Dutch companies	326,980	32.9	23,968	2.9	167,071	83.2	143,885	70.9	661,904	29.6
Other companies	154,829	15.6	138,938	16.6	.....	.....	8,834	4.3	302,601	13.6
Subtotal	994,342	100.0	186,225	22.3	200,793	100.0	193,443	95.3	1,574,803	70.5
Russian government	.....	.....	650,000	77.7	.....	.....	9,465	4.7	659,465	29.5
Total foreign	994,342	100.0	836,225	100.0	200,793	100.0	202,908	100.0	2,234,268	100.0
% of total foreign	44.5		37.4		9.0		9.1		100.0	

TABLE 16.—CRUDE-OIL PRODUCTION IN FOREIGN COUNTRIES, BY MAJOR NATIONALITIES—Continued

(In barrels daily)

	Western Hemisphere	% of area	Europe and Africa	% of area	Near and Middle East	% of area	Far East	% of area	Total foreign	% of area
1942										
American companies	319,908	43.7	5	....	35,124	12.5	2,928	3.7	357,965	18.7
British-Dutch companies	275,083	37.6	23,892	2.9	245,394	87.5	15,942	20.3	560,311	29.3
Other companies	136,542	18.7	174,547	21.2	....	....	51,003	65.0	362,092	18.9
Subtotal	731,533	100.0	198,444	24.1	280,518	100.0	69,873	89.0	1,280,368	66.9
Russian government	....	....	625,000	75.9	....	....	8,600	11.0	633,600	33.1
Total foreign	731,533	100.0	823,444	100.0	280,518	100.0	78,473	100.0	1,913,968	100.0
% of total foreign	38.2		43.0		14.7		4.1		100.0	
1943										
American companies	399,381	48.4	4	....	39,022	12.3	....	....	438,407	19.9
British-Dutch companies	284,281	34.4	26,890	3.1	278,408	87.7	7,000	3.7	596,579	27.0
Other companies	142,155	17.2	173,825	19.8	....	....	172,700	91.7	488,680	22.1
Subtotal	825,817	100.0	200,719	22.9	317,430	100.0	179,700	95.4	1,523,666	69.0
Russian government	....	....	675,000	77.1	....	....	8,600	4.6	683,600	31.0
Total foreign	825,817	100.0	875,719	100.0	317,430	100.0	188,300	100.0	2,207,266	100.0
% of total foreign	37.4		39.7		14.4		8.5		100.0	
1944										
American companies	601,489	56.3	4	....	51,760	12.8	....	....	653,253	26.6
British-Dutch companies	316,648	29.6	27,758	3.2	353,407	87.2	9,500	8.7	707,313	28.8
Other companies	150,115	14.1	143,060	16.4	....	....	90,250	82.4	383,425	15.6
Subtotal	1,068,252	100.0	170,822	19.6	405,167	100.0	99,750	91.1	1,743,991	71.0
Russian government	....	....	700,000	80.4	....	....	9,750	8.9	709,750	29.0
Total foreign	1,068,252	100.0	870,822	100.0	405,167	100.0	109,500	100.0	2,453,741	100.0
% of total foreign	43.5		35.5		16.5		4.5		100.0	

TABLE 17.—WORLD REGISTRATIONS OF MOTOR VEHICLES[1]—YEARS 1919, 1920, 1923, AND 1929–1940 (INCLUSIVE)

(In thousands)

Year	Western Hemisphere (excluding U. S. A.)									Europe and Africa (excluding Russia)								
	Private cars			Commercial cars			Total			Private cars			Commercial cars			Total		
	Number	Index	% total	Number	Index	% total	Number	Index	% world	Number	Index	% total	Number	Index	% total	Number	Index	% world
1910	3	....	....	3	....	....	3	....		3	....	....	3	....	....	3	....	
1919	3	....	....	3	....	....	450	21.1	5.0	3	....	....	3	....	....	710	13.9	7.9
1920	3	....	....	3	....	....	541	25.3	4.8	3	....	....	3	....	....	930	18.3	8.3
1923	3	....	....	3	....	....	868	40.6	4.7	3	....	....	3	....	....	1,728	33.9	9.4
1929	1,567	100.0	73.4	569	100.0	26.6	2,136	100.0	5.9	3,341	100.0	65.6	1,751	100.0	34.4	5,092	100.0	14.0
1930	1,611	102.8	71.0	657	115.4	29.0	2,268	106.2	6.1	3,685	110.3	64.8	1,998	114.1	35.2	5,683	111.6	15.3
1931	1,523	97.2	70.7	633	111.1	29.3	2,156	100.9	5.9	3,944	118.1	65.6	2,066	118.0	34.4	6,010	118.0	16.3
1932	1,426	91.0	72.9	529	92.9	27.1	1,955	91.5	5.6	4,054	121.3	65.7	2,117	120.9	34.3	6,171	121.2	17.6
1933	1,349	86.1	70.2	572	100.4	29.8	1,921	89.9	5.4	4,284	128.2	65.9	2,214	126.4	34.1	6,498	127.6	18.4
1934	1,339	85.4	68.9	605	106.3	31.1	1,944	91.0	5.2	4,668	139.7	66.6	2,342	133.8	33.4	7,010	137.7	18.9
1935	1,441	91.9	69.8	623	109.4	30.2	2,064	96.6	5.2	5,200	155.7	68.3	2,416	138.0	31.7	7,616	149.6	19.3
1936	1,518	96.9	68.1	710	124.8	31.9	2,228	104.3	5.2	5,708	170.9	68.9	2,573	146.9	31.1	8,281	162.6	19.4
1937	1,616	103.1	68.3	748	131.4	31.7	2,364	110.6	5.2	6,181	185.0	69.7	2,684	153.3	30.3	8,865	174.1	19.4
1938	1,701	108.5	70.5	711	124.9	29.5	2,412	112.9	5.2	6,641	198.8	70.2	2,818	160.9	29.8	9,459	185.8	20.4
1939	1,756	112.0	69.0	791	138.9	31.0	2,547	119.3	5.3	6,803	203.6	70.8	2,807	160.3	29.2	9,610	188.7	20.0
1940	1,836	117.2	69.6	801	140.7	30.4	2,637	123.4	5.5	5,400	161.7	69.1	2,417	138.0	30.9	7,817	153.5	16.2

For footnotes 1 and 3 see page 219.

TABLE 17.—WORLD REGISTRATIONS OF MOTOR VEHICLES ¹—YEARS 1919, 1920, 1923, AND 1929–1940 (INCLUSIVE)—Continued

(In thousands)

Year	Near, Middle, and Far East ²									Total foreign (excluding U.S.S.R.)								
	Private cars			Commercial cars			Total			Private cars			Commercial cars			Total		
	Number	Index	% total	Number	Index	% total	Number	Index	% world	Number	Index	% total	Number	Index	% total	Number	Index	% world
1910	3	....	....	3	....	....	3	...	...	3	....	....	3	....	....	3	...	...
1919	3	....	....	3	....	....	112	8.8	1.2	3	....	....	3	....	....	1,272	15.0	14.1
1920	3	....	....	3	....	....	201	15.8	1.8	3	....	....	3	....	....	1,672	19.7	14.9
1923	3	....	....	3	....	....	319	25.1	1.7	3	....	....	3	....	....	2,915	34.3	15.8
1929	818	100.0	64.3	454	100.0	35.7	1,272	100.0	3.5	5,726	100.0	67.4	2,774	100.0	32.6	8,500	100.0	23.4
1930	847	103.5	62.2	515	113.6	37.8	1,362	107.1	3.7	6,143	107.3	66.0	3,170	114.3	34.0	9,313	109.6	25.1
1931	809	98.9	61.4	508	111.9	38.6	1,317	103.5	3.6	6,276	109.6	66.2	3,207	115.6	33.8	9,483	111.6	25.8
1932	768	93.8	60.6	499	109.9	39.4	1,267	99.5	3.6	6,248	109.1	66.5	3,145	113.4	33.5	9,393	110.5	26.8
1933	761	93.0	60.1	505	111.4	39.9	1,266	99.6	3.6	6,394	111.7	66.0	3,291	118.6	34.0	9,685	113.9	27.4
1934	786	96.0	60.0	525	115.6	40.0	1,311	103.0	3.5	6,793	118.6	66.2	3,472	125.2	33.8	10,265	120.8	27.6
1935	819	100.1	58.3	585	129.0	41.7	1,404	110.4	3.6	7,460	130.3	67.3	3,624	130.6	32.7	11,084	130.4	28.1
1936	902	110.2	59.0	626	138.0	41.0	1,528	120.2	3.6	8,128	141.9	67.5	3,909	140.9	32.5	12,037	141.6	28.2
1937	940	114.9	56.1	735	161.9	43.9	1,675	131.6	3.7	8,737	152.6	67.7	4,167	150.2	32.3	12,904	151.8	28.3
1938	1,009	123.3	57.8	737	162.4	42.2	1,746	137.2	3.8	9,351	163.3	68.7	4,266	153.8	31.3	13,617	160.1	29.4
1939	1,104	134.9	58.3	789	173.9	41.7	1,893	148.7	3.9	9,663	168.7	68.8	4,387	158.1	31.2	14,050	165.3	29.2
1940	1,095	133.8	58.8	768	169.4	41.2	1,863	146.5	3.9	8,331	145.5	67.6	3,986	143.7	32.4	12,317	144.9	25.6

For footnotes ¹ and ² see page 219.

TABLE 17.—WORLD REGISTRATIONS OF MOTOR VEHICLES [1]—YEARS 1919, 1920, 1923, AND 1929–1940 (INCLUSIVE)—Continued

(In thousands)

Year	Russia (U.S.S.R.)									Total foreign (including U.S.S.R.)								
	Private cars (estimated)			Commercial cars			Total			Private cars			Commercial cars			Total		
	Number	Index	% total	Number	Index	% total	Number	Index	% world	Number	Index	% total	Number	Index	% total	Number	Index	% world
1910	[3]	....	....	[3]	....	....	3	....	....	[3]	....	....	[3]	....	....	[3]	....	....
1919	[3]	....	....	[3]	....	....	15	23.4	0.2	[3]	....	....	[3]	....	....	1,287	15.0	14.3
1920	[3]	....	....	[3]	....	....	15	23.4	0.1	[3]	....	....	[3]	....	....	1,687	19.7	15.1
1923	[3]	....	....	[3]	....	....	16	24.2	0.1	[3]	....	....	[3]	....	....	2,931	34.2	15.9
1929	3	100.0	3.9	61	100.0	96.1	64	100.0	0.2	5,729	100.0	66.9	2,835	100.0	33.1	8,564	100.0	23.6
1930	3	104.4	2.0	127	206.6	98.0	130	202.6	0.3	6,146	107.3	65.1	3,297	116.3	34.9	9,443	110.3	25.4
1931	3	108.0	1.7	158	257.6	98.3	161	251.8	0.4	6,279	109.6	65.1	3,365	116.7	34.9	9,644	112.6	26.2
1932	3	112.0	1.4	202	328.9	98.6	205	320.1	0.6	6,251	109.1	65.1	3,347	118.0	34.9	9,598	112.1	27.4
1933	3	120.0	1.0	302	490.8	99.0	305	476.6	0.9	6,397	111.5	64.0	3,593	126.7	36.0	9,990	116.6	28.3
1934	3	128.0	0.7	453	736.3	99.3	456	712.5	1.2	6,796	118.6	63.4	3,925	138.4	36.6	10,721	125.2	28.8
1935	4	140.0	0.6	602	979.0	99.4	606	946.3	1.5	7,464	130.3	63.9	4,226	149.0	36.1	11,690	136.5	29.6
1936	4	160.0	0.5	774	1,258.5	99.5	778	1,215.6	1.7	8,132	141.9	63.5	4,683	165.2	36.5	12,815	149.6	29.9
1937	5	200.0	0.5	963	1,566.6	99.5	968	1,513.7	2.1	8,742	152.6	63.0	5,130	180.9	37.0	13,872	162.0	30.4
1938	6	240.0	0.5	1,150	1,869.8	99.5	1,156	1,806.2	2.5	9,357	163.3	63.3	5,416	191.0	36.7	14,773	172.5	31.9
1939	6	240.0	0.5	1,295	2,105.7	99.5	1,301	2,032.8	2.7	9,669	168.7	63.0	5,682	200.4	37.0	15,351	179.2	31.9
1940	6	240.0	0.4	1,554	2,526.8	99.6	1,560	2,437.5	3.2	8,337	145.5	60.1	5,540	195.4	39.9	13,877	162.0	28.8

For footnotes [1] and [3] see page 219.

TABLE 17.—WORLD REGISTRATIONS OF MOTOR VEHICLES[1]—YEARS 1919, 1920, 1923, AND 1929–1940 (INCLUSIVE)—*Continued*

(In thousands)

| Year | United States | | | | | | | | | Total world | | | | | | | |
| | Private cars | | | Commercial cars | | | Total | | | Private cars | | | Commercial cars | | | Total | |
	Number	Index	% total	Number	Index	% total	Number	Index	% world	Number	Index	% total	Number	Index	% total	Number	Index
1910	459	2.0	95.8	20	0.4	4.2	479	1.7	....	[3]	....	....	[3]	....	....	[3]	....
1919	6,751	29.0	87.4	974	21.8	12.6	7,725	27.8	85.7	[3]	....	....	[3]	....	....	9,012	24.8
1920	8,201	35.2	86.5	1,277	28.6	13.5	9,478	34.1	84.8	[3]	....	....	[3]	....	....	11,165	30.7
1923	13,439	57.7	86.7	2,053	46.0	13.3	15,492	55.8	84.1	[3]	....	....	[3]	....	....	18,423	50.7
1929	23,299	100.0	83.9	4,463	100.0	16.1	27,762	100.0	76.4	29,028	100.0	79.6	7,298	100.0	20.4	36,326	100.0
1930	23,164	99.4	83.3	4,653	104.2	16.7	27,817	100.2	74.6	29,310	101.0	78.7	7,950	108.9	21.3	37,260	102.6
1931	22,448	96.3	82.7	4,695	105.2	17.3	27,143	97.8	73.8	28,727	99.0	78.1	8,060	110.4	21.9	36,787	101.3
1932	20,976	90.0	82.4	4,489	106.0	17.6	25,465	91.7	72.6	27,227	93.8	77.7	7,836	107.4	22.3	35,063	96.5
1933	20,757	89.1	82.2	4,501	100.8	17.8	25,258	91.0	71.7	27,154	93.5	77.0	8,094	110.9	23.0	35,248	97.0
1934	21,691	93.1	82.1	4,717	105.7	17.9	26,408	95.1	71.2	28,487	98.1	76.7	8,642	118.4	23.3	37,129	102.2
1935	22,722	97.5	81.8	5,057	113.3	18.2	27,779	100.1	70.4	30,186	104.0	76.5	9,283	127.3	23.5	39,469	108.6
1936	24,458	105.0	81.6	5,518	123.6	18.4	29,976	108.0	70.1	32,590	112.3	76.3	10,201	139.8	23.7	42,791	117.8
1937	25,746	110.5	81.2	5,972	133.8	18.8	31,718	114.2	69.6	34,488	118.8	75.6	11,102	152.1	24.4	45,590	125.5
1938	25,331	108.7	80.2	6,237	139.8	19.8	31,568	113.7	68.1	34,688	119.5	74.9	11,653	159.7	25.1	46,341	127.6
1939	26,262	112.7	80.1	6,543	146.6	19.9	32,805	118.2	68.1	35,931	123.8	74.6	12,225	167.5	25.4	48,156	132.6
1940	27,519	118.1	80.1	6,849	153.5	19.9	34,368	123.8	71.2	35,856	123.5	74.3	12,389	169.7	25.7	48,245	132.8

[1] Private cars—private passenger cars only. Commercial cars—government passenger cars, taxis, trucks, busses, tractors (motorcycles not included). Tractor figures are incomplete for foreign areas. For the United States an estimate for tractors has been added. 1919, 1920, and 1923 foreign exclude tractors. Taxi and government passenger cars are not completely segregated from "Private" in some of the above data. Source: U. S. Foreign and Domestic Commerce Bureau, *American Automobile*, overseas edition.

[2] *Near East*   *Middle East*   *Far East*
Palestine   Aden   China, Indo-China, Thailand (Siam), Malaya, Philippines
Syria   Saudi Arabia   Japan
Turkey   Iran   India, Burma, Ceylon
Iraq   Bahrein   Oceania (Australia, New Zealand, and islands)

[3] Not available.

TABLE 18.—WORLD RETAIL PRICES AND TAXES (EXCLUDING RUSSIA)—GASO

(In cents per

Country and city	Gasoline					Kerosene				
	Retail price	Includes				Retail price	Includes			
		Duty	Taxes	Total	% of retail price		Duty	Taxes	Total	% of retail price
Western Hemisphere										
Canada, Saskatoon.................	26.0	....	5.8	5.8	22.3	19.4	....	....	....	....
British Honduras, Belize............	28.0	8.3	....	8.3	29.6	26.0	3.3	....	3.3	12.7
Costa Rica, San José...............	t 44.4	12.7	1.8	14.5	32.7	34.0	10.9	....	10.9	32.1
Honduras, San Pedro Sula...........	40.0	1.6	11.5	13.1	32.8	t 45.0	9.3	14.5	23.8	52.9
Panama, Panama City..............	25.0	10.0	0.7	10.7	42.8	14.0	1.5	0.4	1.9	13.6
Nicaragua, Managua...............	39.0	6.0	4.0	10.0	25.6	t 29.0	8.6	0.5	9.1	31.4
Salvador, El Salvador..............	46.0	20.0	4.0	24.0	52.2	40.0	14.0	0.4	14.4	36.0
Mexico, Durango..................	15.2	....	6.2	6.2	40.8	10.1	....	....	....	....
Newfoundland, Saint John's.........	29.0	9.0	....	9.0	31.0	21.0	7.5	....	7.5	35.7
Bermuda, Hamilton................	20.8	7.2	....	7.2	34.6	36.0	1.5	....	1.5	4.2
British West Indies, Barbados.......	32.0	2.2	14.5	16.7	52.2	35.0	8.8	....	8.8	25.1
Cuba, Havana.....................	30.0	16.6	d	16.6	55.3	26.0	14.3	d	14.3	55.0
Dutch West Indies, Curaçao.........	22.1	....	6.6	6.6	29.9	17.1	....	o	....	....
French West Indies, Martinique.....	25.8	11.6	1.5	13.1	50.8	17.5	4.5	o	4.5	25.7
Haiti, Port-au-Prince..............	32.0	15.6	....	15.6	48.8	27.5	10.6	....	10.6	38.5
Argentina, Buenos Aires...........	20.5	....	4.5	4.5	22.0	15.1	....	....	....	....
Bolivia, La Paz...................	t 27.3	....	....	....	....	24.3	....	....	....	....
Brazil, Bahia.....................	28.5	6.2	1.3	7.5	26.3	18.1	4.2	....	4.2	23.2
Chile, Santiago...................	32.6	13.2	1.3	14.5	44.5	21.1	10.7	0.8	11.5	54.5
Colombia, Cali....................	21.3	....	5.7	5.7	26.8	17.7	....	....	....	....
Ecuador, Quito...................	14.0	....	3.8	3.8	27.1	t 19.0	....	3.8	3.8	20.0
Peru, Lima.......................	13.2	....	5.4	5.4	40.9	7.5	....	..i.	....	....
Uruguay, Montevideo..............	21.6	10.6	....	10.6	49.1	14.4	5.3	....	5.3	36.8
Venezuela, Maracaibo..............	12.0	....	....	....	....	8.0	....	....	....	....
Trinidad, Port-of-Spain............	29.0	....	15.0	15.0	51.7	20.0	....	6.0	6.0	30.0
Europe										
Norway, Oslo.....................	29.3	....	10.6	10.6	36.2	16.7	....	0.2	0.2	1.2
Sweden, Lulea....................	29.7	o	9.5	9.5	32.0	t 21.1	....	....	....	....
Denmark, Copenhagen.............	26.3	....	11.0	11.0	41.8	13.9	....	....	....	....
Belgium, Antwerp.................	42.0	20.0	3.5	23.5	56.0	35.0	14.0	0.9	14.9	42.6
United Kingdom, London...........	30.9	14.6	o	14.6	47.2	22.0	1.6	o	1.6	7.3
France, Lyon.....................	31.4	15.8	d	15.8	50.3	29.3	16.2	d	16.2	55.3
Portugal, Lisbon..................	36.1	20.1	1.0	21.1	58.4	19.4	5.1	0.5	5.6	28.9
Germany, Berlin..................	64.0	31.0	5.0	36.0	56.3	47.4	26.0	4.0	30.0	63.3
Poland, Warsaw...................	39.0	....	11.0	11.0	28.2	36.0	....	5.0	5.0	13.9
Czechoslovakia, Brno..............	42.9	4.7	15.7	20.4	47.6	25.3	5.6	6.0	11.6	45.8
Austria, Innsbruck................	49.6	5.2	18.1	23.3	47.0	22.7	5.0	o	5.0	22.0
Hungary, Budapest................	35.0	8.0	18.0	26.0	74.3	19.0	4.0	8.0	12.0	63.2
Italy, Rome......................	108.0	d	79.0	79.0	73.1	94.0	d	68.0	68.0	72.3
Jugoslavia, Belgrade..............	39.2	5.6	14.0	19.6	50.0	39.9	3.1	21.5	24.6	61.7
Rumania, Bucharest...............	23.8	....	18.4	18.4	77.3	9.4	....	2.8	2.8	29.8
Switzerland, Zurich...............	46.8	20.2	o	20.2	43.2	25.5	2.5	o	2.5	9.8

t, sold in tins.
d, included with duties/taxes.
o, original source gives no data.
s, surcharge tax payable.
Source of data: Quarterly issue on this subject by Bureau of Mines.

LINE, KEROSENE, AND MOTOR LUBRICATING OILS—IN EFFECT DURING 1939

U. S. gallon)

	Motor lubricating oils—Grades 1, 2, and 3														
	Grade 1					Grade 2					Grade 3				
		Includes					Includes					Includes			
Retail price	Duty	Taxes	Total	% of retail price	Retail price	Duty	Taxes	Total	% of retail price	Retail price	Duty	Taxes	Total	% of retail price
133.3	....	....	....	....	100.0	....	....	....	....	66.6				
90.0	5.0	....	5.0	5.6	o	....	....	....	....	o				
140.0	10.2	....	10.2	7.3	135.0	8.2	....	8.2	6.1	135.0	6.2	....	6.2	4.6
180.0	16.0	13.0	29.0	16.1	120.0	16.0	13.0	29.0	24.2	100.0	16.0	13.0	29.0	29.0
128.0	16.0	3.7	19.7	15.4	90.0	16.0	2.6	18.6	20.7	o				
109.0	29.3	16.7	46.0	42.2	82.0	29.3	16.7	46.0	56.1	o				
210.0	75.0	2.1	77.1	36.7	197.5	75.0	2.0	77.0	39.0	145.0	75.0	1.4	76.4	52.7
117.2	7.0	....	7.0	6.0	73.8	....	....	....	....	48.6				
o					o					o				
81.3	8.1	....	8.1	10.0	o					o				
128.0	13.2	....	13.2	10.3	112.0	13.2	....	13.2	11.8	88.0	13.2	....	13.2	15.0
120.0	26.7	d	26.7	22.3	80.0	19.7	d	19.7	24.6	40.0	17.1	d	17.1	42.8
110.3	0.6	o	0.6	0.5	110.3	0.6	o	0.6	0.5	63.1	1.8	o	1.8	2.9
80.4	2.0	o	2.0	0.2	49.5	2.0	o	2.0	4.0	o				
135.0	26.3	....	26.3	19.5	120.0	23.8	....	23.8	19.8	80.0	17.1	....	17.1	21.4
120.2	28.8	1.5	30.3	25.2	102.4	28.8	1.3	30.1	29.4	98.0	28.8	1.2	30.0	30.6
o					o					o				
81.5	3.7	0.5	4.2	5.2	o					o				
116.5	13.9	4.0	17.9	15.4	57.7	13.9	4.0	17.9	31.0	o				
120.5	11.5	11.4	22.9	19.0	109.8	11.5	11.4	22.9	20.9	102.9	....	11.4	11.4	11.1
133.5	10.5	8	10.5	7.9	87.0	10.5	8	10.5	12.1	59.5	10.5	8	10.5	17.6
104.0	11.8	5.9	17.7	17.0	77.3	10.6	4.4	15.0	19.4	53.8	9.8	3.0	12.8	23.8
144.2	23.3	....	23.3	16.2	93.7	23.3	....	23.3	24.9	57.7	23.3	....	23.3	40.4
o					148.0	38.8	....	38.8	26.2	o				
147.0	38.0	....	38.0	25.9	140.0	38.0	....	38.0	27.1	84.0	38.0	....	38.0	45.2
139.0	3.0	1.4	4.4	3.2	95.0	3.0	1.0	4.0	4.2	o				
182.0	....	....	....	....	130.0	....	....	....	....	85.0				
128.0	3.8	o	3.8	3.0	124.0	3.8	o	3.8	3.1	124.0	3.8	o	3.8	3.1
152.0	2.0	3.7	5.7	3.8	88.0	2.0	2.1	4.1	4.7	o				
136.5	1.6	o	1.6	1.2	97.6	1.6	o	1.6	1.6	58.5	1.6	o	1.6	2.7
122.5	19.8	d	19.8	16.2	75.0	19.8	d	19.8	26.4	o				
122.5	8.7	1.3	10.0	8.2	77.3	8.8	1.3	10.1	13.1	47.6	8.9	1.3	10.2	21.4
310.0	16.0	1.0	17.0	5.5	199.0	16.0	1.0	17.0	8.5	o				
290.0	....	5.0	5.0	1.7	142.0	....	....	....	....	107.0	....	5.0	5.0	4.7
t 223.0	7.6	16.7	24.3	10.9	t 125.4	7.6	16.7	24.3	19.4	t 99.5	7.6	16.7	24.3	24.4
237.5	20.8	o	20.8	8.8	93.6	18.9	o	18.9	20.2	o				
181.0	12.0	27.0	39.0	21.5	101.0	5.0	27.0	32.0	31.7	63.0	....	25.0	25.0	39.7
233.0	d	72.0	72.0	30.9	....					169.0	d	72.0	72.0	42.6
119.0	6.8	13.6	20.4	17.1	66.3	6.8	13.6	20.4	30.8	o				
334.1	106.5	53.2	159.7	47.8	134.4	....	53.2	53.2	39.6	112.1	....	51.7	51.7	46.1
127.4	1.4	o	1.4	1.1	70.0	1.4	o	1.4	2.0	50.0	1.4	o	1.4	2.8

TABLE 18.—WORLD RETAIL PRICES AND TAXES (EXCLUDING RUSSIA)—GASOLINE,

(In cents per

Country and city	Gasoline					Kerosene				
	Retail price	Includes				Retail price	Includes			
		Duty	Taxes	Total	% of retail price		Duty	Taxes	Total	% of retail price
Europe—Continued										
Bulgaria, Sofia..................	45.0	28.0	10.0	38.0	84.4	25.0	12.0	*o*	12.0	48.0
Greece, Athens..................	31.9	18.6	1.2	19.8	62.1	32.6	23.0	*o*	23.0	70.6
Azores, St. Michael.............	40.0	16.2	11.7	27.9	69.8	23.0	4.5	2.4	6.9	30.0
Madeira, Funchal................	39.4	21.5	0.9	22.4	56.9	24.7	6.5	0.5	7.0	28.3
Eire, Dublin....................	32.0	11.0	*o*	11.0	34.4	*o*	....	....	....	....
Estonia, Tallinn................	*t* 53.0	7.0	30.0	37.0	69.8	13.0	2.0	*o*	2.0	15.4
Latvia, Riga....................	43.0	10.0	11.7	21.7	50.5	14.0	1.1	1.9	3.0	21.4
Lithuania, Kaunas...............	64.2	15.5	....	15.5	24.1	39.8	5.1	16.0	21.1	53.0
Africa										
Algeria, Algiers................	28.0	6.0	6.0	12.0	42.9	21.0	8.0	2.0	10.0	47.6
Tunisia, Tunis..................	22.4	1.2	8.9	10.1	45.1	13.7	1.2	1.9	3.1	22.6
Canary Islands, Las Palmas........	27.0	4.4	5.5	9.9	36.7	23.0	4.4	0.1	4.5	19.6
Egypt, Cairo....................	28.8	4.4	13.1	17.5	60.8	8.9	1.1	0.7	1.8	20.2
Liberia, Monrovia...............	*t* 46.0	5.0	5.0	10.0	21.7	*t* 36.0	4.0	4.0	8.0	22.2
Morocco, Casablanca.............	19.0	8.0	*d*	8.0	42.1	18.0	6.0	*d*	6.0	33.3
Nigeria, Lagos..................	*t* 46.4	16.2	*o*	16.2	34.9	*t* 39.0	9.7	*o*	9.7	24.9
Kenya, Nairobi..................	29.6	4.9	4.4	9.3	31.4	25.9	3.3	*o*	3.3	12.7
Mozambique, Lourenço............	38.6	4.8	23.5	28.3	73.3	15.8	4.0	....	4.0	25.3
Angola, Loanda..................	46.0	14.9	*o*	14.9	32.4	40.6	14.2	*o*	14.2	35.0
Union of South Africa, Cape Town...	20.6	6.8	....	6.8	33.0	9.7	Free	....	....	....
Other British South Africa, Durban..	19.5	6.6	....	6.6	33.8	10.0	Free	....	....	....
Near and Middle East										
Palestine, Jerusalem............	33.2	18.3	*o*	18.3	55.1	14.7	3.1	....	3.1	21.1
Syria, Beirut...................	21.6	2.2	7.7	9.9	45.8	15.1	2.8	1.8	4.6	30.5
Iran, Teheran...................	11.2	....	4.3	4.3	38.4	9.7	....	4.3	4.3	44.3
Iraq, Bagdad....................	23.9	12.7	*o*	12.7	53.1	9.8	0.8	*o*	0.8	8.2
Turkey, Ankara..................	52.8	13.1	12.0	25.1	47.5	*t* 49.0	14.6	5.0	19.6	40.0
Far East										
India, Delhi....................	40.8	13.6	*d*	13.6	33.3	22.6	6.8	*o*	6.8	30.1
Malaya, Singapore...............	29.3	13.7	....	13.7	46.8	*t* 21.5	2.0	....	2.0	9.3
Burma, Rangoon.................	36.0	19.5	*d*	19.5	54.2	*t* 27.5	4.5	*o*	4.5	16.4
Ceylon, Colombo................	32.0	18.0	*o*	18.0	56.3	*t* 26.5	5.0	*o*	5.0	18.9
China, Shanghai.................	21.4	5.2	1.9	7.1	33.2	18.6	4.4	1.7	6.1	32.8
Dutch East Indies, Batavia........	44.5	....	26.0	26.0	58.4	*t* 24.5	1.0	7.0	8.0	32.7
Indo-China, Saigon..............	28.0	5.9	1.2	7.1	25.4	20.7	6.0	1.2	7.2	34.8
Hong Kong, China...............	22.7	6.2	*o*	6.2	27.3	*o*	....	....	....	....
Japan, Yokohama................	18.0	4.5	1.3	5.8	32.2	17.0	2.9	....	2.9	17.1
Philippines, Manila.............	30.3	0.7	9.5	10.2	33.7	*t* 27.0	0.8	2.8	3.6	13.3
Thailand, Bangkok..............	34.1	14.6	*o*	14.6	42.8	21.0	7.0	*o*	7.0	33.3
Australia, Adelaide.............	28.4	9.6	2.6	12.2	43.0	20.0	....	1.8	1.8	9.0
French Oceania, Tahiti..........	26.8	*o*	6.0	6.0	22.4	*t* 5.8	0.6	1.1	1.7	6.6
New Zealand, Wellington.........	30.0	9.0	7.0	16.0	53.3	15.0	0.4	..	0.4	2.7

t, sold in tins.
d, included with duties/taxes.
o, original source gives no data.
s, surcharge tax payable.
Source of data: Quarterly issue on this subject by Bureau of Mines.

KEROSENE, AND MOTOR LUBRICATING OILS—IN EFFECT DURING 1939—*Continued*
U. S. gallon)

Motor lubricating oils—Grades 1, 2, and 3

	Grade 1					Grade 2					Grade 3			
		Includes					Includes					Includes		
Retail price	Duty	Taxes	Total	% of retail price	Retail price	Duty	Taxes	Total	% of retail price	Retail price	Duty	Taxes	Total	% of retail price
114.0	35.0	o	35.0	30.7	110.0	35.0	o	35.0	31.8	102.0	35.0	o	35.0	34.3
95.4	20.4	o	20.4	21.4	63.6	20.4	o	20.4	32.1	43.4	20.4	o	20.4	47.0
137.7	0.6	0.3	0.9	0.7	100.3	0.6	0.2	0.8	0.8	58.5	0.6	0.2	0.8	1.4
101.8	10.3	o	10.3	10.1	74.6	10.3	o	10.3	13.8	54.2	10.3	o	10.3	19.0
o	....	....	....	....	o	....	....	....	....	o				
165.0	4.0	o	4.0	2.4	89.0	4.0	o	4.0	4.5	67.0	4.0	o	4.0	6.0
217.0	14.0	10.0	24.0	11.1	184.5	14.0	10.0	24.0	13.0	o				
225.0	5.6	....	5.6	2.5	161.0	5.6	....	5.6	3.5	129.0	5.6	....	5.6	4.3
125.0	19.0	o	19.0	15.2	110.0	19.0	o	19.0	26.0	73.0	19.0	o	19.0	26.0
113.6	30.6	2.0	32.6	28.7	86.6	30.6	1.1	31.7	36.6	o				
100.0	5.5	0.1	5.6	5.6	46.0	5.5	1.1	6.6	14.3	33.0	5.5	0.1	5.6	17.0
106.2	4.4	3.6	8.0	7.5	77.2	4.4	3.6	8.0	10.4	53.0	4.4	3.6	8.0	15.1
156.0	8.0	8.0	16.0	10.3	o	....	....	....	....	o				
104.0	10.0	d	10.0	9.6	56.0	7.0	d	7.0	12.5	36.0	6.0	d	6.0	16.7
107.2	4.9	o	4.9	4.6	68.2	4.9	o	4.9	7.2	43.9	4.9	o	4.9	11.1
88.9	6.6	o	6.6	7.4	44.4	6.6	o	6.6	14.9	o				
77.1	1.5	....	1.5	1.9	o	....	....	....	....	o				
126.6	15.7	o	15.7	12.4	80.4	9.5	o	9.5	11.8	o				
74.2	4.1	....	4.1	5.5	49.4	4.1	....	4.1	8.3	32.9	4.1	....	4.1	12.5
75.0	4.5	....	4.5	6.0	50.0	4.5	....	4.5	9.0	33.0	4.5	....	4.5	13.6
90.9	4.1	o	4.1	4.5	71.1	4.1	o	4.1	5.8	45.1	4.1	o	4.1	9.1
114.3	4.8	0.6	5.4	4.7	65.0	4.8	0.3	5.1	7.8	44.8	4.8	0.2	5.0	11.2
37.9	....	1.8	1.8	4.7	36.2	....	1.8	1.8	5.0	34.5	....	1.8	1.8	5.2
117.0	15.3	o	15.3	13.1	98.0	12.8	o	12.8	13.1	65.0	8.5	o	8.5	13.1
112.0	3.0	7.0	10.0	8.9	72.0	3.0	6.0	9.0	12.5	48.0	3.0	3.0	6.0	12.5
145.9	4.5	o	4.5	3.1	47.9	4.5	o	4.5	9.4	39.8	4.5	o	4.5	11.3
105.6	....	....	....	....	39.1	....	....	....	....	17.6				
124.0	4.2	o	4.2	3.4	50.7	4.2	o	4.2	8.3	34.2	4.2	o	4.2	12.3
80.0	14.0	o	14.0	17.5	53.0	14.0	o	14.0	26.4	36.0	14.0	o	14.0	38.9
97.6	0.1	8.9	9.0	9.2	69.4	0.1	6.3	6.4	9.2	29.6	0.1	2.7	2.8	9.5
125.5	10.4	o	10.4	8.3	101.0	8.3	o	8.3	8.2	55.5	4.6	o	4.6	8.3
88.7	7.9	o	7.9	8.9	44.3	7.9	o	7.9	17.8	35.5	7.9	o	7.9	22.3
o	....	....	....	....	o	....	....	....	....	o				
84.0	6.9	....	6.9	8.2	53.0	6.9	....	6.9	13.0	37.0	6.9	....	6.9	18.6
160.0	0.9	7.6	8.5	5.3	80.0	0.9	7.6	8.5	10.6	50.0	0.9	7.6	8.5	17.0
141.9	4.9	o	4.9	3.5	o	....	....	....	....	o				
133.0	10.2	17.3	27.5	20.7	99.7	10.2	13.0	23.2	23.3	70.0	10.2	9.1	19.3	27.6
169.0	44.5	11.0	55.5	32.8	102.5	26.0	7.0	33.0	32.2	57.0	14.6	4.0	18.6	32.6
134.0	13.0	24.6	37.6	28.1	107.0	13.0	19.7	32.7	30.6	80.0	13.0	14.7	27.7	34.6

TABLE 19.—ESTIMATED CRUDE AND PRODUCT DEMAND IN FOREIGN COUNTRIES, BY AREAS, 1938 [1]

(In thousand barrels of 42 U. S. gal.)

World area	1938	% total foreign
North America.....................	87,402	9.5
South America....................	90,636	9.9
Western Hemisphere...............	178,038	19.4
Europe...........................	339,690	37.0
Africa............................	46,672	5.1
Europe and Africa................	386,362	42.1
Russia...........................	205,231	22.3
Near and Middle East.............	26,080	2.8
South and East Asia...............	77,742	8.5
Oceania..........................	45,197	4.9
Near, Middle, and Far East........	149,019	16.2
Eastern Hemisphere..............	740,612	80.6
Total foreign....................	918,650	100.0

[1] Source: Private information and estimates.

TABLE 20.—INDICATED TOTAL DOMESTIC CRUDE AND PRODUCT DEMAND IN ALL FOREIGN COUNTRIES (INCLUDING RUSSIA) AND QUANTITIES SUPPLIED BY EXPORTS FROM UNITED STATES, 1865–1942 [1]

(In thousand barrels of 42 U. S. gal.)

Year	Indicated total foreign domestic demand	Total exports from United States of crude and products		Year	Indicated total foreign domestic demand	Total exports from United States of crude and products	
	Barrels	Barrels	% total demand		Barrels	Barrels	% total demand
1865	825	607	73.6	1904	125,203	24,336	19.4
1866	1,515	1,214	80.1	1905	110,460	30,086	27.2
1867	2,035	1,673	82.2	1906	118,218	31,449	26.6
1868	2,236	1,892	84.6	1907	130,168	32,306	24.8
1869	2,877	2,396	83.3	1908	145,393	38,633	26.6
1870	3,246	2,708	83.4	1909	154,435	39,042	25.3
1871	4,149	3,624	87.3	1910	155,550	37,958	24.4
1872	4,020	3,436	85.5	1911	166,008	43,851	26.4
1873	6,667	5,723	85.8	1912	168,106	45,619	27.1
1874	6,604	5,598	84.8	1913	175,372	52,251	29.8
1875	6,844	5,655	82.6	1914	177,570	54,359	30.6
1876	8,191	6,273	76.6	1915	190,290	56,449	29.7
1877	11,020	8,616	78.2	1916	201,056	62,459	31.1
1878	11,338	8,318	73.4	1917	201,120	64,503	32.1
1879	13,728	10,041	73.1	1918	176,655	68,012	38.5
1880	11,989	8,257	68.9	1919	194,079	63,848	32.9
1881	16,583	12,251	73.9	1920	226,329	79,576	35.2
1882	17,342	11,988	69.1	1921	245,856	71,652	29.1
1883	19,499	12,694	65.1	1922	245,951	74,344	30.2
1884	24,715	12,964	52.5	1923	290,813	101,981	35.1
1885	28,258	13,352	47.3	1924	329,158	117,144	35.6
1886	33,270	14,092	42.4	1925	342,221	113,834	33.3
1887	33,358	13,834	41.5	1926	393,149	131,950	33.6
1888	38,072	13,519	35.5	1927	428,276	141,649	33.1
1889	42,443	16,100	37.9	1928	486,644	154,957	31.8
1890	47,215	16,406	34.7	1929	538,660	163,120	30.3
1891	52,695	15,888	30.2	1930	573,248	156,499	27.3
1892	55,865	17,641	31.6	1931	562,099	124,394	22.1
1893	64,363	20,756	32.2	1932	570,739	103,275	18.1
1894	61,299	21,306	34.8	1933	610,381	106,727	17.5
1895	70,913	20,313	28.6	1934	675,840	114,507	16.9
1896	75,424	22,185	29.4	1935	722,949	128,987	17.8
1897	85,191	23,674	27.8	1936	795,848	131,994	16.6
1898	93,103	23,488	25.2	1937	883,486	172,834	19.6
1899	96,719	22,643	23.4	1938	918,650	193,728	21.1
1900	108,733	23,217	21.4	1939	955,774	188,959	19.8
1901	123,743	25,692	20.8	1940	907,076	130,466	14.4
1902	118,381	25,339	21.4	1941	932,337	108,830	11.7
1903	116,720	22,302	19.1	1942	871,126	116,907	13.4

[1] Source: Total exports from United States (1865–1942), U. S. Geological Survey and Bureau of Mines. Indicated total foreign domestic demand (1865–1942). Private information and estimates.

TABLE 21.—U. S. EXPORTS, IMPORTS OF CRUDE AND PRODUCTS,

(In thousand barrels

Year	Exports from United States							Imports	
	Crude oil			Refined products		Total		Crude oil	
	Barrels	% U. S. crude production, Col. (18)	% total U. S. petroleum exports, Col. (6)	Barrels	% total U. S. petroleum exports, Col. (6)	Barrels	% total U. S. production, Col. (20)	Barrels	% total U. S. petroleum imports, Col. (12)
	(1)	(2)	(3)	(4)	(5)	(6)	(7)	(8)	(9)
1910	6,026	2.9	15.9	31,932	84.1	37,958	18.1	557	90.7
1911	6,353	2.9	14.5	37,498	85.5	43,851	19.9	1,710	97.4
1912	4,624	2.1	10.1	40,995	89.9	45,619	20.4	7,383	94.5
1913	5,408	2.2	10.4	46,843	89.6	52,251	21.0	17,809	97.7
1914	2,970	1.1	5.5	51,389	94.5	54,359	20.4	16,913	98.1
1915	3,768	1.3	6.7	52,681	93.3	56,449	20.0	18,139	99.7
1916	4,098	1.4	6.6	58,361	93.4	62,459	20.6	20,797	97.9
1917	4,901	1.5	7.6	59,602	92.4	64,503	18.9	30,163	95.6
1918	5,884	1.7	8.7	62,128	91.3	68,012	18.7	37,736	96.9
1919	6,348	1.7	9.9	57,500	90.1	63,848	16.4	52,822	97.5
1920	9,295	2.1	11.7	70,281	88.3	79,576	17.5	106,175	97.6
1921	9,627	2.0	13.4	62,025	86.6	71,652	14.8	125,364	97.3
1922	10,805	1.9	14.5	63,539	85.5	74,344	13.0	127,308	93.6
1923	17,534	2.4	17.2	84,447	82.8	101,981	13.5	82,015	82.3
1924	18,239	2.6	15.6	98,905	84.4	117,144	15.9	77,775	82.2
1925	13,337	1.7	11.7	100,497	88.3	113,834	14.4	61,824	79.1
1926	15,407	2.0	11.7	116,543	88.3	131,950	16.4	60,382	74.3
1927	15,844	1.8	11.2	125,805	88.8	141,649	15.0	58,383	81.4
1928	18,966	2.1	12.2	135,991	87.8	154,957	16.4	79,767	87.1
1929	26,401	2.6	16.2	136,719	83.8	163,120	15.4	78,933	72.6
1930	23,705	2.6	15.1	132,794	84.9	156,499	16.4	62,129	58.8
1931	25,535	3.0	20.5	98,859	79.5	124,394	13.9	47,250	54.9
1932	27,393	3.5	26.5	75,882	73.5	103,275	12.6	44,682	60.0
1933	36,584	4.0	34.3	70,143	65.7	106,727	11.3	31,893	70.3
1934	41,127	4.5	35.9	73,380	64.1	114,507	12.1	35,558	70.4
1935	51,430	5.2	39.9	77,557	60.1	128,987	12.4	32,239	61.3
1936	50,313	4.6	38.1	81,681	61.9	131,994	11.5	32,327	56.6
1937	67,234	5.3	38.9	105,600	61.1	172,834	13.0	27,484	48.1
1938	77,254	6.4	39.9	116,474	60.1	193,728	15.3	26,412	48.6
1939	72,076	5.7	38.1	116,883	61.9	188,959	14.3	33,095	56.0
1940	51,496	3.8	39.5	78,970	60.5	130,466	9.2	42,662	50.9
1941	33,238	2.4	30.5	75,592	69.5	108,830	7.3	50,606	52.1
1942	33,834	2.4	28.9	83,073	71.1	116,907	7.9	12,297	34.2

1 Source of data: U. S. Geological Survey and Bureau of Mines.
* Denotes deficit.

AND DOMESTIC CRUDE PRODUCTION, 1910–1942 [1]

of 42 U. S. gal.)

into United States				Excess/deficit * of exports over imports				U. S. domestic production		
Refined products		Total		Crude oil	Refined products	Total		Crude oil	Natural gasoline /benzol	Total
Barrels	% total U. S. petroleum imports, Col. (12)	Barrels	% total U. S. production Col. (20)	Barrels	Barrels	Barrels	% total U. S. production, Col. (20)	Barrels	Barrels	Barrels
(10)	(11)	(12)	(13)	(14)	(15)	(16)	(17)	(18)	(19)	(20)
57	9.3	614	0.3	5,469	31,875	37,344	17.8	209,557	......	209,557
45	2.6	1,755	0.8	4,643	37,453	42,096	19.1	220,449	177	220,626
426	5.5	7,809	3.5	2,759 *	40,569	37,810	16.9	222,935	288	223,223
422	2.3	18,231	7.3	12,401 *	46,421	34,020	13.7	248,446	573	249,019
334	1.9	17,247	6.5	13,943 *	51,055	37,112	13.9	265,763	1,016	266,779
53	0.3	18,192	6.4	14,371 *	52,628	38,257	13.5	281,104	1,556	282,660
447	2.1	21,244	7.0	16,699 *	57,914	41,215	13.6	300,767	2,464	303,231
1,400	4.4	31,563	9.3	25,262 *	58,202	32,940	9.7	335,316	5,188	340,504
1,227	3.1	38,963	10.7	31,852 *	60,901	29,049	8.0	355,928	8,000	363,928
1,376	2.5	54,198	14.0	46,474 *	56,124	9,650	2.5	378,367	9,867	388,234
2,647	2.4	108,822	24.0	96,880 *	67,634	29,246 *	6.4 *	442,927	10,932	453,859
3,428	2.7	128,792	26.6	115,737 *	58,597	57,140 *	11.8 *	472,183	12,061	484,244
8,665	6.4	135,973	23.8	116,503 *	54,874	61,629 *	10.8 *	557,531	13,732	571,263
17,638	17.7	99,653	13.2	64,481 *	66,809	2,328	0.3	732,407	21,761	754,168
16,806	17.8	94,581	12.8	59,536 *	82,099	22,563	3.1	713,940	24,438	738,378
16,376	20.9	78,200	9.9	48,487 *	84,121	35,634	4.5	763,743	28,164	791,907
20,938	25.7	81,320	10.1	44,975 *	95,605	50,630	6.3	770,874	34,417	805,291
13,353	18.6	71,736	7.6	42,539 *	112,452	69,913	7.4	901,129	41,219	942,348
11,790	12.9	91,557	9.7	60,801 *	124,201	63,400	6.7	901,474	45,135	946,609
29,777	27.4	108,710	10.2	52,532 *	106,942	54,410	5.1	1,007,323	55,318	1,062,641
43,489	41.2	105,618	11.1	38,424 *	89,305	50,881	5.3	898,011	55,320	953,331
38,837	45.1	86,087	9.6	21,715 *	60,022	38,307	4.3	851,081	45,443	896,524
29,812	40.0	74,494	9.1	17,289 *	46,070	28,781	3.5	785,159	37,312	822,471
13,501	29.7	45,394	4.8	4,691	56,642	61,333	6.5	905,656	35,178	940,834
14,936	29.6	50,494	5.3	5,569	58,444	64,013	6.8	908,065	38,264	946,329
20,396	38.7	52,635	5.1	19,191	57,161	76,352	7.4	996,596	41,204	1,037,800
24,777	43.4	57,104	5.0	17,986	56,904	74,890	6.5	1,099,687	45,272	1,144,959
29,673	51.9	57,157	4.3	39,750	75,927	115,677	8.7	1,279,160	51,967	1,331,127
27,896	51.4	54,308	4.3	50,842	88,578	139,420	11.0	1,214,355	53,111	1,267,466
25,965	44.0	59,060	4.5	38,981	90,918	129,899	9.8	1,264,962	54,148	1,319,110
41,089	49.1	83,751	5.9	8,834	37,881	46,715	3.3	1,353,214	58,867	1,412,081
46,536	47.9	97,142	6.5	17,368 *	29,056	11,688	0.8	1,402,228	84,290	1,486,518
23,669	65.8	35,966	2.4	21,537	59,404	80,941	5.5	1,386,645	85,719	1,472,364

Table 22.—U. S. Exports of Crude Oil and Finished Petroleum

(In thousand barrels

Countries	Year	Crude oil			Motor fuel			Kerosene			Gas oil distillate and residual fuel oil [3]		
		Barrels	% total crude	% total exports, Col. (25)	Barrels	% total motor fuel	% total exports, Col. (25)	Barrels	% total kerosene	% total exports, Col. (25)	Barrels	% total gas and fuel oil	% total exports, Col. (25)
		(1)	(2)	(3)	(4)	(5)	(6)	(7)	(8)	(9)	(10)	(11)	(12)
United Kingdom and Ireland	1938	89	0.1	0.5	10,209	21.2	54.2	1,574	21.7	8.4	4,061	9.3	21.5
	1937	753	1.1	5.5	5,862	16.1	43.2	1,349	15.6	9.9	2,462	5.9	18.1
	1936	160	0.3	1.6	4,895	18.2	49.6	978	14.6	9.9	1,371	4.3	13.9
	1929	92	0.3	0.3	17,757	29.2	65.9	2,976	15.0	11.0	3,599	10.1	13.4
	1925	145	1.1	0.8	8,308	27.1	45.5	2,692	12.8	14.7	4,405	13.6	24.1
	1913	27	0.6	0.3	464	10.6	5.2	4,031	16.2	44.8	3,009	36.3	33.5
	1910	.....	.....	.....	403	21.8	4.6	4,624	19.4	52.3	2,510	84.9	28.4
France	1938	16,743	21.7	77.5	3,835	8.0	17.8	9	0.1	.....	240	0.5	1.1
	1937	10,066	15.0	70.4	2,607	7.2	18.2	1	.....	.....	978	2.3	6.8
	1936	7,463	14.8	78.2	1,302	4.8	13.6	2	.....	.....	104	0.3	1.1
	1929	4	.....	.....	8,738	14.3	71.7	1,255	6.3	10.3	249	0.7	2.0
	1925	.....	.....	.....	6,143	20.1	62.8	1,357	6.4	13.9	515	1.6	5.3
	1913	584	12.5	19.8	476	10.9	16.2	1,261	5.1	42.8	.....	.....	.....
	1910	312	7.8	15.0	157	8.5	7.6	1,117	4.7	53.7	.....	.....	.....
Germany	1938	1,287	1.7	14.4	2,313	4.8	25.9	1	.....	.....	4,025	9.2	45.1
	1937	1,430	2.1	21.0	1,179	3.2	17.3	104	1.2	1.5	2,690	6.4	39.5
	1936	1,176	2.4	18.5	983	3.7	15.4	1	.....	.....	2,841	9.0	44.6
	1929	33	0.1	0.6	1,770	2.9	31.5	737	3.7	13.1	1,351	3.8	24.1
	1925	548	4.2	12.0	1,103	3.6	24.2	751	3.6	16.5	982	3.0	21.5
	1913	.....	.....	.....	354	8.1	10.0	2,476	9.9	70.2	71	0.8	2.0
	1910	.....	.....	.....	271	14.6	6.2	3,616	15.1	82.1	26	0.9	0.6
Italy	1938	6,751	8.7	76.8	432	0.9	4.9	.....	.....	.....	1,201	2.7	13.7
	1937	4,544	6.8	70.5	597	1.6	9.3	94	1.1	1.4	721	1.7	11.2
	1936	1,863	3.7	40.4	508	1.9	11.0	9	0.1	0.2	1,689	5.4	36.7
	1929	.....	.....	.....	1,319	2.2	52.1	171	0.9	6.7	311	0.9	12.3
	1925	165	1.3	4.7	1,052	3.4	29.7	542	2.6	15.3	1,139	3.5	32.2
	1913	.....	.....	.....	186	4.3	17.3	504	2.0	46.7	206	2.5	19.1
	1910	.....	.....	.....	84	4.5	9.3	621	2.6	68.8	17	0.6	1.9
Belgium and Netherlands	1938	675	0.9	6.4	3,794	7.9	35.9	747	10.3	7.1	4,217	9.6	39.9
	1937	755	1.1	6.2	4,457	12.2	36.4	1,121	12.9	9.2	4,299	10.3	35.2
	1936	360	0.7	4.6	2,925	10.9	37.7	736	11.0	9.5	2,538	8.0	32.7
	1929	.....	.....	.....	3,942	6.5	47.3	1,604	8.1	19.3	1,378	3.8	16.5
	1925	38	0.3	0.6	2,181	7.1	31.8	2,560	12.1	37.3	970	3.0	14.1
	1913	.....	.....	.....	427	9.8	7.1	4,597	18.4	77.2	314	3.8	5.3
	1910	.....	.....	.....	202	10.9	4.3	3,883	16.2	82.6	133	4.5	2.8
Denmark, Finland, Norway, Sweden	1938	1,024	1.3	12.3	3,581	7.4	43.0	1,089	15.0	13.1	2,074	4.7	24.9
	1937	405	0.6	8.3	1,560	4.3	31.9	506	5.8	10.3	1,857	4.5	38.0
	1936	557	1.1	19.0	627	2.3	21.4	567	8.5	19.4	803	2.5	27.4
	1929	47	0.2	0.7	3,421	5.6	52.5	1,446	7.3	22.2	985	2.7	15.1
	1925	.....	.....	.....	1,239	4.1	29.9	1,323	6.3	32.0	977	3.0	23.6
	1913	1	.....	0.1	56	1.3	2.8	1,750	7.0	90.6	.....	.....	.....
	1910	.....	.....	.....	12	0.6	0.8	1,367	5.7	95.0	.....	.....	.....
Spain	1938	54	0.1	1.8	2,095	4.4	68.8	12	0.2	0.4	771	1.8	25.3
	1937	134	0.2	10.2	828	2.3	63.2	.....	.....	.....	301	0.7	23.0
	1936	37	0.1	1.1	2,065	7.7	60.9	.....	.....	.....	1,252	4.0	37.0
	1929	148	0.1	6.9	1,370	2.2	64.1	88	0.5	4.1	210	0.6	9.8
	1925	11	0.1	0.9	674	2.2	53.7	157	0.7	12.5	210	0.6	16.7
	1913	307	6.6	84.1	.....	.....	.....	.....	.....	.....	.....	.....	.....
	1910	231	5.7	86.8	.....	.....	.....	.....	.....	.....	.....	.....	.....
Canada and Newfoundland	1938	24,845	32.2	80.3	3,287	6.8	10.6	231	3.2	0.7	1,528	3.5	4.9
	1937	28,080	41.8	86.8	1,747	4.8	5.4	86	1.0	0.3	1,323	3.2	4.1
	1936	25,683	51.1	87.0	1,279	4.7	4.3	57	0.8	0.2	1,632	5.2	5.5
	1929	22,412	84.9	72.1	5,235	8.6	16.9	120	0.6	0.4	2,126	6.6	6.8
	1925	8,916	67.9	54.2	2,521	8.2	15.3	135	0.6	0.8	4,527	13.9	27.5
	1913	2,970	63.8	47.2	1,282	29.3	20.4	434	1.7	6.9	1,406	17.0	22.3
	1910	934	23.2	49.9	397	21.5	21.2	243	1.0	13.0	209	7.1	11.1

[1] 1910 and 1913, fiscal year ending June 30.
[2] Source: Foreign Commerce and Navigation, Department of Commerce.

	Lubricants			Wax			Asphalt, coke, etc.			Total finished products			Total U. S. exports crude and products
Barrels	% total lubes	% total exports, Col. (25)	Barrels	% total wax	% total exports, Col. (25)	Barrels	% total asphalt, coke, etc.	% total exports, Col. (25)	Barrels	% total finished products	% total exports, Col. (25)	
(13)	(14)	(15)	(16)	(17)	(18)	(19)	(20)	(21)	(22)	(23)	(24)	(25)
2,519	26.0	13.4	170	23.6	0.9	217	10.6	1.1	18,750	16.8	99.5	18,839
2,594	23.0	19.1	218	26.4	1.7	344	17.5	2.5	12,829	12.7	94.5	13,582
2,120	23.7	21.5	206	30.8	2.1	138	8.3	1.4	9,708	12.7	98.4	9,868
1,866	16.7	6.9	298	26.1	1.2	345	9.2	1.3	26,841	20.3	99.7	26,933
2,146	21.6	11.7	350	29.3	1.9	223	21.8	1.3	18,124	18.8	99.2	18,269
1,462	28.7	16.2	4	.....	...	4	.....	...	8,966	21.0	99.7	8,993
1,303	32.1	14.7	4	.....	...	4	.....	...	8,840	27.0	100.0	8,840
549	5.7	2.5	4	0.5	...	221	10.8	1.1	4,858	4.4	22.5	21,601
461	4.1	3.2	2	0.2	...	181	9.2	1.4	4,230	4.2	29.6	14,296
495	2.5	5.2	2	0.3	...	180	10.8	1.9	2,085	2.7	21.8	9,548
1,667	14.9	13.7	5	0.4	0.1	270	7.2	2.2	12,184	9.2	100.0	12,188
1,732	17.4	17.7	8	0.7	0.1	22	2.2	0.2	9,777	10.2	100.0	9,777
622	12.2	21.2	4	.....	...	4	.....	...	2,359	5.5	80.2	2,943
492	12.1	23.7	4	.....	...	4	.....	...	1,766	5.4	85.0	2,078
1,259	13.0	14.1	15	2.1	0.2	32	1.6	0.3	7,645	6.8	85.6	8,932
1,271	11.3	18.6	107	12.9	1.6	33	1.7	0.5	5,384	5.3	79.0	6,814
1,308	14.6	20.5	36	5.4	0.6	27	1.6	0.4	5,196	6.8	81.5	6,372
1,343	12.0	23.9	56	4.9	1.0	326	8.7	5.8	5,583	4.2	99.4	5,616
1,011	10.2	22.1	87	7.3	1.9	83	8.1	1.8	4,017	4.2	88.0	4,565
629	12.4	17.8	4	.....	...	4	.....	...	3,530	8.3	100.0	3,530
489	12.0	11.1	4	.....	...	4	.....	...	4,402	13.4	100.0	4,402
315	3.2	3.6	79	11.0	0.9	9	0.4	0.1	2,036	1.8	23.2	8,787
386	3.4	6.0	75	9.1	1.2	25	1.3	0.4	1,898	1.9	29.5	6,442
269	3.0	5.8	100	14.9	2.3	168	10.1	3.6	2,743	3.6	59.6	4,606
386	3.4	15.2	128	11.2	5.1	219	5.8	8.6	2,534	1.9	100.0	2,534
452	4.6	12.8	183	15.4	5.2	4	0.4	0.1	3,372	3.5	95.3	3,537
182	3.6	16.9	4	.....	...	4	.....	...	1,078	2.5	100.0	1,078
181	4.5	20.0	4	.....	...	4	.....	...	903	2.8	100.0	903
1,024	10.6	9.7	76	10.5	0.7	32	1.6	0.3	9,890	8.9	93.6	10,565
1,502	13.3	12.3	69	8.3	0.5	22	1.1	0.2	11,470	11.4	93.8	12,225
1,120	12.5	14.4	50	7.5	0.6	34	2.0	0.5	7,403	9.7	95.4	7,763
1,103	9.9	13.2	86	7.6	1.0	225	6.0	2.7	8,339	6.3	100.0	8,339
996	10.0	14.5	103	8.6	1.5	13	1.3	0.2	6,823	7.1	99.4	6,861
618	12.2	10.4	.....	.....	.....	.....	.....	...	5,956	13.9	100.0	5,956
482	11.9	10.3	.....	.....	.....	.....	.....	...	4,700	14.3	100.0	4,700
429	4.4	5.2	43	6.0	0.5	85	4.2	1.0	7,301	6.5	87.7	8,325
427	3.8	8.7	48	5.8	1.0	86	4.4	1.8	4,484	4.4	91.7	4,889
303	3.4	10.3	31	4.6	1.1	42	2.5	1.4	2,373	3.1	81.0	2,930
403	3.6	6.2	47	4.1	0.7	169	4.5	2.6	6,471	4.9	99.3	6,518
548	5.5	13.2	27	2.3	0.7	23	2.2	0.6	4,137	4.3	100.0	4,137
125	2.5	6.5	.....	.....	.....	.....	.....	...	1,931	4.5	99.9	1,932
60	1.5	4.2	.....	.....	.....	.....	.....	...	1,439	4.4	100.0	1,439
108	1.1	3.5	7	1.0	0.2	.....	.....	...	2,993	2.7	98.2	3,047
39	0.3	3.0	6	0.7	0.5	1	0.1	0.1	1,175	1.2	89.8	1,309
30	0.3	0.8	2	0.3	0.1	2	0.1	0.1	3,351	4.4	98.9	3,388
109	1.0	5.1	27	2.4	1.4	184	4.9	8.6	1,988	1.5	93.1	2,136
148	1.5	11.8	50	4.2	4.0	5	0.5	0.4	1,244	1.3	99.1	1,255
58	1.1	15.9	.....	.....	...	.....	.....	...	58	0.1	15.9	365
35	0.9	13.2	.....	.....	...	.....	.....	...	35	0.1	13.2	266
511	5.3	1.7	40	5.6	0.2	490	24.0	1.6	6,087	5.5	19.7	30,932
468	4.2	1.4	8	1.0	...	635	32.2	2.0	4,267	4.2	13.2	32,347
436	4.9	1.5	6	0.9	...	435	26.0	1.5	3,845	5.0	13.0	29,528
606	5.4	2.0	11	1.0	...	557	14.9	1.8	8,655	6.6	27.9	31,067
275	2.8	1.7	3	0.3	...	76	7.4	0.5	7,537	7.8	45.8	16,453
201	4.0	3.2	.....	.....	...	.....	.....	...	3,323	7.8	52.8	6,293
88	2.2	4.8	.....	.....	...	.....	.....	...	937	2.9	50.1	1,871

[3] For 1910 and 1913, include residuum, tar, and all other from which light bodies have been distilled.
[4] Included in gas-oil distillate and residual fuel oil. See note [3].

TABLE 22.—U. S. EXPORTS OF CRUDE OIL AND FINISHED PETROLEUM PRODUCTS

(In thousand barrels

Countries	Year	Crude oil			Motor fuel			Kerosene			Gas oil distillate and residual fuel oil [3]		
		Barrels	% total crude	% total exports, Col. (25)	Barrels	% total motor fuel	% total exports, Col. (25)	Barrels	% total kerosene	% total exports, Col. (25)	Barrels	% total gas and fuel oil	% total exports, Col. (25)
		(1)	(2)	(3)	(4)	(5)	(6)	(7)	(8)	(9)	(10)	(11)	(12)
Dutch West Indies	1938	.....	.....	....	4,852	10.1	43.4	1,209	16.6	10.8	5,111	11.7	45.7
	1937	842	1.3	7.6	3,629	10.0	32.8	1,293	14.9	11.7	5,280	12.6	47.8
	1936	.....	.....	....	832	3.1	26.6	1,301	19.4	41.7	983	3.1	31.5
	1929	.....	.....	....	1,416	2.3	60.0	4	.....	0.2	932	2.6	39.5
	1925	.....	.....	....	3	.....	10.8	2	.....	7.1	21	0.1	75.0
	1913	.....	.....	....	1	.....	16.7	5	.....	83.3	.....	.....	....
	1910	.....	.....	....	.....	.....	....	5	.....	100.0	.....	.....	....
Argentine, Brazil, Chile	1938	1,537	2.0	21.5	1,724	3.6	24.1	429	5.9	6.0	3,028	6.9	42.2
	1937	1,554	2.3	21.8	1,610	4.4	22.6	546	6.3	7.6	2,947	7.0	41.3
	1936	1,317	2.6	24.3	1,507	5.6	27.8	508	7.6	9.4	1,695	5.4	31.3
	1929	179	0.7	1.4	4,005	6.6	30.8	832	4.2	6.3	7,073	19.8	54.4
	1925	57	0.4	0.6	1,775	5.8	18.0	1,002	4.8	10.2	6,371	19.6	64.8
	1913	204	4.4	4.7	519	11.9	11.9	1,480	5.9	34.0	1,895	22.9	43.5
	1910	594	14.8	26.5	130	7.0	5.8	1,343	5.6	60.0	10	0.3	0.4
Japan and Kwantung	1938	22,189	28.7	66.6	2,121	4.4	6.4	221	3.0	0.6	8,327	19.0	25.0
	1937	16,668	24.9	55.3	1,821	5.0	6.0	471	5.4	1.6	10,621	25.4	35.2
	1936	10,467	20.8	48.9	1,245	4.6	5.8	4	0.1	.....	9,308	29.5	43.5
	1929	2,476	9.4	22.8	1,010	1.6	9.3	1,604	8.1	14.8	5,233	14.7	48.1
	1925	836	6.4	18.9	235	0.8	5.3	1,490	7.1	33.6	1,585	4.9	35.8
	1913	.....	.....	....	20	0.5	0.8	2,325	9.3	95.2	.....	.....	....
	1910	.....	.....	....	3	0.2	0.2	1,434	6.0	95.7	.....	.....	....
Australia and New Zealand	1938	.....	.....	....	2,929	6.1	71.2	231	3.2	5.6	218	0.5	5.3
	1937	12	.....	0.3	2,555	7.0	64.4	316	3.7	8.0	295	0.7	7.4
	1936	1	0.2	.....	2,480	9.2	61.7	197	2.9	4.9	849	2.7	21.1
	1929	61	.....	0.8	4,673	7.7	61.6	1,062	5.4	14.0	795	2.2	10.5
	1925	.....	.....	....	2,336	7.6	56.6	693	3.3	16.8	723	2.2	17.5
	1913	.....	.....	....	255	5.8	25.4	607	2.4	60.5	2	.....	0.2
	1910	.....	.....	....	105	5.7	12.7	627	2.6	76.0	2	0.1	0.3
Philippines	1938	.....	.....	....	954	2.0	33.7	509	7.0	18.0	1,210	2.8	42.7
	1937	.....	.....	....	783	2.2	36.8	412	4.8	19.4	734	1.8	34.5
	1936	.....	.....	....	945	3.5	38.4	513	7.6	20.8	866	2.7	35.1
	1929	.....	.....	....	463	0.8	23.9	462	2.3	23.9	887	2.5	45.9
	1925	56	0.4	3.7	125	0.4	8.3	341	1.6	22.6	931	2.9	61.6
	1913	.....	.....	....	37	0.8	10.3	311	1.3	86.4	.....	.....	....
	1910	1	.....	0.6	3	0.2	1.9	149	0.6	91.4	.....	.....	....
China and Hong Kong	1938	166	0.2	14.1	105	0.2	8.9	116	1.6	9.9	619	1.4	52.7
	1937	.....	.....	....	829	2.3	25.5	1,142	13.2	35.2	769	1.8	23.8
	1936	8	.....	0.4	485	1.8	23.7	680	10.1	33.3	520	1.6	25.4
	1929	.....	.....	....	411	0.7	7.5	3,726	18.8	68.0	872	2.4	15.9
	1925	80	0.6	1.5	311	1.0	5.8	3,733	17.7	69.2	987	3.0	18.3
	1913	.....	.....	....	1	.....	....	2,196	8.8	97.7	.....	.....	....
	1910	.....	.....	....	5	0.3	0.2	1,990	8.3	99.0	.....	.....	....
Other countries	1938	1,894	2.4	10.5	5,862	12.2	32.5	883	12.2	4.9	7,203	16.4	39.9
	1937	1,884	2.8	10.2	6,332	17.4	34.2	1,223	14.1	6.6	6,544	15.7	35.3
	1936	1,221	2.4	8.5	4,840	18.0	33.7	1,159	17.3	8.1	5,153	16.3	35.9
	1929	942	3.6	4.2	5,331	8.8	23.9	3,732	18.8	16.7	9,714	27.2	43.6
	1925	2,273	17.3	11.8	2,632	8.6	13.6	4,297	20.4	22.2	8,166	25.1	42.3
	1913	565	12.1	9.6	292	6.7	5.1	2,997	12.0	51.0	1,383	16.7	23.5
	1910	1,950	48.5	35.0	77	4.2	1.4	2,910	12.2	52.2	47	1.6	-0.9
Total exports excluding noncontiguous	1938	77,254	100.0	40.9	48,093	100.0	25.5	7,261	100.0	3.8	43,833	100.0	23.2
	1937	67,127	100.0	39.9	36,396	100.0	21.6	8,664	100.0	5.2	41,821	100.0	24.9
	1936	50,313	100.0	39.7	26,918	100.0	21.2	6,712	100.0	5.3	31,604	100.0	24.9
	1929	26,394	100.0	16.6	60,861	100.0	38.3	19,820	100.0	12.5	35,715	100.0	22.5
	1925	13,125	100.0	12.0	30,638	100.0	28.0	21,075	100.0	19.2	32,509	100.0	29.7
	1913	4,658	100.0	9.8	4,370	100.0	9.2	24,974	100.0	52.7	8,286	100.0	17.5
	1910	4,022	100.0	10.9	1,849	100.0	5.0	23,929	100.0	65.1	2,954	100.0	8.0

1 1910 and 1913, fiscal year ending June 30.
2 Source: Foreign Commerce and Navigation, Department of Commerce.

Lubricants			Wax			Asphalt, coke, etc.			Total finished products			Total U.S. exports crude and products
Barrels	% total lubes	% total exports, Col. (25)	Barrels	% total wax	% total exports, Col. (25)	Barrels	% total asphalt, coke, etc.	% total exports, Col. (25)	Barrels	% total finished products	% total exports, Col. (25)	
(13)	(14)	(15)	(16)	(17)	(18)	(19)	(20)	(21)	(22)	(23)	(24)	(25)
13	0.1	0.1	.....	.....	...	2	0.1	...	11,187	10.0	100.0	11,187
8	0.1	0.1	.....	.....	...	.....	.....	...	10,210	10.1	92.4	11,052
6	0.1	0.2	.....	.....	...	.....	.....	...	3,122	4.1	100.0	3,122
6	0.1	0.3	.....	.....	...	.....	.....	...	2,358	1.8	100.0	2,358
2	.....	7.1	.....	.....	...	.....	.....	...	28	.....	100.0	28
.....	.....	.....	.....	.....	...	.....	.....	...	6	.....	100.0	6
.....	.....	.....	.....	.....	...	.....	.....	...	5	.....	100.0	5
349	3.6	4.9	35	4.9	0.5	59	2.9	0.8	5,624	5.0	78.5	7,161
388	3.4	5.4	33	4.0	0.5	60	3.0	0.8	5,584	2.5	78.2	7,138
310	3.5	5.7	36	5.4	0.6	46	2.8	0.9	4,102	5.4	75.7	5,419
687	6.2	5.3	82	7.2	0.6	139	3.7	1.2	12,818	9.7	98.6	12,997
531	5.4	5.4	73	6.1	0.7	25	2.4	0.3	9,777	10.1	99.4	9,834
253	5.0	5.9	.....	.....	...	.....	.....	...	4,147	9.7	95.3	4,351
163	4.0	7.3	.....	.....	...	.....	.....	...	1,646	5.0	73.5	2,240
397	4.1	1.2	.....	.....	...	82	4.0	0.2	11,148	10.0	33.4	33,337
511	4.5	1.7	6	0.7	...	46	2.3	0.2	13,476	13.4	44.7	30,144
352	3.9	1.6	8	1.2	...	33	2.0	0.2	10,950	14.3	51.1	21,417
387	3.5	4.6	52	4.6	0.5	109	2.9	1.0	8,395	6.3	77.2	10,871
210	2.1	4.7	31	2.6	0.7	44	4.3	1.0	3,595	3.7	81.1	4,431
98	1.9	4.0	.....	.....	...	.....	.....	...	2,443	5.7	100.0	2,443
62	1.5	4.1	.....	.....	...	.....	.....	...	1,499	4.6	100.0	1,499
508	5.2	12.3	3	0.4	0.1	225	11.0	5.5	4,114	3.7	100.0	4,114
624	5.5	15.7	3	0.4	0.1	164	8.3	4.1	3,957	3.9	99.7	3,969
431	4.8	10.7	3	0.4	0.1	62	3.7	1.5	4,022	5.2	100.0	4,023
619	5.5	8.2	5	0.4	0.1	369	9.8	4.9	7,523	5.7	99.2	7,584
256	2.6	6.2	4	0.3	0.1	116	11.4	2.8	4,128	4.3	100.0	4,128
139	2.7	13.9	.....	.....	...	.....	.....	...	1,003	2.4	100.0	1,003
91	2.2	11.0	.....	.....	...	.....	.....	...	825	2.5	100.0	825
91	1.0	3.2	2	0.3	0.1	64	3.1	2.3	2,830	2.5	100.0	2,830
125	1.1	5.9	3	0.4	0.2	68	3.4	3.2	2,125	2.1	100.0	2,125
76	0.9	3.1	5	0.8	0.2	59	3.5	2.4	2,464	3.2	100.0	2,464
73	0.7	3.8	4	0.4	0.2	44	1.2	2.3	1,933	1.4	100.0	1,933
41	0.4	2.7	6	0.5	0.3	12	1.2	0.8	1,456	1.5	96.3	1,512
12	0.2	3.3	.....	.....	...	.....	.....	...	360	0.9	100.0	360
10	0.2	6.1	.....	.....	...	.....	.....	...	162	0.5	99.4	163
119	1.2	10.1	23	3.2	2.0	27	1.3	2.3	1,009	0.9	85.9	1,175
424	3.8	13.1	18	2.2	0.5	63	3.2	1.9	3,245	3.2	100.0	3,245
271	3.0	13.3	29	4.3	1.4	52	3.1	2.5	2,037	2.7	99.6	2,045
283	2.5	5.2	96	8.4	1.7	94	2.5	1.7	5,482	4.1	100.0	5,482
149	1.5	2.8	60	5.0	1.1	71	7.0	1.3	5,311	5.5	98.5	5,391
51	1.0	2.3	.....	.....	...	.....	.....	...	2,248	5.3	100.0	2,248
15	0.4	0.8	.....	.....	...	.....	.....	...	2,010	6.1	100.0	2,010
1,502	15.5	8.1	222	30.9	1.3	498	24.4	2.8	16,170	14.5	89.5	18,064
2,059	18.2	11.1	231	27.9	1.2	242	12.3	1.4	16,631	16.5	89.8	18,515
1,428	15.9	10.0	155	23.2	1.1	393	23.5	2.7	13,128	17.1	91.5	14,349
1,629	14.6	7.3	243	21.3	1.2	700	18.7	3.1	21,349	16.1	95.8	22,291
1,432	14.4	7.4	208	17.4	1.1	304	29.8	1.6	17,039	17.7	88.2	19,312
637	12.5	10.8	.....	.....	...	.....	.....	...	5,309	12.4	90.4	5,874
587	14.5	10.5	.....	.....	...	.....	.....	...	3,621	11.0	65.0	5,571
9,693	100.0	5.1	719	100.0	0.4	2,043	100.0	1.1	111,642	100.0	59.1	188,896
11,287	100.0	6.7	827	100.0	0.5	1,970	100.0	1.2	100,965	100.0	60.1	168,092
8,955	100.0	7.1	669	100.0	0.5	1,671	100.0	1.3	76,529	100.0	60.3	126,842
11,167	100.0	7.0	1,140	100.0	0.7	3,750	100.0	2.4	132,453	100.0	83.4	158,847
9,929	100.0	9.1	1,193	100.0	1.1	1,021	100.0	0.9	96,365	100.0	88.0	109,490
5,087	100.0	10.8	.....	.....	...	.....	.....	...	42,717	100.0	90.2	47,375
4,058	100.0	11.0	.....	.....	...	.....	.....	...	32,790	100.0	89.1	36,812

³ For 1910 and 1913, include residuum, tar, and all other from which light bodies have been distilled.

TABLE 23.—INDICATED DOMESTIC DEMAND FOR CRUDE AND PRODUCTS IN ALL FOREIGN COUNTRIES—UNITED STATES, AND TOTAL WORLD, 1912–1942 [1]

(In thousand barrels of 42 U. S. gal.)

Year	Indicated total foreign domestic demand		United States domestic demand		Total world
	Barrels	% total world	Barrels	% total world	Barrels
1912	168,106	45.7	200,009	54.3	368,115
1913	175,372	44.9	215,579	55.1	390,951
1914	177,570	45.7	210,926	54.3	388,496
1915	190,290	44.3	239,109	55.7	429,399
1916	201,056	43.0	266,219	57.0	467,275
1917	201,120	40.8	291,658	59.2	492,778
1918	176,655	33.8	345,400	66.2	522,055
1919	194,079	34.1	374,541	65.9	568,620
1920	226,329	33.2	455,764	66.8	682,093
1921	245,856	35.0	457,521	65.0	703,377
1922	245,951	31.7	530,990	68.3	776,941
1923	290,813	30.8	652,027	69.2	942,840
1924	329,158	32.4	687,742	67.6	1,016,900
1925	342,221	32.0	726,797	68.0	1,069,018
1926	393,149	33.5	780,487	66.5	1,173,636
1927	428,276	34.8	802,499	65.2	1,230,775
1928	486,644	36.1	859,759	63.9	1,346,403
1929	538,660	36.4	940,083	63.6	1,478,743
1930	573,248	38.2	927,016	61.8	1,500,264
1931	562,099	38.4	902,920	61.6	1,465,019
1932	570,739	40.6	835,482	59.4	1,406,221
1933	610,381	41.3	868,487	58.7	1,478,868
1934	675,840	42.3	920,165	57.7	1,596,005
1935	722,949	42.4	983,685	57.6	1,706,634
1936	795,848	42.1	1,092,754	57.9	1,888,602
1937	883,486	43.0	1,169,682	57.0	2,053,168
1938	918,650	44.7	1,137,122	55.3	2,055,772
1939	955,774	43.7	1,231,076	56.3	2,186,850
1940	907,076	40.6	1,326,620	59.4	2,233,696
1941	932,337	38.6	1,483,392	61.4	2,415,729
1942	871,126	38.0	1,420,756	62.0	2,291,882

[1] Source: Indicated total foreign domestic demand (1912–1942), private information and estimates. U. S. domestic demand (1912–1917 incl.), Osborne, "Oil Economics," and "Commerce Yearbook," 1928. 1918–1939, A.P.I. *Statistical Bulletin*, Mar. 20, 1941. 1940–1942, Bureau of Mines.

TABLE 24.—WORLD TANKERS,[1] 1914–1926 [2]

(500 gross tons and over)

Flag	June 30, 1914						June 30, 1926					
	Steam and gas		Sail and barge		Total		Steam and gas		Sail and barge		Total	
	No.	Gross	No.	Gross	No.	Gross	No.	Gross	No.	Gross	No.	Gross
American [3]...	26	94,466	28	56,219	54	150,685	392	2,305,566	88	116,307	480	2,421,873
Argentine....	...	....	..	....	...	....	7	23,123	2	2,643	9	25,766
Belgian......	8	25,811	..	....	8	25,811	9	49,092	...	....	9	49,092
Brazilian....	...	....	..	....	...	....	1	2,347	...	....	1	2,347
British.......	181	815,849	7	21,561	188	837,410	355	1,918,901	4	14,593	359	1,933,494
Chinese......	...	....	..	....	...	....	3	2,385	...	....	3	2,385
Cuban........	...	....	..	....	...	....	4	11,176	4	4,125	8	15,301
Danish.......	...	....	1	735	1	735	3	12,660	1	731	4	13,391
Danzig.......	...	....	..	....	...	....	10	88,197	...	....	10	88,197
Dominican...	...	....	..	....	...	....	1	1,970	...	....	1	1,970
Dutch........	27	72,766	8	8,642	35	81,408	47	156,309	3	2,207	50	158,516
Ecuadorian...	...	....	..	....	...	....	1	2,210	...	....	1	2,210
Estonian.....	...	....	..	....	...	....	1	614	...	....	1	614
Finnish......												
French.......	3	11,232	..	....	3	11,232	24	131,986	...	....	24	131,986
German.......	46	215,844	1	728	47	216,572	16	57,346	...	....	16	57,346
Greek........	1	1,633	..	....	1	1,633						
Italian.......	3	16,007	..	....	3	16,007	35	157,784	...	....	35	157,784
Japanese.....	4	19,808	..	....	4	19,808	12	36,080	...	....	12	36,080
Mexican.....	4	13,464	..	....	4	13,464	2	11,716	4	3,014	6	14,730
Moroccan....												
Norwegian...	9	48,042	1	1,254	10	49,296	53	326,225	...	....	53	326,225
Panamanian..	...	....	..	....	...	....	1	6,163	...	....	1	6,163
Peruvian.....												
Philippine....	...	....	..	....	...	....	2	3,284	...	....	2	3,284
Portuguese...	...	....	..	....	...	....	2	2,822	...	....	2	2,822
Rumanian....	...	....	..	....	...	....	3	9,270	...	....	3	9,270
Russian......	6	14,371	..	....	6	14,371	2	6,505	...	....	2	6,505
Spanish......	1	672	..	....	1	672	9	31,270	...	....	9	31,270
Swedish......	1	2,092	..	....	1	2,092	3	16,270	...	....	3	16,270
Uruguayan...	...	....	..	....	...	....	1	630	...	....	1	630
Venezuelan...	...	....	..	....	...	....	2	3,953	...	....	2	3,953
Total......	320	1,352,057	46	89,139	366	1,441,196	1,001	5,375,854	106	143,620	1,107	5,519,474

[1] Exclusive of Navy, Admiralty, and other government tankers.
[2] Authority: All figures, except for American tankers, are prepared from Lloyd's Register.
[3] Including tankers on Great Lakes.

TABLE 25.—WORLD TANKER FLEET, BY COUNTRIES, JUNE 30, 1939 [1]

Country	Motor ships		Steamers		Total tankers [2]		Total world merchant fleet [3]	
	No.	Gross tons	No.	Gross tons	No.	Gross tons	No.	Gross tons
United States...	72	361,267	349	2,439,513	421	2,800,780	2,853	11,361,533
British Empire:								
Great Britain, Ireland....	224	1,748,815	211	1,170,751	435	2,919,566	6,722	17,819,134
Canada......	11	86,601	20	42,913	31	129,514	792	1,223,961
Other Dominions....	8	45,266	24	169,895	32	215,161	1,463	1,886,830
Belgium........	9	65,559	...	....	9	65,559	200	408,418
Denmark.......	12	96,802	2	9,670	14	106,472	705	1,174,944
France........	19	152,334	31	165,579	50	317,913	1,231	2,933,933
Germany.......	21	128,055	16	128,038	37	256,093	2,459	4,482,662
Italy..........	17	110,350	67	315,652	84	426,002	1,227	3,424,804
Japan.........	33	307,613	14	122,177	47	429,790	2,337	5,629,845
Netherlands....	62	400,311	45	137,253	107	537,564	1,523	2,969,578
Norway........	223	1,758,792	49	358,589	272	2,117,381	1,987	4,833,813
Panama........	42	398,087	12	71,577	54	469,664	159	717,525
Spain.........	9	49,837	6	20,813	15	70,649	777	902,251
Sweden........	19	158,815	...	....	19	158,815	1,231	1,577,120
U.S.S.R........	25	124,955	3	7,898	28	132,853	699	1,305,959
Other countries.	9	22,084	67	261,020	76	283,104	3,398	5,785,122
World total...	815	6,015,543	916	5,421,337	1,731	11,436,880	29,763	68,509,432

[1] Authority: U. S. Maritime Commission, from Lloyd's Register.
[2] All tank vessels 1,000 gross tons and over.
[3] Does not include sailing vessels and barges.

TABLE 26.—TOTAL CRUDE RUNS TO STILLS IN FOREIGN REFINERIES, 1939–1944
INCLUSIVE [1]

(In barrels of 42 U. S. gal. per day)

	1939	1940	1941	1942	1943	1944
North and Central America						
All refineries...........	207,788	222,087	254,306	237,721	256,335	275,811
American-owned [2]......	90,792	103,359	120,384	111,515	118,587	130,328
Per cent runs American	43.7	46.5	47.3	46.9	46.3	47.3
Caribbean Area						
All refineries...........	485,857	458,719	557,195	431,513	516,914	628,668
American-owned.......	255,137	230,646	293,546	192,185	267,304	331,718
Per cent runs American	52.5	50.3	52.7	44.5	51.7	52.8
Other South America						
All refineries...........	88,767	92,259	101,622	115,773	119,604	[3]
American-owned.......	36,678	30,838	36,175	48,618	[3]	[3]
Per cent runs American	41.3	33.4	35.6	42.0	[3]	[3]
Middle East						
All refineries [4].........	241,825	238,055	207,185	316,708	338,312	403,254
American-owned......	28,556	31,437	30,749	29,971	30,997	38,468
Per cent runs American	11.8	13.2	14.8	9.5	9.2	9.5

[1] Source: Bureau of Mines and Petroleum Administration for War.
[2] Roughly estimated.
[3] Data not available.
[4] Includes refineries at Hurghada, Egypt, at Morgha and Digboi, India, as well as at Abadan, Iran, Ras Tanura, Saudi Arabia, and Bahrein Island, but excludes refinery runs for Haifa, Palestine, refinery as no data were available.

REFINERIES INCLUDED IN TOTALS OF TABLE 26

North and Central America

Company   Location

AMERICAN OWNERSHIP

Company	Location
Imperial Oil, Ltd............................	Imperoyal, N.S., Canada
Imperial Oil, Ltd............................	Montreal, Que., Canada
McColl-Frontenac Oil Co., Ltd...............	Montreal East, Que., Canada
Imperial Oil, Ltd............................	Sarnia, Ont., Canada
Imperial Oil, Ltd............................	Regina, Sask., Canada
Imperial Oil, Ltd............................	Calgary, Alb., Canada
Standard Oil Co. of British Columbia...........	Burnaby, B.C., Canada
Imperial Oil, Ltd............................	Fort Norman, Northwest Territory, Canada
McColl-Frontenac Oil Co., Ltd................	Toronto, Ont., Canada
Imperial Oil, Ltd............................	Ioco, B.C., Canada
Standard Oil Co. of Cuba.....................	Belot, Cuba

REFINERIES INCLUDED IN TOTALS OF TABLE 26—*Continued*

Company	Location
OTHER OWNERSHIP	

Petroleos Mexicanos............................	7 refineries in Mexico
British American Oil Co., Ltd..................	5 refineries in Canada
Shell Oil Co. of Canada, Ltd..................	2 refineries in Canada
Other companies.............................	20 refineries in Canada

Caribbean Area

AMERICAN OWNERSHIP

Colombia Petroleum Co........................	La Petrolea, Colombia
Tropical Oil Co...............................	Barranca Bermeja, Colombia
Lago Oil and Transport Co., Ltd. (of Canada)....	St. Nicholas, Aruba
Creole Petroleum Corp........................	Caripito, Venezuela
Compania de Petrolea........................	La Salina, Venezuela

OTHER OWNERSHIP

N.V Arend Petroleum Maatschappij............	Druif, Aruba
Curacaosche Petroleum Industrie Maatschappi....	Emmastad, Curaçao
United British Oilfields of Trinidad, Ltd.........	Pt. Fortin, Trinidad
Trinidad Leaseholds, Ltd......................	Pointe-a-Pierre, Trinidad
Caribbean Petroleum Company, Ltd.............	San Lorenzo, Venezuela

Other South America

AMERICAN OWNERSHIP

Cia. Nativa de Petroleos, S.A..................	Bahia Blanca, Argentina
Cia. Nativa de Petroleos, S.A..................	Campana, Argentina
Standard Oil Co., S.A.........................	Dadin, Argentina
Standard Oil Co., S.A.........................	Manuel Elordi, Argentina
Ultramar, S.A., Petrolea......................	Dock Sud, Argentina
International Petroleum Co., Ltd...............	Talara, Peru
Compania de Petroleo Ganso Azul..............	Aguas Calientes, Peru

OTHER OWNERSHIP

Y.P.F., government refineries..................	Argentina
Diadema Argentina S.A., de Petroleo...........	Buenos Aires, Argentina
Y.P.F.B. (government)........................	Sanandita, Bolivia
Y.P.F.B. (government)........................	Camiri, Bolivia
Anglo-Ecuadorian Oilfields, Ltd................	La Libertad, Ecuador
Ecuadorian Oilfields, Ltd......................	Cautivo, Ecuador
ANCAP (government).........................	Uruguay
Peruvian government refinery..................	Villar, Peru

Middle East

AMERICAN OWNERSHIP

Arabian American Oil Co......................	Ras Tanura, Saudi Arabia
The Bahrein Petroleum Co. Ltd...............	Bahrein Island

OTHER OWNERSHIP

Anglo-Egyptian Oilfields, Ltd..................	Hurghada, Suez, Egypt
Attock Oil Co., Ltd...........................	Morgha, India
Assam Oil Co., Ltd...........................	Digboi, India
Anglo-Iranian Oil Co., Ltd....................	Abadan, Iran
Consolidated Refineries, Ltd..................	Haifa, Palestine

TABLE 27.—AMERICAN INTEREST IN FOREIGN REFINERIES
LOCATION, OWNERSHIP, AND DAILY CRUDE INPUT CAPACITY

Location	Ownership	Map symbol [1]	Daily average crude input capacity
Canada			
Ioco, Vancouver, B. C...	Imperial Oil Co. (S.O.N.J.)	◑	16,000
Calgary...............	Imperial Oil Co. (S.O.N.J.)	◑	8,000
Regina...............	Imperial Oil Co. (S.O.N.J.)	◑	9,500
Sarnia...............	Imperial Oil Co. (S.O.N.J.)	●	41,500
Montreal.............	Imperial Oil Co. (S.O.N.J.)	●	25,000
Halifax..............	Imperial Oil Co. (S.O.N.J.)	●	34,000 (T) [2]
Fort Norman..........	Imperial Oil Co. (S.O.N.J.)	▲	840
Montreal.............	McColl-Frontenac Oil Co. (Texas—49 per cent)	●	7,800 [3]
Toronto..............	McColl-Frontenac Oil Co. (Texas—49 per cent)	●	5,880 [3]
North Burnaby, Vancouver..........	Standard Oil Co. Calif.	◑	4,300
Pt. Moody, Vancouver..	Union Oil Co. Calif.	●	1,500
	Total Canada (11 refineries)		154,320
Cuba			
Havana...............	Standard Oil Co. of Cuba (S.O.N.J.)	●	4,200
Brazil			
São Paulo.............	Standard Oil Co. of Brazil (S.O.N.J.)	◑	2,160
Bolivia			
Sanandita.............	Standard Oil Co. of Bolivia (S.O.N.J.)	◑	800
Camiri...............	Standard Oil Co. of Bolivia (S.O.N.J.)	◑	400
	Total Bolivia (2 refineries)		1,200
Colombia			
Barranca Bermeja......	Tropical Oil Co. (S.O.N.J.)	▲	14,000
Petrolea..............	Colombian Pet. Co. (50/50 Socony-Vacuum and Texas)	▲	500
	Total Colombia (2 refineries)		14,500

[1] ▲ Refineries located near or at large producing fields.
● Refineries erected to operate largely on imported crude.
[2] T = topping.
[3] Represents 49 per cent Texas Co. interest.

TABLE 27.—AMERICAN INTEREST IN FOREIGN REFINERIES
LOCATION, OWNERSHIP, AND DAILY CRUDE INPUT CAPACITY—*Continued*

Location	Ownership	Map symbol	Daily average crude input capacity
Mexico			
Tampico (Arbol Grande)	Mex. Sinclair Pet. Corp. (Sinclair)	▲	15,000
Tampico (Mata Ratonda)	Pan-American Pet. and Transp. Co. (S.O.N.J.)	▲	8,500
	Total Mexico (2 refineries)		23,500
Dutch West Indies			
Aruba..............	Lago Pet. Co. (S.O.N.J.)	▲	285,000
Peru			
Talara...............	InternationalPet.Co.(S.O.N.J.)	▲	36,000 (T) [2]
Aguas Calientes.......	Ganzo Azul Petrol Co.	▲	1,000 (T) [2]
	Total Peru (2 refineries)		37,000
Venezuela			
La Salina.............	Cia de Pet. Lago (S.O.N.J.)	▲	8,000
Caripito	Standard Oil Co. of Venezuela (S.O.N.J.)	▲	38,000
Cabimas..............	Mene Grande Oil Co. (Gulf)	▲	1,800
Oficina...............	Mene Grande Oil Co. (Gulf)	▲	420
	Total Venezuela (4 refineries)		48,220
Argentina			
Campana.............	Cia Nativa de Petroleos (S.O.N.J.)	●	16,000
Bahia Blanca..........	Cia Nativa de Petroleos (S.O.N.J.)	▲	3,000
Embarcacion..........	Standard Oil Co. of Argentina (S.O.N.J.)	▲	1,000
Plaza Huincul.........	Standard Oil Co. of Argentina (S.O.N.J.)	▲	200
Buenos Aires..........	Ultramar Pet. Co. (50/50 Socony-Vacuum and Texas)	●	6,000
	Total Argentina (5 refineries)		26,200

[2] T = topping.

TABLE 27.—AMERICAN INTEREST IN FOREIGN REFINERIES
LOCATION, OWNERSHIP, AND DAILY CRUDE INPUT CAPACITY—*Continued*

Location	Ownership	Map symbol	Daily average crude input capacity
Trinidad			
Brighton..............	Trinidad Lake Asphalt Co. (Barber Asphalt)	▲	1,000
Point D'Or............	West India Oil Co. (S.O.N.J.)	▲	1,000
	Total Trinidad (2 refineries)		2,000
Austria			
Kagran...............	Vacuum Oil Co. A.G. (Socony-Vacuum)	●	1,500
Belgium			
Hoboken..............	Cie Ind. Atlas (S.O.N.J.)	●	1,500
Terdonck.............	Belgo-Petroleum (S.O.N.J.)	●	(c) [4]
	Total Belgium (2 refineries)		1,500
Bulgaria			
Rousse...............	Petrole Co. (Socony-Vacuum)	●	200 [5]
Czechoslovakia			
Kolin................	Vacuum Oil Co. A.S. (Socony-Vacuum)	●	2,000
France			
Frontignan...........	Cie Industrielle Des Pet. (Socony-Vacuum)	●	4,300
Gravenchon...........	Raff. De La Vacuum Oil (Socony-Vacuum)	●	4,200
Port Jerome..........	Standard Franco-Americaine (S.O.N.J.)	●	25,300
Bec D'Ambes.........	Raff. De Pet. De La Gironde (Texas)	●	7,000
	Total France (4 refineries)		40,800
Germany			
Harburg..............	Ebano Asphaltwerke (S.O.N.J.)	●	8,000
Oslebshausen.........	Deutsche Vacuum Oil Co. (Socony-Vacuum)	●	1,500
Schulau..............	Deutsche Vacuum Oil (Socony-Vacuum)	●	(finishing plant)

[4] (c) = cracking.
[5] Represents 35 per cent Socony-Vacuum interest.

Location	Ownership	Map symbol	Daily average crude input capacity
Germany—Continued			
Hamburg..............	Europaische Tanklager und Transport (Davis)	●	7,500
Bremen................	Mineraloel Raffinerie Vorm A. Kopf (S.O.N.J.)	●	1,000
Wilhelmsburg..........	J. Schindler Oelwerke (Pure Oil)	●	800 [6]
Peine.................	J. Schindler Oelwerke (Pure Oil)	●	295 [6]
	Total Germany (7 refineries)		19,095
Great Britain			
Fawley................	AGWI Pet. Corp., Ltd. (S.O.N.J.)	●	12,000
Hungary			
Almas Fuzito..........	Vacuum Oil Co. (Socony-Vacuum)	●	4,350
Italy			
Trieste...............	S.I.A.P. Raffineria (S.O.N.J.)	●	2,500
Fornovo..............	Sta. Pet. Italiana (S.O.N.J.)	●	1,000
Naples...............	Raff. Di Napoli (Socony-Vacuum)	●	5,000
	Total Italy (3 refineries) [7]		8,500
Norway			
Vallo.................	Norsk Americansk Mineral (S.O.N.J.)	●	1,000
Poland			
Czechowice...........	Vacuum Oil Co. (Socony-Vacuum)	▲	1,600
Libusza..............	Vacuum Oil Co. (Socony-Vacuum)	▲	1,200
	Total Poland (2 refineries)		2,800
Rumania			
Teleajen..............	Romano-Americana (S.O.N.J.)	▲	20,000
Brasov...............	Photogen (Socony-Vacuum)	▲	1,000
	Total Rumania (2 refineries)		21,000

[6] Represents 49 per cent Pure Oil interest.
[7] The short term of general licenses for finished products versus those for crude puts the marketers without refineries in a precarious position compared to those with refineries.

Location	Ownership	Map symbol	Daily average crude input capacity
Yugoslavia			
Bos Brod..............	Standard-Vacuum Oil Co. of Yugoslavia (Socony-Vacuum)	●	2,200
Bahrein			
Bahrein...............	Bahrein Pet. Co. (50/50 S.O. Cal. and Texas)	▲	58,500
Dutch East Indies			
Soengei Gerong.........	N.K.P.M. (50/50 Socony-Vacuum and S.O.N.J. through Standard-Vacuum)	▲	45,000
Kapoean...............	N.K.P.M. (50/50 Socony-Vacuum and S.O.N.J. through Standard-Vacuum)	▲	500
	Total Dutch East Indies (2 refineries)		45,500
Saudi Arabia			
Ras Tanura............	Arabian American (50/50 S.O. Cal. and Texas)	▲	3,000
Ras Tanura (Nejma)....	Arabian American (50/50 S.O. Cal. and Texas)	▲	50,000
	Total Saudi Arabia (2 refineries)		53,000
Japan			
Tsurumi...............	Mitsubishi Oil Co. (Tide Water Assoc. Oil Co.)	●	2,750

Recapitulation

	Map symbol	Number	%	Capacity	%
Total operating on imported crude....	●	40	60.6	280,035	32.0
Total near or at producing fields......	▲	26	39.4	596,060	68.0
Grand total....................		66	100.0	876,095	100.0

[8] Represents 50 per cent interest of Tide Water Assoc. Oil Co.

TABLE 28.—CRUDE DISTILLING CAPACITY OF AMERICAN-OWNED REFINERIES IN FOREIGN COUNTRIES VERSUS TOTAL CAPACITY OF ALL REFINERIES [1]

(In barrels of 42 U. S. gal. per day)

Country	Total all refineries	American-owned refineries	% American to total
Western Hemisphere			
Canada	248,508	154,320	62.1
Mexico	139,500	23,500	16.8
Cuba	4,200	4,200	100.0
Argentina	101,457	26,200	25.8
Bolivia	1,200	1,200	100.0
Brazil	4,560	2,160	47.4
Chile	535		
Colombia	14,500	14,500	100.0
Ecuador	2,388		
Peru	38,000	37,000	97.4
Uruguay	6,300		
Venezuela	86,800	48,220	55.6
Dutch West Indies	550,000	285,000	51.8
Trinidad	78,800	2,000	2.5
Total	1,276,748	598,300	46.9
Europe and Africa			
United Kingdom	91,500	12,000	13.1
Germany	54,285	20,195	37.2
France	152,800	40,800	26.7
Belgium	10,800	1,500	13.9
Holland	20,200		
Denmark	120		
Norway	1,000	1,000	100.0
Sweden	6,000		
Italy, Albania	44,100	8,500	19.3
Spain	700		
Portugal	4,795		
Austria	6,500	1,500	23.1
Hungary	12,700	4,350	34.3
Czechoslovakia	14,200	2,000	14.1
Poland	22,500	2,800	12.4
Rumania	216,500	21,000	9.7
Yugoslavia, Bulgaria	6,379	2,400	37.6
Eire	600		
Canary Islands	11,500		
Egypt, Sudan	23,500		
South Africa	1,000		
Belgian Congo	250		
Total	701,929	118,045	16.8
Russia	670,000		
Near and Middle East			
Iraq	7,000		
Syria	3,500		
Palestine	81,800		
Saudi Arabia	53,000	53,000	100.0
Bahrein	58,500	58,500	100.0
Iran	362,500		
Total	566,300	111,500	19.7
South and East Asia			
Dutch East Indies	176,750	45,500	25.7
Japan and Manchukuo	85,470	2,750	3.2
Thailand	1,400		
Burma	27,150		
India	10,800		
Australia	6,693		
Sarawak	20,000		
Total	328,263	48,250	14.7
Total (excl. Russia)	2,873,240	876,095	30.5
Total (incl. Russia)	3,543,240	876,095	24.7

[1] Source of data: Published sources and private information.   Latest available data.

(Statistical tables are continued on page 244.)

TABLE 29.—AMERICAN DIRECT INVESTMENTS IN FOREIGN COUNTRIES [1]

U. S. Department of Commerce Estimates, End of Year

(In thousands of dollars)

Country	1929				1936				1940			
	Total direct investments	Petroleum Amount	% total petroleum	% total direct investments	Total direct investments	Petroleum Amount	% total petroleum	% total direct investments	Total direct investments	Petroleum Amount	% total petroleum	% total direct investments
Canada and Newfoundland	2,010,320	55,047	4.9	2.8	1,951,641	108,138	10.0	5.5	2,102,694	119,606	9.4	5.7
West Indies												
Cuba	918,957	9,030	0.8	1.0	666,254	6,078	0.6	0.9	559,797	10,195	0.8	1.8
Other West Indies	134,794	25,562	2.3	18.9	86,877	22,715	2.1	26.1	114,136	54,760	4.3	48.0
Total West Indies	1,053,751	34,592	3.1	3.3	753,131	28,793	2.7	3.8	673,933	64,955	5.1	9.6
Mexico and Central America												
Mexico	682,536	205,868	18.5	30.2	479,465	69,039	6.4	14.4	357,927	41,970	3.3	11.7
Other Central America	234,557	3,608	0.3	1.5	148,416	1,670	0.2	1.1	188,094	8,095	0.6	4.3
Total Mexico and Central America	917,093	209,476	18.8	22.8	627,881	70,709	6.6	11.3	546,021	50,065	3.9	9.2
South America												
Argentina	331,819	29,811	2.7	9.0	*	*			*	*		
Brazil	193,606	23,010	2.1	11.9	194,345	32,678	3.0	16.8	240,109	30,717	2.4	12.8
Colombia	123,994	55,835	5.0	45.0	107,549	58,577	5.5	54.5	111,616	75,090	5.9	67.3
Uruguay	27,904	3,260	0.3	11.7	*	*			10,918	2,429	0.2	22.2
Venezuela	232,538	226,171	20.2	97.3	186,266	174,430	16.3	93.6	262,376	249,679	19.5	95.2
Other South America	638,034	34,403	3.0	5.4	977,829	87,374	8.1	8.9	926,463	99,149	7.8	10.7
Total South America	1,547,895	372,490	33.3	24.1	1,465,989	353,059	32.9	24.1	1,551,482	457,064	35.8	29.5
Europe												
Belgium	64,246	18,963	1.7	29.5	34,890	14,374	1.3	41.2	17,004	5,181	0.4	30.5
Denmark	15,824	6,006	0.5	38.0	13,778	5,474	0.5	39.7	19,691	9,626	0.7	48.9
France	145,009	25,108	2.2	17.3	145,683	40,463	3.8	27.8	117,199	42,682	3.3	36.4
Germany [2]	216,514	35,270	3.2	16.3	227,817	49,993	4.7	21.9	349,399	57,391	4.5	16.4
Italy	113,216	25,903	2.3	22.9	*	*			75,493	37,759	3.0	50.0

	1	2	3	4	5	6	7	8	9	10	11	12
Netherlands	43,224	12,144	1.1	28.1	18,836	6,824	0.6	36.2	18,167	4,124	0.3	22.7
Portugal	11,546	7,910	0.7	68.5	*	*	*	*	7,050	3,779	0.3	53.6
Spain	72,230	8,482	0.8	11.7	80,532	1,373	0.1	1.7	73,396	1,890	0.1	2.6
Sweden	*	*	*	*	25,493	8,272	0.8	32.4	26,361	7,181	0.6	27.2
Switzerland	16,804	6,634	0.6	39.5	*	*	*	*	23,852	2,546	0.2	10.7
United Kingdom	485,235	20,960	1.9	4.3	474,130	60,572	5.6	12.8	540,694	71,257	5.6	13.2
Other Europe	160,400	63,591	5.7	37.6	223,793	87,599	8.2	39.1	152,059	62,105	4.9	40.8
Total Europe	1,344,248	230,971	20.7	17.1	1,244,952	274,944	25.6	22.1	1,420,365	305,521	23.9	21.5
Asia												
Arabia, Bahrein, and Iran	*	*	*	*	17,780	17,453	1.6	98.2	57,234	56,266	4.4	98.3
British Malaya, French Indo-China, and Siam	27,103	2,201	0.2	8.1	*	*	*	*	*	*	*	*
China	113,754	42,839	3.8	37.7	*	*	*	*	*	*	*	*
India	*	*	*	*	*	*	*	*	48,775	19,478	1.5	39.9
Cyprus, Iraq, Palestine, and Syria[3]	7,050	1,875	0.2	26.6	29,605	20,911	2.0	70.6	*	*	*	*
Japan	60,700	8,077	0.7	13.3	*	*	*	*	*	*	*	*
Philippine Islands	79,935	10,381	0.9	13.0	*	*	*	*	*	*	*	*
Other Asia	114,503	48,628	4.4	45.9	369,608	108,599	10.1	29.4	315,936	101,138	7.9	32.0
Total Asia	403,045	114,001	10.2	28.9	416,993	146,963	13.7	35.2	421,945	176,882	13.8	41.9
Africa												
British South Africa[4]	76,846	19,199	1.7	25.0	55,127	20,994	2.0	38.1	72,901	24,427	1.9	35.5
Egypt and Anglo-Egyptian Sudan	*	*	*	*	*	*	*	*	22,753	9,395	0.7	41.3
Portuguese Africa	*	*	*	*	*	*	*	*	*	*	*	*
French Africa	*	*	*	*	10,451	10,451	1.0	100.0	9,789	8,937	0.7	91.3
Other Africa	25,383	12,293	1.1	48.4	27,116	8,072	0.7	29.8	25,630	7,176	0.6	28.0
Total Africa	102,229	31,492	2.8	30.8	92,694	39,517	3.7	42.6	131,073	49,935	3.9	38.1
Oceania—Australia and New Zealand	149,154	68,856	6.2	46.2	111,027	42,986	4.0	38.7	120,232	49,365	3.9	41.1
International	*	*	*	*	26,190	8,962	0.8	34.3	32,597	3,780	0.3	11.6
Total world	7,527,735	1,116,925	100.0	14.9	6,690,498	1,074,071	100.0	16.1	7,000,342	1,277,173	100.0	18.2

[1] Source: U. S. Department of Commerce—*Trade Information Bulletin* No. 731 American Direct Investments in 1929; American Direct Investments in Foreign Countries—1936; American Direct Investments in Foreign Countries—1940.

[2] Including Austria in 1940.

[3] Excluding Iraq in 1929.

[4] Including other British Africa in 1929.

* Included in "Other."

TABLE 30.—United States Exports of Crude-oil Producing, Pipe-line, and Refinery Equipment [1]

(In thousands of dollars)

Destination	1930	1931	1932	1933	1934	1935	1936	1937	1938	1939	1940	1941
North America..........	3,546	1,582	915	1,229	2,669	1,006	1,989	4,616	2,908	2,773	3,432	5,750
South America..........	8,798	5,197	2,919	6,089	9,193	10,546	9,317	19,516	25,068	20,331	20,377	15,912
Total Western Hemisphere (excl. United States)	12,344	6,779	3,834	7,318	11,862	11,552	11,306	24,132	27,976	23,104	23,809	21,662
Europe (excl. U.S.S.R.)...	2,987	1,513	879	835	1,955	1,467	3,784	4,412	3,110	2,793	3,765	354
Africa.................	263	90	51	26	127	185	267	1,338	1,228	1,287	675	482
Total Europe and Africa (excl. U.S.S.R.).......	3,250	1,603	930	861	2,082	1,652	4,051	5,750	4,338	4,080	4,440	836
Russia.................	7,773	1,837	488	31	483	564	501	3,346	619	246	5,091	5,694
Total Europe, Africa...	11,023	3,440	1,418	892	2,565	2,216	4,552	9,096	4,957	4,326	9,531	6,530
Near and Middle East...	1,286	229	304	623	883	961	1,185	1,120	6,340	5,909	1,708	252
South and East Asia....	2,766	1,721	582	1,312	2,315	1,093	2,256	3,823	3,475	5,990	5,291	2,903
Oceania...............	2,112	629	76	200	1,051	1,379	2,289	5,316	4,611	6,164	2,647	2,954
Total Eastern Hemisphere....	17,187	6,019	2,380	3,027	6,814	5,649	10,282	19,355	19,383	22,389	19,177	12,639
Total foreign..........	29,531	12,798	6,214	10,345	18,676	17,201	21,588	43,487	47,359	45,493	42,986	34,301
Total foreign (excl. U.S.S.R.).............	21,758	10,961	5,726	10,314	18,193	16,637	21,087	40,141	46,740	45,247	37,895	28,607

[1] 6062 casing and oil-line pipe, seamless
6063 casing and oil-line pipe, welded
7342 petroleum and gas-well drilling apparatus and parts
7349 other petroleum well and refinery machinery and parts

TABLE 31.—ALL PURCHASES [1] INCLUDING PETROLEUM PRODUCTS MADE BY AMERICAN
OIL COMPANIES IN ALL FOREIGN COUNTRIES [2]

(In thousands of dollars)

Year	Western Hemisphere			Eastern Hemisphere			Total foreign (incomplete)
	North America	South America	Total Western Hemisphere	Total Europe and Africa	Total Asia and Oceania	Total Eastern Hemisphere	
1935	41,064	17,451	58,515	24,026	745	24,771	83,286
1936	35,230	13,437	48,667	22,689	851	23,540	72,207
1937	39,454	19,533	58,987	20,678	1,267	21,945	80,932
1938	40,832	27,216	68,048	53,863	1,830	55,693	123,741
1939	36,465	27,754	64,219	55,483	2,889	58,372	122,591
1940	45,950	28,498	74,448	32,658	3,135	35,793	110,241
1941	68,630	36,296	104,926	24,462	4,421	28,883	133,809
1942	78,218	34,483	112,701	16,656	3,939	20,595	133,296
1943	79,026	45,472	124,498	15,397	4,129	19,526	144,024
1944	93,770	60,467	154,237	18,374	5,956	24,330	178,567
10-year total	558,639	310,607	869,246	284,286	29,162	313,448	1,182,694

[1] Source of data: Tabulation of data from 11 American oil companies and their subsidiaries and affiliates.

[2] All countries in which American oil companies have producing, marketing, and other investments are included. Reports were not submitted for some countries because of war conditions.

TABLE 32.—TOTAL ROYALTIES AND TAXES [1] PAID BY AMERICAN OIL COMPANIES
IN ALL FOREIGN COUNTRIES [2]

(In thousands of dollars)

| Year | Western Hemisphere | | | Eastern Hemisphere | | | Total foreign (incomplete) |
	North America	South America	Total Western Hemisphere	Total Europe and Africa	Total Asia and Oceania	Total Eastern Hemisphere	
1935	24,430	37,531	61,961	258,112	260,201	518,313	580,274
1936	28,432	38,827	67,259	233,396	291,138	524,534	591,793
1937	32,315	52,224	84,539	266,241	336,071	602,312	686,851
1938	36,042	58,278	94,320	226,436	284,319	510,755	605,075
1939	33,838	53,606	87,444	218,658	285,262	503,920	591,364
1940	40,875	52,943	93,818	54,777	126,062	180,839	274,657
1941	55,181	74,981	130,162	24,352	94,527	118,879	249,041
1942	55,984	48,412	104,396	23,631	65,884	89,515	193,911
1943	53,476	66,261	119,737	22,341	74,816	97,157	216,894
1944	57,413	97,797	155,210	7,723	89,543	97,266	252,476
10-year total	417,986	580,860	998,846	1,335,667	1,907,823	3,243,490	4,242,336

[1] Source of data: Tabulation of data from 11 American oil companies and their subsidiaries and affiliates.

[2] All countries in which American oil companies have producing, marketing, and other investments are included. Reports were not submitted for some countries because of war conditions.

TABLE 33.—EMPLOYMENT AND WAGES PAID BY AMERICAN OIL COMPANIES IN FOREIGN OIL-PRODUCING COUNTRIES [1]

(In thousand of dollars)

Year	North America				South America [2]				Total Western Hemisphere				Asia and Oceania [3]				Total foreign (incomplete) [4]			
	Number of employees			Total pay roll [5]	Number of employees			Total pay roll [5]	Number of employees			Total pay roll [5]	Number of employees			Total pay roll [5]	Number of employees			Total pay roll [5]
	Nationals	Others	Total		Nationals	Others	Total		Nationals	Others	Total		Nationals	Others	Total		Nationals [6]	Others	Total	
1935	8,106	5	8,111	12,426	21,574	2,197	23,771	22,496	29,680	2,202	31,882	34,922	7,316	938	8,254	4,624	36,996	3,140	40,136	39,546
1936	7,998	5	8,003	12,351	22,376	2,159	24,535	23,234	30,374	2,164	32,538	35,585	11,235	1,272	12,507	5,734	41,609	3,436	45,045	41,319
1937	8,430	205	8,635	13,507	27,793	2,297	30,090	31,867	36,223	2,502	38,725	45,374	12,902	1,602	14,504	6,634	49,125	4,104	53,229	52,008
1938	8,284	404	8,688	14,562	35,806	2,759	38,565	40,288	44,090	3,163	47,253	54,850	15,593	1,015	16,608	6,979	59,683	4,178	63,861	61,829
1939	8,196	505	8,701	13,743	37,741	3,218	40,959	45,069	45,937	3,723	49,660	58,812	18,932	1,009	19,941	8,162	64,869	4,732	69,601	66,974
1940	8,684	415	9,099	14,137	33,031	3,106	36,137	45,987	41,715	3,521	45,236	60,124	18,407	1,018	19,425	8,242	60,122	4,539	64,661	68,366
1941	8,840	208	9,138	16,150	32,046	2,771	34,817	43,664	40,886	3,069	43,955	59,814	15,551	759	16,310	7,152	56,437	3,828	60,265	66,966
1942	9,156	234	9,390	16,998	31,990	2,461	34,451	47,900	41,146	2,695	43,841	64,898	4,215	190	4,405	2,451	45,361	2,885	48,246	67,349
1943	11,033	309	11,342	17,907	34,184	2,207	36,391	49,350	45,217	2,516	47,733	67,257	4,292	781	5,073	3,025	63,215	4,059	67,274	70,282
1944	12,335	321	12,656	23,842	40,007	2,237	42,244	59,965	52,342	2,558	54,900	83,807	10,873	1,501	12,374	6,186				89,993
10-year total	......	......	......	155,623	......	......	......	409,820	......	......	......	565,443	......	......	......	59,189	......	......	......	624,632

[1] Countries in which American oil companies have producing and refining interests, exclusive of European countries for which figures were unobtainable because of war conditions; also, exclusive of U.S.S.R. Source of data: Tabulation of data from 11 American oil companies and their subsidiaries and affiliates.

[2] Includes Aruba, Dutch West Indies.

[3] Includes Near and Middle East and Dutch East Indies.

[4] Does not include European countries or U.S.S.R. (see footnote 1).

[5] Inclusive of allowances, benefits, etc.

[6] For breakdown of native employment see Appendix Table 34.

TABLE 34.—BREAKDOWN OF NATIVE EMPLOYMENT BY AMERICAN OIL COMPANIES
IN FOREIGN PRODUCING COUNTRIES [1]

Area	Skilled and common labor	Supervisory and office personnel	Technical (geologists, engineers, doctors, etc.)	Total employed
North America................	9,187	2,631	456	12,274
South America [2]............	32,451	6,869	460	39,780
Western Hemisphere........	41,638	9,500	916	52,054
Asia......................	10,242	555	76	10,873
Total foreign [3] (incomplete)	51,880	10,055	992	62,927

[1] Countries in which American oil companies have producing and refining interests, exclusive of European countries for which figures were unobtainable because of war conditions; also, exclusive of U.S.S.R.   Figures are for 1944 or for the last year for which figures were available and therefore slightly vary from number of employees shown for 1944, Appendix Table 33.   Source of data: Tabulation of data from 11 American oil companies and their subsidiaries and affiliates.
[2] Includes Aruba, Dutch West Indies.
[3] Does not include Europe or U.S.S.R. (see footnote 1).

TABLE 35.—ALL PURCHASES INCLUDING PETROLEUM PRODUCTS MADE BY AMERICAN
OIL COMPANIES IN FOREIGN PRODUCING COUNTRIES [1]

(In thousands of dollars)

Year	Western Hemisphere			Asia and Oceania [3]	Total foreign (incomplete) [4]
	North America	South America [2]	Total		
1935	40,802	11,804	52,606	717	53,323
1936	34,955	7,468	42,423	791	43,214
1937	39,154	12,698	51,852	1,065	52,917
1938	38,174	13,146	51,320	1,543	52,863
1939	33,459	13,710	47,169	2,316	49,485
1940	42,761	12,985	55,746	2,611	58,357
1941	63,778	17,379	81,157	2,588	83,745
1942	72,988	17,991	90,979	870	91,849
1943	70,540	32,051	102,591	998	103,589
1944	84,225	43,811	128,036	2,955	130,991
10-year total	520,836	183,043	703,879	16,454	720,333

[1] Countries in which American oil companies have producing and refining interests, exclusive of European countries for which figures were unobtainable because of war conditions; also, exclusive of U.S.S.R.   Source of data: Tabulation of data from 11 American oil companies and their subsidiaries and affiliates.
[2] Includes Aruba, Dutch West Indies.
[3] Includes Near and Middle East and Dutch East Indies.
[4] Does not include European countries or U.S.S.R.

TABLE 36.—ROYALTIES AND TAXES PAID BY AMERICAN OIL COMPANIES IN FOREIGN PRODUCING COUNTRIES [1]

(In thousands of dollars)

Year	Western Hemisphere									Asia and Oceania [3]			Total foreign (incomplete) [4]		
	North America			South America [2]			Total Western Hemisphere								
	Royalties	Taxes	Total	Royalties	Taxes	Total	Royalties	Taxes	Total	Royalties	Taxes	Total	Royalties	Taxes	Total
1935	89	20,101	20,190	7,981	20,617	28,598	8,070	40,718	48,788	......	1,881	1,881	8,070	42,599	50,669
1936	138	23,291	23,429	7,610	22,177	29,787	7,748	45,468	53,216	665	8,432	9,097	8,413	53,900	62,313
1937	272	25,939	26,211	12,973	30,556	43,529	13,245	56,495	69,740	1,296	12,386	13,682	14,541	68,881	83,422
1938	227	29,384	29,611	16,389	31,845	48,234	16,616	61,229	77,845	1,629	8,747	10,376	18,245	69,976	88,221
1939	111	26,491	26,602	13,947	29,731	43,678	14,058	56,222	70,280	3,237	10,892	14,129	17,295	67,114	84,409
1940	248	33,903	34,151	12,611	29,483	42,094	12,859	63,386	76,245	5,320	13,639	18,959	18,179	77,025	95,204
1941	385	46,729	47,114	27,957	33,442	61,399	28,342	80,171	108,513	4,369	11,328	15,697	32,711	91,499	124,210
1942	477	47,658	48,135	9,983	30,697	40,680	10,460	78,355	88,815	4,149	......	4,149	14,609	78,355	92,964
1943	528	46,612	47,140	21,363	36,208	57,571	21,891	82,820	104,711	2,109	......	2,109	24,000	82,820	106,820
1944	521	49,849	50,370	33,460	54,472	87,932	33,981	104,321	138,302	4,015	......	4,015	37,996	104,321	142,317
10-year total	2,996	349,957	352,953	164,274	319,228	483,502	167,270	669,185	836,455	26,789	67,305	94,094	194,059	736,490	930,549

[1] Countries in which American oil companies have producing and refining interests, exclusive of European countries for which figures were unobtainable because of war conditions; also, exclusive of U.S.S.R.   Source of data: Tabulation of data from 11 American oil companies and their subsidiaries and affiliates.

[2] Includes Aruba, Dutch West Indies.

[3] Includes Near and Middle East and Dutch East Indies.

[4] Does not include European countries or U.S.S.R.

TABLE 37.—TOTAL PAY ROLL, ALL PURCHASES, AND ROYALTIES AND TAXES PAID BY AMERICAN OIL COMPANIES IN FOREIGN PRODUCING COUNTRIES [1]

(In thousands of dollars)

Year	Total pay roll [2]	All purchases [3]	Royalties	Taxes	Foreign total (incomplete) [4]
1935	39,546	53,323	8,070	42,599	143,538
1936	41,319	43,214	8,413	53,900	146,846
1937	52,008	52,917	14,541	68,881	188,347
1938	61,829	52,863	18,245	69,976	202,913
1939	66,974	49,485	17,295	67,114	200,868
1940	68,366	58,357	18,179	77,025	221,927
1941	66,966	83,745	32,711	91,499	274,921
1942	67,349	91,849	14,609	78,355	252,162
1943	70,282	103,589	24,000	82,820	280,691
1944	89,993	130,991	37,996	104,321	363,301
10-year total...	624,632	720,333	194,059	736,490	2,275,514

[1] Countries in which they have producing and refining interests, exclusive of European countries for which figures were unobtainable because of war conditions; also, exclusive of U.S.S.R. Aruba, Dutch West Indies, is included. Source of data: Tabulation of data from 11 American oil companies and their subsidiaries and affiliates.

[2] Includes allowances, benefits, etc.

[3] Includes petroleum products.

[4] Does not include Europe or U.S.S.R.

TABLE 38.—CREOLE PETROLEUM CORPORATION EXPENDITURES FOR SOCIAL AND EDUCATIONAL PURPOSES

(In U. S. dollars)

Purpose	Capital expenditures	Annual (1944) operating expense
Housing..............................	17,868,297	2,842,164
Hospitals (medical care).................	1,054,464	2,259,327 [1]
Schools...............................	553,467	537,143
Retirement fund.......................	....	4,200
Recreational facilities..................	654,307	376,757
Modern services (lighting, sanitation, etc.)	2,978,073	154,735
Other................................	....	1,239,278
Total............................	23,108,608	7,413,604
Estimated present total annual expenditure for social and educational purposes	7,413,000	
Per cent of annual expenditures present total annual operating expenses........	29.27	

[1] Hospital revenue for 1944 was $63,456, and in addition contributions of $22,959 were made to other hospitals. Therefore, the net cost of operating company-owned hospitals after revenue was $2,172,912. The company is obligated to defray the cost of accidents but has gone far beyond this obligation in providing medical attention for its employees.

TABLE 39.—MENE GRANDE OIL COMPANY EXPENDITURES FOR SOCIAL AND EDU-
CATIONAL PURPOSES

(In U. S. dollars)

Purpose	Capital expenditures	Annual (1944) operating expense
Housing	8,317,251	1,149,956
Hospitals (medical care) [1]	1,058,030	689,469
Schools	251,639	144,686
Retirement fund		
Recreational facilities	506,731	97,854
Modern services (lighting, sanitation, etc.)	3,357,845	258,467
Other	....	650,754
Total	13,491,496	2,991,186
Estimated present total annual expenditures for social and educational purposes	2,991,000	
Per cent of annual expenditures present total annual operating expenses	22.2	

[1] Gross operating costs have totaled $6,271,271, of which $2,169,000 was voluntary and $4,102,000 required by law; revenue has totaled $612,000, of which $365,000 was voluntary and $247,000 required by law. Thus, net operating costs were $5,659,000, of which $1,804,000 was voluntary and $3,855,000 required by law. It will be noted that revenue received from patients is less than 10 per cent of the company's total cost of operating hospitals and dispensaries. In addition, the company contributed about $18,000 to hospitals not directly connected with the oil industry.

TABLE 40.—TROPICAL OIL COMPANY AND ANDIAN NATIONAL CORPORATION ESTIMATED EXPENDITURES FOR SOCIAL AND EDUCATIONAL PURPOSES SINCE 1922

(In U. S. dollars)

Housing	2,700,000 [1]
Hospitals (medical care)	5,700,000 [2]
Schools	300,000 [3]
"Cesantia" fund	2,400,000 [4]
Recreational facilities	600,000 [5]
Other	2,000,000 [6]
Depreciation on the above items	4,600,000 [7]
Total	18,300,000

[1] Exclusive of depreciation but inclusive of proportionate charge for water, light, and gas provided for all quarters.
[2] Net expense, exclusive of depreciation, and includes both dental and sanitation expense. No revenue was provided by the patients. The company's hospitals are organized on a voluntary basis. Although the company is obligated by law to defray the cost of accidents, it has gone far beyond this obligation in providing medical attention for its employees.
[3] Includes school and church expense exclusive of depreciation.
[4] By law, the company is to pay one month's wage for each year of service known as "cesantia." Included in the total paid for this reason are death and accident claims paid. The amount shown is that paid to nationals of the country only as being a direct social benefit.
[5] Represents welfare expense, club houses, sports, etc., exclusive of depreciation.
[6] Represents expense for messes, boardinghouses, etc. Depreciation on buildings and equipment is excluded.
[7] This item is added to indicate the total depreciation excluded from expenditures listed above.

TABLE 41.—N. V. NEDERLANDSCHE KOLONIALE PETROLEUM MAATSCHAPPIJ EXPENDITURES FOR EDUCATIONAL AND SOCIAL PURPOSES PRIOR TO 1942

(In U. S. dollars)

Housing	2,576,000
Hospitals (medical care)	163,000
Schools	28,000
Recreational facilities	226,000
Modern services (lighting, sanitation, etc.)	205,000
Total	3,198,000

TABLE 42.—ESTIMATED N. V. NEDERLANDSCHE KOLONIALE PETROLEUM MAATSCHAPPIJ ANNUAL EXPENDITURES FOR EDUCATIONAL AND SOCIAL PURPOSES DURING THE LAST YEARS PRIOR TO JAPANESE INVASION, 1942

(In U. S. dollars)

Medical and hospital	151,000
Annuities and insurance	131,000
School allowance, burial expense, etc	22,000
Contributions to schools and other charitable institutions not connected with the oil business	15,000
Total	319,000

TABLE 43.—WORLD CRUDE-OIL PRODUCTION BY COUNTRIES AND YEARS, 1857 TO 1943 INCLUSIVE [1]

(In barrels of 42 U. S. gal. per day)

Year	Rumania	United States	Italy	Canada	Russia	Poland	Japan and Taiwan	Germany	India	Burma[2]	Dutch East Indies	Peru	Mexico	Argentina	Trinidad	Egypt	British Borneo	Iran (Persia)
1857–1860	13	344																
1861	47	5,791																
1862	63	8,375		33														
1863	77	7,154		227	112													
1864	90	5,781	5	246	178													
1865	107	6,844	3	301	184													
1866	115	9,858	3	479	227													
1867	140	9,169	3	521	329													
1868	153	9,963		546	240													
1869	162	11,548		603	553													
1870	230	14,414		685	559													
1871	247	14,260		740	452													
1872	249	17,194		842	505													
1873	285	27,107		1,000	1,301													
1874	282	29,937		463	1,597	411												
1875	296	24,075		603	1,910	433	14											
1876	303	24,955	8	852	3,609	448	19											
1877	296	36,576	8	855	4,934	466	27											
1878	299	42,184	11	855	6,578	482	49											
1879	301	54,560	8	1,575	7,564	589	63											
1880	314	71,820	5	956	8,199	626	71	25										
1881	334	75,784	3	753	9,866	786	47	79										
1882	373	83,151	5	753	12,433	904	41	159										
1883	381	64,246	5	685	16,444	1,000	55	74										
1884	577	66,168	8	688	29,522	1,115	77	126										
1885	529	59,888	5	685	38,151	1,274	82	112										
1886	460	76,891	5	1,600	49,332	838	104	203										
1887	499	77,488	3	1,441	50,323	942	79	203										
1888	598	75,443	3	1,899	62,975	975	101	232										
1889	816	96,339	3	1,932	67,422	1,411	145	186	258									
1890	1,049	125,547	8	2,178	78,605	1,805	142	296	323									
1891	1,337	148,746	22	2,069	94,721	1,729	145	299	521									
1892	1,620	138,019	49	2,131	97,746	1,765	189	276	661									
1893	1,466	132,688	52	2,186	110,841	1,899	290	274	819		1,644							
1894	1,392	135,188	58	2,271	99,658	2,600	474	337	896		1,885							
1895	1,578	144,909	71	1,989	126,411	3,981	466	332	1,019		3,332							
1896	1,494	166,557	49	1,986	129,019	6,678	648	396	1,175		3,899	128						
1897	1,564	165,687	38	1,945	149,038	6,099	718	455	1,496		6,992	195						
1898	2,126	151,680	41	2,077	168,795	6,510	874	504	1,485		8,121	195						
1899	3,907	156,357	44	2,214	180,699	6,340	1,477	526	2,578		4,921	244						
1900	4,463	174,305	33	2,501	207,616	6,430	2,386	981	2,956		6,173	751						

1901	4,597	190,108	44	2,074	233,337	8,907	3,060	860	3,921	......	10,997	753	27	......	......	......	......	......
1902	5,644	243,196	52	1,455	220,658	11,348	2,729	970	4,430	......	6,658	786	110	......	......	......	......	......
1903	7,570	275,236	49	1,334	207,099	14,342	3,312	1,222	6,877	......	15,808	762	205	......	......	......	......	......
1904	9,833	319,894	71	1,511	214,582	16,249	3,331	1,740	9,249	......	17,781	792	344	......	......	......	......	......
1905	12,112	369,088	121	1,737	150,575	15,797	3,690	1,537	11,334	......	21,507	1,022	688	......	......	......	......	......
1906	17,474	346,558	148	1,559	161,362	14,981	4,285	1,586	11,003	......	22,414	1,455	1,375	......	......	......	......	......
1907	22,241	455,056	164	2,162	169,455	23,167	4,707	2,074	11,901	......	27,350	2,058	2,753	......	......	......	......	......
1908	22,546	487,778	139	1,443	169,910	34,459	5,112	2,757	13,790	......	28,096	2,582	10,746	33	......	......	......	......
1909	25,553	501,839	115	1,153	180,740	40,912	5,170	2,792	18,293	......	30,252	3,866	7,436	49	156	......	......	......
1910	26,641	574,128	140	866	192,704	34,721	5,011	2,827	16,816	......	30,222	3,447	9,956	55	392	......	......	......
1911	30,433	603,969	205	797	181,326	28,819	4,759	2,786	17,674	......	33,351	4,014	34,392	36	781	58	......	......
1912	35,453	609,111	148	664	185,844	23,320	4,533	2,817	19,445	......	31,788	4,787	45,241	128	1,194	585	......	......
1913	37,136	680,673	129	625	183,159	21,419	5,315	2,348	21,726	......	31,797	5,674	70,401	359	1,381	269	386	5,088
1914	35,141	728,117	110	589	178,824	17,633	7,222	2,140	20,301	......	32,459	5,033	71,878	756	1,765	2,063	871	7,973
1915	32,959	770,148	121	589	189,482	14,663	8,022	1,926	22,471	......	34,004	7,066	90,166	1,406	2,055	581	1,074	9,907
1916	24,440	821,768	139	541	195,430	17,997	8,096	1,792	23,199	......	35,741	7,085	102,213	2,368	2,538	1,104	1,719	12,232
1917	10,195	918,674	112	586	172,750	17,063	7,838	1,759	22,134	......	37,343	7,060	151,671	3,337	4,390	2,584	1,485	19,581
1918	23,918	975,145	96	836	72,012	16,526	6,688	740	22,433	......	36,360	6,923	175,899	3,706	5,704	5,301	1,381	23,624
1919	18,508	1,036,622	96	660	88,233	16,701	6,132	726	23,934	......	43,984	7,200	253,288	3,646	5,044	4,156	1,633	27,778
1920	20,736	1,210,189	96	536	75,842	15,320	6,041	672	22,883	......	47,877	7,697	445,462	4,511	5,691	2,847	2,787	33,415
1921	23,391	1,293,652	88	515	79,364	14,156	5,950	751	23,929	......	47,992	10,134	549,544	5,634	6,450	3,438	3,866	45,679
1922	27,465	1,527,482	85	490	97,786	14,321	5,519	874	23,367	......	48,442	14,559	508,455	7,850	6,700	3,255	7,805	60,951
1923	30,487	2,006,595	93	466	107,252	14,800	4,796	948	23,030	......	57,387	15,614	415,242	9,137	8,359	2,888	10,795	69,123
1924	37,127	1,950,656	107	440	123,921	15,456	4,784	1,109	22,995	......	58,904	21,344	384,300	12,729	11,085	3,066	11,374	88,451
1925	46,585	2,092,447	167	910	143,359	16,329	4,924	1,482	22,668	......	62,012	24,507	317,628	16,406	12,019	3,359	11,663	95,994
1926	65,181	2,111,984	112	998	174,958	16,011	4,759	1,789	21,948	......	61,432	28,843	247,408	21,506	13,620	3,255	13,540	98,197
1927	73,541	2,468,847	129	1,306	208,943	14,389	4,365	1,816	22,005	......	72,718	27,260	175,739	23,672	14,740	3,471	13,542	108,734
1928	86,180	2,463,044	126	1,715	239,571	14,757	4,844	1,721	23,883	......	84,450	32,283	137,099	24,782	20,994	4,906	14,270	118,746
1929	98,209	2,759,789	135	3,070	282,194	13,383	5,357	2,104	23,965	......	104,228	36,723	122,345	25,730	23,786	5,059	14,917	115,466
1930	119,075	2,460,304	185	4,268	370,782	13,290	5,233	3,520	24,347	......	110,159	34,107	108,231	24,662	24,989	5,229	13,766	125,570
1931	136,900	2,331,729	397	4,338	446,685	12,642	5,165	5,044	23,876	......	93,913	27,641	90,335	32,080	26,635	5,276	10,511	121,578
1932	149,700	2,145,243	663	2,888	421,544	11,132	4,370	4,732	24,091	......	100,698	27,049	89,443	35,883	27,639	4,899	10,369	135,164
1933	151,032	2,481,249	568	2,676	419,408	11,042	3,878	4,715	23,927	......	110,277	36,321	92,822	37,496	26,194	4,301	12,230	148,066
1934	172,353	2,487,849	440	2,767	470,425	10,611	4,173	6,138	25,216	......	120,817	44,600	104,123	38,428	29,847	3,976	13,219	157,271
1935	170,943	2,730,400	343	2,597	497,554	10,322	6,177	8,241	25,280	......	120,856	46,753	109,775	39,167	31,934	3,267	14,304	156,523
1936	177,983	3,004,609	283	2,491	532,607	10,211	6,678	8,504	26,282	......	128,288	48,074	111,527	42,227	36,167	3,283	13,259	170,904
1937	145,625	3,504,548	314	6,368	555,951	10,090	6,835	8,697	5,929	21,433	145,843	47,854	127,918	44,811	42,474	3,081	15,466	212,548
1938	134,050	3,327,000	291	17,521	579,596	10,232	6,806	10,587	6,679	20,663	148,025	43,391	104,874	46,784	47,463	4,550	17,756	213,737
1939	127,141	3,465,649	241	20,664	600,718	9,058	6,471	12,823	6,375	21,570	160,554	37,007	117,203	50,999	53,541	12,796	19,383	202,611
1940	116,789	3,697,306	224	23,078	624,000	9,600	6,331	19,433	7,500	21,795	159,821	33,134	119,982	56,314	58,000	17,788	19,619	178,628
1941	109,749	3,841,721	225	26,957	647,000	8,950	6,300	20,000	8,000	20,959	141,918	32,702	117,488	60,315	60,000	23,343	13,731	138,704
1942	105,822	3,799,027	225	27,697	625,000	11,300	6,438	20,000	7,500	3,562	43,973	37,338	95,113	64,942	65,000	22,241	5,000	199,433
1943	100,000	4,118,290	225	26,447	675,000	10,000	6,100	18,000	7,000	2,500	144,000	40,149	95,595	68,063	60,000	24,596	15,000	212,000
1944	63,000	4,584,025	110	26,580	700,000	10,000	6,000	17,000	9,500	2,500	70,000	39,307	103,863	66,205	60,000	25,850	10,000	280,000

[1] Commencing in 1939, figures for many countries in the Eastern Hemisphere reflect assumed approximations. Source: Bureau of Mines and private information.
[2] Included with India up to 1935.

TABLE 43.—WORLD CRUDE-OIL PRODUCTION BY COUNTRIES AND YEARS, 1857 TO 1943 INCLUSIVE [1]—*Continued*

(In barrels of 42 U. S. gal. per day)

Year	Vene-zuela	Ecua-dor	France	Czecho-slovakia	Great Britain	Colom-bia	Sak-halin	Bolivia	Iraq	Austria	Bahrein	Albania	Hun-gary	Saudi Arabia	China	Yugo-slavia	Other coun-tries	Total foreign	Total world
1857–1860																		13	357
1861																		47	5,838
1862																		96	8,471
1863																		416	7,570
1864																		514	6,295
1865																		597	7,441
1866																		824	10,682
1867																		993	10,162
1868																		939	10,902
1869																		1,318	12,866
1870																		1,474	15,888
1871																		1,439	15,699
1872																		1,596	18,790
1873																		2,586	29,693
1874																		2,756	32,693
1875																		3,259	27,334
1876																		5,239	30,194
1877																		6,586	43,162
1878																		8,274	50,458
1879																		10,100	64,660
1880																		10,196	82,016
1881																		11,868	87,652
1882																		14,668	97,819
1883																		18,644	82,890
1884																		32,108	98,276
1885																		40,838	100,726
1886																		52,542	129,433
1887																		53,490	130,978
1888																		67,084	142,527
1889																		72,173	168,512
1890																		84,406	209,953
1891																		100,843	249,589
1892																		104,437	242,456
1893																		119,471	252,159
1894																		109,571	244,759
1895																		139,179	284,088
1896																		145,462	312,019
1897																		168,540	334,227
1898																		190,728	342,408
1899																		202,950	359,307
1900																		234,290	408,595

Year																			
1901																	55	268,632	458,740
1902																	71	254,911	498,107
1903																	99	258,679	533,915
1904																	109	275,592	595,486
1905																	82	220,202	589,290
1906																	82	237,724	584,282
1907																	82	268,114	723,170
1908																	55	291,695	779,473
1909																	55	316,542	818,381
1910																	55	323,853	897,981
1911																	55	339,486	943,455
1912																	55	356,002	965,113
1913																	58	387,267	1,067,940
1914																	37	384,816	1,112,933
1915																		416,529	1,186,677
1916																	90	436,724	1,258,492
1917	618	156															104	460,766	1,379,440
1918	1,006	164	995														87	404,399	1,540,334
1919	708	164	915	132	5												69	503,712	
1920	1,437	164	973	189	8												64	695,248	1,905,437
1921	4,104	164	1,066	258	8	182	6	60									62	826,731	2,120,383
1922	6,569	164	1,359	329	8	887	19	71									84	837,338	2,364,820
1923	13,032	238	1,353	203	3	1,164	25	33									90	786,525	2,793,120
1924	25,014	273	1,358	208	3	1,215	219	151									95	825,579	2,776,235
1925	55,915	459	1,258	433	8	2,758	486	152									96	841,425	2,933,872
1926	101,178	1,042	1,310	411	5	17,654	600										71	895,888	3,007,872
1927	173,087	1,339	1,381	307	5	40,912	1,305		926								58	985,761	3,454,608
1928	288,966	2,967	1,399	257	3	53,695	2,276		1,948								62	1,161,933	3,624,977
1929	376,809	3,701	1,537	258	3	54,947	3,288		2,186								89	1,319,640	4,079,429
1930	375,308	4,269	1,410	426	3	54,670	6,073		2,002								89	1,431,816	3,892,120
1931	325,696	4,812	1,419	411	3	48,815	6,938	69	2,000								90	1,433,269	3,764,998
1932	322,705	4,358	1,404	344	3	43,844	8,230	121	2,000								130	1,433,403	3,578,646
1933	329,978	4,536	1,512	359		35,217	9,341	307	2,501	37	86						163	1,468,990	3,950,239
1934	373,592	4,555	1,535	527		46,410	8,976	435	21,896	67	784							1,663,181	4,151,030
1935	407,915	4,806	1,574	404		47,218	7,672	449	76,359	110	3,465							1,794,008	4,524,408
1936	425,992	5,330	1,456	397		50,502	8,832	286	83,089	110	12,691							1,908,453	4,913,062
1937	511,934	6,013	1,367	337		54,944	9,300	203	88,000	572	21,267	1,000	55					2,096,832	5,901,380
1938	521,841	6,264	1,364	337		58,925	9,315	250	88,877	1,089	22,734	1,603	908	1,370				2,128,654	5,455,654
1939	562,829	6,461	1,370	326	88	64,835	10,601	589	82,079	2,580	20,791	2,315	3,069	10,778				2,228,578	5,694,227
1940	508,562	6,532	1,037	500	358	69,136	11,270	647	51,498	6,508	19,388	3,027	5,339	14,000				2,170,811	5,868,117
1941	625,017	4,385	1,350	525	632	66,816	12,000	644	31,632	12,000	18,600	4,000	8,944	11,800			75	2,234,268	6,075,989
1942	405,436	6,418	1,350	575	1,656	28,732	11,000	844	51,570	16,000	17,100	3,507	13,500	12,400	1,000	1,000	28	1,913,968	5,712,995
1943	491,505	6,518	1,500	600	2,298	36,316	11,000	1,082	74,430	24,000	18,000	4,775	15,500	13,000	1,500	2,700	142	2,207,266	6,325,556
1944	702,278	8,107	1,400	550	1,912	60,904	10,000	833	86,899	32,500	17,000	2,500	16,500	21,268	2,000	1,500	175	2,453,741	7,037,766

¹ Commencing in 1939, figures for many countries in the Eastern Hemisphere reflect assumed approximations.   Source: Bureau of Mines and private information.

INDEX